AF423014

"This is a valuable resource written in a way that theological students will understand, and supervisors will appreciate! It takes the student "by the hand" from the formulation of the research topic through methodological positioning and choices and closes with a chapter on supervision expectations. I look forward to prescribing it to my own postgraduate students."

NADINE BOWERS DU TOIT, Professor - Theology and Development, University of Stellenbosch, editor of *Race, Faith and Inequality amongst Young Adults in South Africa*

"It is very good to see the use of social science methods being developed to aid religious studies and theological research. My hope is that this very practical book, using up-to-date resources, will help to develop this important form of study further."

ROBIN GILL, Emeritus Professor of Applied Theology, University of Kent, author of the trilogy on *Sociological Theology*

"Upon launching out on research, students and scholars are always on the lookout for good books on research methodology. In Dr Iyadurai's book, they will find an excellent manual spanning the length and breadth of what they are looking for. I strongly recommend this book to all those engaged in research."

FRANCIS GONSALVES SJ, President, Jnana Deepa: Pontifical Athenaeum of Philosophy & Theology, author of *God of Our Soil: Towards Subaltern Trinitarian Theology*

"Joshua Iyadurai has been teaching research methods to PhD students in Christian Studies for over a decade. He is an expert facilitator in this hybrid field, helping both theology and religious studies students use social research methods more rigorously and effectively. This book will be immensely helpful to anyone wanting to do research in the field of religion, as well as to those in classes focused on research methods. I highly recommend it."

ROBERT K. JOHNSTON, Professor of Theology and Culture, Fuller Theological Seminary, co-author of *Deep Focus: Film and Theology in Dialogue*

"*Social Research Methods for Students and Scholars of Theology and Religious Studies* is a masterpiece that draws from Joshua's experience of teaching social research for two decades. The book aims to catalyze theological scholarship using social research methods with scientific precision. Scholars, educators, and graduate students will find this text a welcome resource. I highly recommend it!"

DAVID TARUS, Executive Director, Association for Christian Theological Education in Africa (ACTEA), author of *A Different Way of Being*

"This textbook fills an important niche for postgraduate researchers embarking on empirical research in Practical Theology or Religious Studies. Those who have little or no background in the social sciences will find this a clear and well-structured introduction on how to conceive a research project and what methods are available to answer their research questions. Reading this before they embark on their journey could save a lot of problems further down the road."

ANDREW VILLAGE, Professor of Practical and Empirical Theology, York St John University, author of *The Church of England in the First Decade of the 21st Century*

SOCIAL
RESEARCH
METHODS

SOCIAL RESEARCH METHODS

For Students and Scholars of Theology and Religious Studies

JOSHUA IYADURAI

Marina Centre for Interdisciplinary Studies in Religion
Chennai

SOCIAL RESEARCH METHODS

For Students and Scholars of Theology and Religious Studies

Copyright ©2023 Joshua Iyadurai.

All rights reserved. Except for brief quotations in critical publications or reviews, no part of this book may be reproduced in any manner without prior written permission from the publisher.

Published by

Joshua Iyadurai

Marina Centre for Interdisciplinary Studies in Religion

Chennai India

https://mcisr.org

ISBN 978-93-5620-482-9 (paper)

ISBN 978-93-5627-844-8 (eBook)

Cataloguing-in-Publication Data

Author: Iyadurai, Joshua

Social research methods: for students and scholars of theology and religious studies / Joshua Iyadurai.

Includes bibliographical references and index.

1. Social sciences–Research–Methodology 2. Religion–Methodology–Research 3. Theology–Research

The website URLs mentioned in this book are offered as resources for research. The author and publisher do not vouch for the contents of those sites and are not intended in any way to be or imply an endorsement by them.

Book Cover and Interior Design by Jerusha Joshem
https://jerushajoshem.com

To
3Js

Brief Contents

Detailed Contents

8. WRITING A RESEARCH REPORT   191

9. THE ROLE OF SUPERVISORS AND EXAMINERS   217

Acknowledgement

I thank my students who have taken my course on research methodology, students who have completed their research projects, and those currently doing their research under my supervision. Your questions, challenges, and inspiration have shaped the book.

Although, I have cherished the idea of writing this book for many years, the grant from the Langham Partnership UK set the project in motion with a residency at the Trinity College of Bristol, UK in 2018. The Nagel Institute of Calvin University, Grand Rapids, provided a grant so I could continue the writing project at the Prophet's Chamber. Langham Literature made a grant towards the publication of this book. I am grateful to these institutions for their grants.

Special thanks to Joel Carpenter for his inspiration and help in bringing out this book and Paul Fields, Theological Librarian at Calvin, for his help with accessing the titles that I wanted to consult. I am indebted to Krysia Lear for her scrupulous editing and polishing the manuscript, Thilagavathy Joseph and Jedidah Joshem for copy editing, and Hema Joshua for proof reading. I thank Jerusha Joshem, a multidisciplinary designer, who designed the book cover and interior.

The families of Chris and Warren and Rosemary provided social and pastoral support during my stay in Bristol. Donna, Nellie, Peter and

Hepzi, Sam, and Mike made my stay comfortable amid snowstorms in Grand Rapids. I am grateful to these friends.

This book project separated me physically and emotionally from my family for the past few years. I am thankful to my wife, Hema, for taking the full load at home and sparing me to focus on writing and the 3Js (Jed, Jeru, and Jem), my daughters, who sacrificed their time with dad. Most importantly, I thank Jesus for his grace.

Preface

"Research can be your hobby if you master research methods," said Dr Sebastian Perriannan in his workshop on social research methodology in 2002 at the University of Madras, Chennai. This statement is contrary to the common perception among students that research is not for everyone but can be done only by top-ranking students, as it is difficult to master research methods. Periannan's idea that research could be a hobby removed my mental blocks against research methods and motivated me to explore in depth the use of social research methods for theology and religious studies. Teaching research methodology became my passion after that.

In his introduction to social research for Christian Studies, Perriannan also led me to realize that people's experiences could be a valid source for sound theological and religious research. Researching lived experiences is common among many disciplines in human sciences and now scholars of religious studies and theology have turned to researching lived religion, lived theology, and lived experience.

Contextual theologies shifted the loci of theological research from the speculative/philosophical to contextual, with a liberative approach. However, contextual theologians assumed the role of patrons of the marginalized and oppressed communities and articulated theologies on their behalf, rather than making them partners in their theological reflection. Their intentions were well meant and their attempt to see text and reality from below is greatly appreciated. However, most contextual theologians have stopped short of achieving their goals of producing relevant theologies that emancipated the communities because they failed to engage the lived realities of the marginalized and oppressed. These scholars needed to bring data from lived realities to their theological reflection.

Researching lived experience shifts the methodological paradigm from rhetoric and speculation to constructivism in theologizing. Researching lived reality makes one enter the complex social world, where reality is perceived differently by different players. Its hermeneutical tools differ. For theologians to enter the social world to study lived realities, they must adopt the expertise of social sciences. Therefore, studying lived experience leads one to adopt an interdisciplinary approach.

An interdisciplinary approach can open ways to innovate ideas for research, because it lets scholars think originally and be creative. Scholars can move beyond their disciplinary order to create something new.

But what is the need for theology to engage other sciences, one might ask, when its focus is the study of God? Theology is not like other disciplines, it has been argued, because it focuses on God, who cannot be the subject of analysis similar to social structure, a subject of analysis in sociology, or kinship in anthropology. Even so, theology necessarily ranges beyond the nature of God's being to ask: what are God's ways and God's will? These questions force theologians to reflect on human experience in order to understand the activity of God or the Spirit. Theology aims at understanding God's activity in relation to human community and the world. Therefore, theology cannot isolate itself but must engage social sciences to study lived theology or lived religion.

In an interdisciplinary approach, theology does not abandon its unique perspectives but incorporates insights from other disciplines to improve its own perspective and offers insights to other disciplinary perspectives. When theology engages social sciences, it retains its position while being open to interacting with the perspectives of social sciences. Theology's primary lens is to understand the social world in relation to God, through Christ. When theology engages social sciences from this position, it guards itself against reductionism, while considering insights from social sciences to have a holistic understanding of the social world in relation to God. Through interdisciplinary approaches, theology can be more intelligible in engaging the world.

Religious studies have turned to researching lived religion by shifting the focus away from defining the universal phenomenon of religion or macro-level questions and looking for universal definitions or normative positions on beliefs and practices. Now scholars of religious studies and social scientists who study religion are interested in exploring how religion is practiced in different cultural contexts. This also paves the way for understanding individuals' experiences and interpretations.

Some theological scholars think that they are not social scientists and hence assume that their field-based study in theology does not require the level of scientific rigor expected in social sciences. But research in every discipline is a scientific endeavor and scientific rigor cannot be compromised in any research.

Field-based studies lacking scientific rigor have little value. Although field-based studies are common in theology and religious studies, the scientific rigor employed in such studies has often been found deficient, as the proficiency of theological scholars in executing social scientific research is a matter of debate. While some field-based studies in theology and religious studies are excellent, many fall short in terms of quality. Let me give you some examples. I was once asked to review a master's thesis on differing views on the doctrine of eschatology. This thesis was a theological study that analyzed various theologians' viewpoints on eschatology. Yet, to my surprise, the methodology chapter was all about qualitative research, with both the student and the supervisor erroneously assuming that an analysis of a theological concept or doctrine equated to a qualitative study. Similarly, I once witnessed a public defense of a PhD dissertation based on a phenomenological study that was filled with statistical analyses. All three examiners questioned the inconsistency between the chosen approach and analysis. These examples underscore the need of providing both students and scholars with clear and reliable information on using social research methods for theology and religious research.

Social Research Methods for Students and Scholars of Theology and Religious Studies results from teaching research methods for more than a decade and supervising and examining a number of dissertations. Teaching research methodology at various institutions has enabled me to understand the minds of students from different cultures.

My students taught me and inspired me to write this book. Keeping the expectations of students from across cultures in mind, I have written this book from the students' point of view so that they could gain the confidence to design and conduct a study using social research methods and acquire the needed research skills. Therefore, this book will demystify designing and executing a research project and make their research journey enjoyable.

For professors, this book will be a reference tool in supervising and examining dissertations/theses that use social research methods. At the end of a workshop on supervising social research methods, one professor commented to me, "if social research involves all these steps, then we have not produced any scientific research until now." Scholars and professors will find this book helpful in maintaining scientific rigor in their research projects and helping their students in producing dissertations/theses with scientific rigor to contribute knowledge beyond the fields of theology and religious studies.

By writing this book, I would like to achieve the following purposes:

1. To help students and scholars of theology and religious studies to engage in research that would be relevant to the faith communities and society at large
2. To facilitate researching "lived religion" or "lived theology" of the people where religion thrives
3. To encourage interdisciplinary research in the fields of theology and religious studies to contribute knowledge across disciplines
4. To introduce scientific rigor in theological and religious studies research

To achieve the above purposes, *Social Research Methods* is intended to be a guide to students and scholars in designing and carrying out theological/religious studies research using social research methods with scientific rigor. The book follows the process of producing sound research from choosing a topic to writing a research report. It discusses the role of professors in supervising and examining dissertations/ theses that use social research methods. I envisage this title being used as a textbook in courses on research methods in the fields of theology, religious studies, and across social sciences dealing with religion.

Chapter 1 provides an overview of research fundamentals and explores the process of selecting a topic for investigation. Chapter 2 is designed to enhance your ability to critically engage with existing literature for your research. In Chapter 3, you will be introduced to various research strategies, including qualitative, quantitative, and mixed methods, and explore different paradigms employed in social research. Chapters 4, 5, and 6 provide guidance on designing qualitative, quantitative, and mixed methods studies, respectively. In Chapter 7, you will learn the art of crafting a compelling research proposal, while Chapter 8 delves into the intricacies of writing a dissertation/thesis or article for publication. Chapter 9 offers practical guidelines on supervising and examining dissertations/theses that use social research methods and provides insight into the roles played by supervisors and examiners in facilitating a successful research journey.

I hope this book will inspire you to adopt "research as a hobby" to make this world a better place!

Joshua Iyadurai

About the Author

Joshua Iyadurai, PhD
is the founder and director of Marina Centre for Interdisciplinary Studies in Religion (MCISR), Chennai. He is a theological educator and social scientist who is passionate about teaching social research methods in hopes of bringing a paradigm shift in theological research to engage people as a source of constructing theology. His ability to generate a passion for social research among students is one hallmark of his lectures. He has been teaching research methods for more than a decade and supervising students using social research methods for their theological research in several institutions that included the University of Roehampton-online, London, University of Madras, Chennai, and South Asia Institute of Advanced Christian Studies (SAIACS), Bangalore. He has been a resource person for research methods seminars that equip seminary students in using social research methods and workshops to equip faculty for supervising students in using social research methods for their dissertations.

He authored *Transformative Religious Experience: A Phenomenological Understanding of Religious Conversion* and has contributed several book chapters and articles on religious conversion.

He is available for leading research methods seminars for students and workshops for faculty to supervise and examine dissertations/theses using social research methods. He can be contacted at https://jiyadurai.com

Chapter 1

CHOOSING A TOPIC

Theology was once considered the queen of sciences but is now largely confined within its domain, with a few exceptions. For centuries, theological research methods have been confined largely to reflection and speculation; a common perception is that theological research stays largely disconnected from the church and the followers of the faith. More recently, theological researchers have found that social research methods make it possible for them to be relevant. They can address real-world problems because the methods enable them to engage people as a source of theological research.

Field-based studies in theology and religious studies have lacked scientific precision. Steve Bruce (2018), Professor of Sociology at the University of Aberdeen, finds quantitative studies dealing with religion, lacking in scientific accuracy. This is also true of the quantitative studies done in theology. Only in the recent past, has some interest been shown to use qualitative research in theology and religious studies; however, this is being challenged by many who are influenced by the positivist paradigm.

Using social research methods also enables theological and religious scholars to readily work across disciplines, a current trend in research, and so pursue interdisciplinary or cross-disciplinary or multidisciplinary approaches to solve problems. Social research methods can provide bridges for theology and religious studies to interact with other disciplines.

The goal of education is passing on knowledge and the goal of research is advancing knowledge. Advancing knowledge is a scientific process that requires scientific rigor; scientific rigor in research requires researchers to know the basics of research and the research process. Students and scholars from the fields of theology and religious studies cannot compromise on scientific rigor. This chapter will help you with the basics of research and the steps involved in choosing a topic.

Research

The term research could mean different things to different people: People use Google to search for information, companies conduct market survey to launch a product, organizations do research to solve a problem, journalists do research to report to the public, and so on. But academic research is a scientific process to produce knowledge. Before we continue, let us be clear about what research is not.

- Research is not collecting information on a topic.
- Research is not finding information that is hard to find.
- Research is not logically compiling information on a topic by referencing the sources.
- Research is not covering all aspects of a topic and writing a book on it.
- Research is not solving a practical problem.

Research may include some of these steps, but research is much more (Booth et al. 2016; Leedy and Ormrod 2015). Therefore, it is critical to understand what research is.

Research is an investigation designed to solve a problem, or to discover something that is not known in a field of study by answering a question or a set of questions. The steps in a criminal investigation have some helpful parallels to the steps in academic research. An officer investigating a murder would collect and analyze evidence from various sources to solve the mystery. She would try to find answers to the following questions:

- Who was the victim?
- Who committed the murder?
- When was the crime committed?
- How was the crime committed?
- What was the motive for the crime?
- How does the murder compare to other murders in the area?

To collect evidence, she would visit the crime scene, interview eyewitnesses and anyone else connected to the crime, have crime technicians gather items and other forms of evidence from the crime scene, and take photographs of it. The investigator would examine databases and social media for relevant information. She would then examine the autopsy report, the forensic report, and the evidence. Then she would analyze the data seeking to answer the questions and assemble the facts that let her solve the mystery. Finally, she would write a report so the case could be argued in a court of law.

Similarly, a researcher investigates a particular issue in a field of study to find a solution or answers, but this time, to a conceptual problem or to questions, which have not been explored. A researcher often undertakes a study because they have begun to wonder about an issue or a phenomenon and were unable to find satisfactory answers in the existing literature. To resolve the mystery of the unknown, the researcher asks a question or a set of questions about the unknown and collects data and analyses them to answer the questions.

Denise F. Polit and Cheryl T. Beck, in *Essentials of Nursing Research*, (2010, 4), define research as a "systematic inquiry that uses disciplined methods to answer questions and solve problems. The ultimate goal of the research is to develop, refine, and expand a body of knowledge." This definition of research is common to all disciplines.

"Systematic inquiry" in the above definition means scientific study, the use of methodical steps and procedures to collect credible data and analyze it. Scientific inquiry is objective; in other words, is free of personal biases. However, no research is free from subjectivity because "subjectivity is an integral part of your way of thinking that is 'conditioned' by your educational background, discipline, philosophy, experience and skills." Contrarily, bias is a "deliberate attempt to either conceal or highlight something" (Ranjit Kumar 2011, 5-7). Scientific inquiry requires researchers to guard against bias at every stage of the research process to maintain objectivity.

Researchers must use the procedures that are accepted as methods in their field of study. Researchers in natural sciences follow experimental methods accepted in their disciplines. Biblical scholars adopt suitable approaches that are accepted in biblical studies to examine a text. Similarly, when you use social science methods for theological or religious studies, you are bound by the approaches and methods that are used in social sciences to maintain scientific rigor. For interdisciplinary research, you can creatively combine methods from other disciplines.

The goal of academic research is to produce knowledge. Your research may develop or refine or expand the current knowledge in your field of study, as stated in the above definition. In addition, research may lead to a better understanding of the practices and advancement of knowledge in a profession (Kumar 2011). Denise F. Polit and Cheryl T. Beck (2018, 33) revised their definition: "The ultimate goal of formal research is to gain knowledge that would be *useful for many people*" [emphasis added]. Now researchers are also interested in the application of new knowledge in their academic pursuit.

New knowledge offers new ways of understanding a practical problem. Therefore, research solves "a conceptual problem not by doing something to change the world but by answering a question that helps us understand it better" (Booth, Colomb, and Williams 2008, 53). In turn, researchers or practitioners could apply the new knowledge to resolve a practical problem.

Therefore, research is an investigation that deploys scientific methods for collecting credible data and analyzing them to answer questions and solve conceptual problems by producing new knowledge. The new knowledge could be new insights or modified or refined forms of the current knowledge presented in the literature, to enhance human life.

Social Research

In theological circle, "empirical research" is a term commonly used to refer to social research or field-based research. Theoretically, "empirical research" refers to quantitative research because of its philosophical foundation on empiricism. However, "social research" is a broader term that embraces quantitative, qualitative, and mixed methods research strategies.

Social research studies people and their world and produces new knowledge concerning the social world by adopting approaches and methods that are accepted in the social sciences. Social research is a scientific investigation that collects and analyzes data from the field to answer questions with evidence. This method is valuable for scholars of theological and religious studies because it lends itself to producing knowledge that may be applied to make life better.

However, social research may be undermined by theological scholars because theological research has generally been confined to analyzing theological concepts rhetorically or philosophically or reflectively.

Theology is preoccupied with defining abstract theological concepts accurately. A story about the irrelevance of theological research to lay people was attributed to Tony De Mello, a Catholic spiritual trainer. The story goes like this. There was an emergency in an aircraft and the pilot asked everyone to pick up a parachute and jump as the plane was about to crash. Everyone jumped. One man landed on a tree. He felt relieved that he was alive and had landed safely. But he did not know where he was. He called out to a passerby. The man stopped and looked up to see where the voice was coming from. The man on the tree asked, "Could you please tell me where I have landed?" The passerby replied, "You have landed on top of a tree." Immediately the man on the tree asked, "Are you a theologian?" The passerby wondered how a stranger could have recognized him to be a theologian. So, he asked, "Yes! I am a theologian. But how did you, a foreigner, recognize me?" The man on the tree answered him, "You gave me an accurate answer but not a useful one." This story reflects the condition of theological research, which is preoccupied with offering definitions of theological terms and doctrines. But many times, they are not relevant to the real life of people.

Modernity had enthroned reason as the only arbiter of knowledge, and it was largely guided by positivism and empiricism. The emergence of postmodernism opened the way for scholars to consider lived experience, art, and intuition as the sources of knowledge for which social research methods provide the needed approaches and techniques. Thus, theological/religious studies incorporating social research can contribute knowledge to fill in gaps in knowledge and solve real-world problems.

Because people practice religion in social contexts, theologians and religious studies scholars are called to research them in their social world to understand religion. When we research the social world, we interact with social sciences to conceptualize the topic. Therefore, the current trend in theological research is studying real-life issues and human problems to understand them and offer theological perspectives.

Still, social research is not new to the field of theology. As early as 1933, J. Waskom Pickett (1933) did a study on the conversion movements in India by using social research methods and published his book, *Christian Mass Movements in India*. Social research enables theological scholars to address issues related to the context and examine them to enlighten the academia and public with a better understanding and improve human life. A discussion for the need to engage social research for theology and religious studies is beyond the scope of this chapter.

Research in theology and religious studies cannot continue to be done as pure research aiming only to produce knowledge for the sake of knowledge. Rather, it must aim at producing new knowledge that could be applied to improve the services offered to the faithful and enhance the religious beliefs and practices of a religion. A field-based study enables scholars to produce this type of knowledge because it allows the researcher to learn from the participants of the study in their natural environment. Field-based research involves collecting and analyzing numerical or narrative data from the field. Field-based research, if used in theology and religious studies, will lead to a better understanding of the world of the followers of a religion, cater to their needs effectively, and make the world a better place. For example, a pastoral theology student could do social research to understand the effects of alcoholism in a family by interviewing the spouse and children who are affected. This may allow the student to come up with deeper insights when designing a model to provide pastoral care to such families. Such a model would be relevant to the cultural context because it was developed based on the lived experience of the families.

In academic research, the end result—producing knowledge that could be applied to enhance human life—depends on the quality of the researcher's starting point. It depends on the quality of the research topic.

Starting with Research Interest

In order to sustain your motivation through to the end of the research, your research topic must emerge out of your interests (Kumar 2011). Before you start any research, you may already know what area of interest you want to explore. If you have multiple areas of interest, you will want to assess in consultation with the literature, which one is most likely to let you find a suitable topic. You may identify your interest in a practical problem from a social/cultural context. Your research interest might relate to your church, institution, ministry context or workplace, socio-cultural or political context, personal experience, course work, or the literature.

Once you identify your interest, locate it in a broad field of study or subject area and then choose an area of the subject and identify a topic. Then do a preliminary search to determine the viability of pursuing your research interest further. Identify the key terms associated with your topic and search in Google Scholar and online encyclopedias to get an overview of what research has been done on your topic. Explore your topic for intellectual controversies, relevancy to your context, and viability. Search journals, conference papers, and reviews of the latest books to ascertain trends in researching your interest.

Narrowing Down Research Interest

If you have a broad topic, it may not be viable, so you will need to narrow it down to help you determine the direction of the topic and identify the focal point of your research. Funneling exercises are useful for helping narrow your research interest. The first level of funneling is identifying the general area of your interest and the second level deals with the particular interest related to the general interest. The third level brings out the specific aspect of the particular interest. The fourth narrows the topic to the essential aspect to be focused on in the study, while the fifth locates the precise aspect of the study. With this information, you can create a title that captures all levels of the funnel to indicate the focal point of your research topic. See examples in the figure.

In addition to using the funneling exercise, you can ask several questions to further focus your topic. This will help you identify subareas associated with your topic, so you can choose specific aspects for your investigation. The following questions could help you:

- What would I like to know about this topic?
- What are some controversies about this issue in my social/cultural/political context?
- What aspects of the literature are fascinating to me?
- What aspects of the literature are unimpressive to me?
- What would scholars want to know about this topic?
- What would religious leaders/priests/missionaries/preachers/anyone involved in religious activities want to know about this topic?
- What do I not yet know about this topic?
- How can I extend my knowledge on this topic?

The answers will also help you think through your research topic from different angles and gain more clarity in formulating your research questions. Once you are clear about the focus and the aspects to be covered in your research, you can formulate research questions.

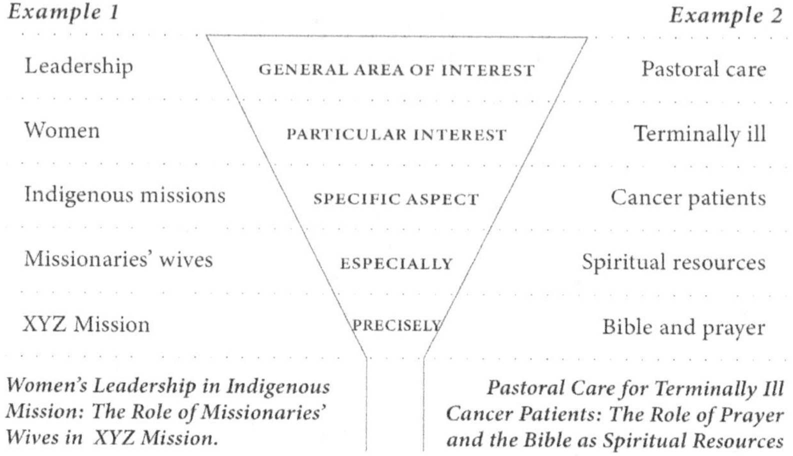

Figure: Funneling Exercise for Narrowing Topics

Formulating Research Questions

Research questions are conceptual or abstract questions that a research project intends to answer and are generally formulated based on the literature. As a first step, you raise a question on the topic of your interest. A good research question with a single focus will help you to collect appropriate data for answering the question and solve a problem (Booth, Colomb, and Williams 2008). If you start your research without a research question, you may end up finding many answers without knowing what the question is.

A research question is a question that is researchable, precise, and able to produce theoretical knowledge (Alvesson and Sandberg 2013). A precise research question defines the focal point of the study and avoids ambiguity. A research question that is formulated from literature can produce new knowledge in the context of the existing knowledge. It is advisable to develop one primary or central question and four or five sub-questions. A research question cannot be answered with a yes or no and it should set a stage for investigation.

The research question determines the path and the destination of your research. Research questions will guide you in searching the literature, choosing a research design, determining the kinds of data required, identifying participants for your study, analyzing the data, and writing up your findings and results (Bryman 2016). In addition, research questions will keep you focused. Without a research question, you will collect a range of data related to your topic and will find it difficult to reach a conclusion (Bryman 2016). Research questions determine the questions you will ask your research participants in interviews or surveys; their answers, in turn will help you answer your research question (Smith, Flowers, and Larkin 2009). Thus, research questions are crucial for the successful completion of your research project. In addition, they help readers understand the essence of your research.

There is no one way to develop a question on a topic. You are free to raise a question in your own way, either drawn from the literature or context, but it must mirror the focus of your study. You might turn the title developed from the funneling exercise into a primary/main question. Based on the chosen research strategy, you may need one primary research question with several sub questions or several main questions.

The sub-questions relate to the different aspects or areas to be covered in your study. To develop them, first identify the sub-areas and aspects from the literature that you want to investigate and formulate sub-questions related to the primary question. Do not try to cover all aspects of the topic but choose only three or four and base the sub-questions on your interest or theory. You could also break the primary question into sub-questions that guide your study of various sub-areas such as perspectives, concepts, and groups of people. At the end of the research, the answers to the sub-questions, taken together, will answer the primary question (Punch 2016). Box 1 presents examples of research questions.

Developing your primary research question and sub-questions is not a linear but a cyclical process. Because the literature plays a key role in formulating the questions, as you read, you may prefer to shift your focal point or cover the aspects that you had not thought of earlier. In that case, you may need to modify the title, primary questions, and sub-questions accordingly.

You can be creative in formulating your research questions. You can challenge the assumptions of the existing studies to generate alternative explanations. You can compare different theoretical assumptions and identify the inconsistencies among them through the lens of your preferred position. Such inconsistencies might provide a lead to formulating research questions that might generate interesting theories (Alvesson and Sandberg 2013). This approach is relevant for interdisciplinary theological/religious research, where researchers critically engage literature from social sciences and come across inconsistencies from a

Box 1: Examples of Research Questions

Example1

Women's Leadership in Indigenous Mission: The Role of Missionaries Wives in XYZ Mission

The primary research question could be one of the following:
- What is the role of missionaries' wives in indigenous missions?
- How do missionaries' wives contribute to indigenous mission leadership?
- What is the role of women in indigenous missions?

The sub-questions could be:
- How do missionaries' wives perceive indigenous missions?
- How do they perceive their role as missionaries' wives?
- How do they perceive their role as a homemaker?
- How do they get involved in indigenous missions?
- What is the leadership structure created by indigenous mission agencies for missionaries' wives to involve in the mission?
- How are missionaries' wives being perceived by the indigenous people?

Example 2:

Pastoral Care for Terminally Ill Cancer Patients: The Role of Prayer and the Bible as Spiritual Resources.

The primary research question could be one of the following:
- What is the role of prayer and the Bible as spiritual resources for terminally ill cancer patients?
- How do prayer and the Bible help terminally ill cancer patients?
- How do terminally ill cancer patients find prayer and the Bible as spiritual resources?

For this topic, we could have the following sub-questions:
- How do terminally ill cancer patients perceive their condition?
- How do they make sense of their faith in this condition?
- How do they use the Bible while facing the eventuality of death?
- How and what do they pray?
- How could a pastoral care model be developed by incorporating the Bible and prayer as spiritual resources for terminally ill cancer patients?

All the sub-questions in these two examples directly relate to the primary questions.

theological or religious perspective. It can also work in reverse, where inconsistencies are found among theological/religious assumptions from social scientific perspectives. Such approaches may open a new direction for generating interesting theories/theologies based on alternative assumptions.

It is not always necessary to base your research questions on the literature; you can base them on observation or intuition (Vanderstoep and Johnston 2009), your experience, concerns, context, and so on. If you find aspects that apply to your cultural context but are not found in the literature, you may formulate suitable research questions to examine in your research. "Producing new and good research questions means that there are no predefined answers available; new questions offer starting points for new answers" (Alvesson and Sandberg 2013, 63). By engaging social sciences, theological research has ample avenues to raise new questions, break new ground, set new directions, and find new theories or answers.

See Chapter 7 for formulating research questions for qualitative, quantitative, and mixed methods research.

Hypothesis

A hypothesis is a prediction of the relationship between variables. A variable is a measurable attribute or characteristic of an individual or object or a phenomenon. Quantitative research uses a hypothesis to test a theory or to generalize the results to the population. Experimental studies, which measure variables and compare the results between two groups, begin with hypotheses. However, survey research and qualitative research, which are the more commonly used methods in the fields of theology and religious studies do not require the use of hypotheses.

To test a hypothesis, you need to create a research or alternative hypothesis that predicts that a relationship exists between the variables and a null hypothesis that claims that there is no statistically significant relationship between the variables. The research/alternative hypothesis is the one that you aim to support in your research. The null hypothesis is denoted as H_0 and we denote the alternative hypothesis as H_1. The alternative hypothesis is assumed to be false until the null hypothesis is rejected. See Chapter 5 for more on hypothesis testing.

Qualitative research does not start with a hypothesis but rather ends with generating several hypotheses. In the fields of theology and religious studies survey research and qualitative research are common, which do not require hypotheses.

Defining a Research Problem

Once you have formulated the research questions, you will need to define a research problem, a statement that identifies the gaps in the literature and justifies the need for your study. Without defining the research problem, you may come up with several solutions, without knowing what the problem is. In such instances, researchers end up with a data dump and struggle to conclude (Booth et al. 2016).

As noted, your research does not solve a practical problem or resolve an issue in the real world, because a practical problem is not a research problem. If you have identified a practical problem you want to address, you must conceptualize it by critically engaging the literature.

A research problem is a conceptual statement based on the literature about the issue under investigation, such as missing or inadequate information on a topic. Ronald Jacobs (2011, 127) defines research problems as "artificial entities that come together only through the intense efforts of the researcher, who has identified a gap in information or understanding within a topic." A research problem is a statement about a concern related to the gaps in the literature.

As you engage with the literature keep in mind that various types of gaps exist. Anthony Miles (2017, 2) identifies seven gaps. I have relied on Miles' taxonomy of research gaps to offer the following classification.

Knowledge Gap

The absence of information about a phenomenon or a particular aspect of a topic or deficient information in the literature. This occurs because either no studies have been done or the number done was insufficient to explain a problem. You may have a hunch about a problem from your experience and find that no study offers the expected explanation.

Disciplinary Gap

The absence of holistic understanding of a problem because of the absence of studies from a particular disciplinary perspective. With the growing interest among scholars to provide a holistic understanding of a phenomenon, identifying disciplinary gaps is vital. Unlike social sciences, which examine real-world problems, few studies in theology or religious studies examine real-world problems. Therefore, you are likely to find a disciplinary gap from the perspective of theology or religious studies for many real-world problems.

Theoretical Gap

A lack of theories explaining a phenomenon or conflicting explanations about a phenomenon that arc offered by various theories. A discrepancy among the theories provides a gap to examine the "explanatory power of one theory over the other" (Jacobs 2011, 133). A theoretical gap is found when a theory fails to explain a current phenomenon or is not pertinent for addressing a particular aspect of the phenomenon. For example, social influence theory explains religious conversion as a social process in a group context minus spiritual dimension, but it failed to explain conversion in isolation where the convert does not join any group (Iyadurai 2015).

Relationship Gap

A lack of research about relationship among certain variables in existing studies. This may occur because the studies have not identified certain variables or had considered them insignificant. But you may want to consider them significant enough to be worth investigating by establishing a relationship gap in the literature.

Methodological Gap

The absence of a philosophical worldview in examining a problem. A methodology is based on a philosophical assumption or worldview that guides research. In other words, a methodology is an approach or paradigm or perspective, or lens adopted by researchers in researching a problem. The philosophical worldview includes broad approaches such as a) deductive or inductive reasoning; b) the four paradigms of social research (postpositivist, constructivist, transformative, and pragmatic); and c) other theoretical approaches like feminism or indigenous. You can look for worldview gaps among the current studies and then investigate the issue using a different lens.

Analytical Gap

A lack of sufficient analysis of a problem because not enough methods were used. When studies have used only one type of analysis, for example, quantitative (statistical) or qualitative (thematic), then an analytical gap exists and usually results in an insufficient understanding of the problem. A different method of analysis could yield a better understanding of a problem.

Sampling Gap

A lack of diverse sampling, which occurs when studies have used similar samples but not with different people or different kinds of data. When a theory is tested or extended by adopting the same type of samples, it may not offer any breakthroughs or establish the relevance of the theory to a different set of people. A study using a different kind of sample could show whether a theory is relevant for a different sample, which could yield new insights into understanding a phenomenon or pave a new direction for future research.

Contextual Gap

The lack of diverse enough findings, which occurs when the research sites of studies are narrow. To find possible contextual gaps, search the literature to see whether the studies were largely conducted in North America or Europe or Asia or Africa. With the postmodern turn in research, contextual factors became key elements in generating knowledge. Now theories based on the Western context are being challenged from postmodern perspectives such as indigenous, transformative, pragmatic, feminist, postcolonial viewpoints, and so on. Designing a study to take contextual factors into consideration could result in new ways of understanding a problem.

Theory-Praxis Gap

A difference between the claims of theories and the actual practice in real life. A theory, for example, may say pastors as counselors should not offer prescriptive suggestions to members. However, in practice, in the non-Western world, people look up to pastors as an authority to tell them what to do. You can look for such inconsistencies between the claims of a theory and practices in real-world.

By critically engaging the literature you can identify any one or more of the gaps mentioned above. You might identify these kinds of gaps by reflecting on your experience or observation in view of the literature. The greater the number of gaps you identify, the greater the significance of your research is likely to be.

Research problem for professional doctoral research is a real-world problem in ministry practice. Therefore, you describe the problem or issue in ministry with details of contextual factors to offer clarity on what your research is about. Also, you must present the theory/theology/ explanation that you plan to apply in your research to solve this problem by referring to the literature.

Developing a Title

A title guides the researcher in advancing to the intended destination. The research title is an "orienting device" (Creswell and Creswell 2018, 63) for the reader and the researcher. In the early stages, you may want to adopt a working title to help you and others understand the focal point of the study. You may modify the title as you progress in reviewing the literature.

Formulate a title that indicates one or more of the following:
- A specific focus of research
- Relationship among variables
- Significance
- Methodological approach
- Location of the study

Use keywords in the main title and the subtitle should expand the main idea to identify a specific aspect of the study.

A title should not be too broad or too narrow. You must have a valid reason for every word that appears in your title. Your title must be precise and clear. Avoid starting a title with phrases like: "A study of," "A critical study," "An Examination of," "An Analysis of," and so on. Avoid redundant words and use only the keywords (Creswell and Creswell 2018).

Considering the Feasibility of a Study

Assessing the feasibility of your intended research involves foreseeing the hurdles you may encounter at different stages in the process. If you cannot resolve an obstacle at a later stage, it will be difficult for you to change the topic. Therefore, you must be very clear about the viability of your proposed study in its early stages. To assess the feasibility of your research topic, ask the following questions:
- Can I find the necessary literature?
- Will I have access to the data?

- Are there any ethical/moral issues that would hinder data collection?
- Do I have the needed skills? If not, will I be able to acquire them to execute the research successfully?
- Is it possible to complete the research within the available period?
- Do I have the financial resources to complete the research?
- Will the topic remain "alive" over the period of research and beyond?

If you can answer these questions satisfactorily, you will reduce the risk of facing hurdles in executing your research.

Research Ethics

Research ethics are the principles that govern how researchers treat participants, the data, and the works of others. The fundamental principle in research ethics is honesty. Ethics in social research is about the relationship between the researcher and the participants when engaging with people as the primary source of collecting data. Research ethics are concerned with how participants are treated, and how the data are managed to avoid causing any harm to people. While your research may not harm participants physically, it might embarrass them because of the disclosures of their private life or disturb them emotionally or violate their privacy (Booth et al. 2016). Observing the principles of research ethics will help you avoid any potential risk for participants.

Principles of Research Ethics

The basic principles of research ethics are:

1. The researcher must inform the potential participants about the purpose and nature of the research in non-specialist's language to obtain informed consent. "Informed consent means that participants have adequate information about the study, comprehend the information, and have the power of free choice, enabling them to consent to or decline participation voluntarily" (Polit and Beck 2018, 139).
2. Participants must be given the right to withdraw from the research at any time.
3. Participants must be given the right to decline to answer any question.

4. Steps must be taken to avoid intrusion into participants' privacy by not collecting sensitive information that is beyond the scope of the research.
5. All deceptive practices used to obtain data are unacceptable.
6. Anonymity and confidentiality must be protected.
7. Participants must not be exposed to any risk or harm due to the research.
8. Extra care and protection to be taken to avoid harming vulnerable participants.

Ethical Parameters for Collecting Data

For collecting data through a survey or interviews or observation, the following parameters are to be followed:

- Obtaining informed consent from adults participating in research.
- Obtaining permission from a responsible person to have vulnerable persons participate in your research. Vulnerable persons include children or terminally/seriously ill patients or victims of substance abuse or survivors of other forms of abuse.
- Considering your subordinates or your students or anyone under your supervision as potentially vulnerable persons. The possibility of being coerced into participating in your research is high. Therefore, take special care to include them in your research without using any form of coercion.
- Obtaining prior permission from authorities or gatekeepers to conduct a study in an institution/church/community.
- Not sharing recordings of raw data with anyone else.
- Protecting identifiable information.
- Storing research project data safely and securely for a minimum of 5 years.
- Not disrupting participants' activities while doing participant observation.
- Respecting the cultural beliefs and practices of the community or institution or church while collecting data.
- Omitting names from field notes.
- Obtaining ethical approval for doing covert research. Such research is permitted to understand a problem, which is otherwise not possible to study.

For using existing data, the following parameters apply:

- You may use documents, reports, statistics, and so on that are available in the public domain or provided by government and institutions with open access.
- You must obtain written permission from appropriate authorities to access and use data that are protected by an authority.
- You must maintain confidentiality and proprietary requirements set by the authority.

Many institutions have an ethics committee to approve the research proposals of students. The purpose is to ensure that your research causes no harm to research participants and to protect the institution. It also prevents you from researching without addressing ethical issues that may damage the value of your research and your reputation.

In cases where an institution does not have a separate ethics committee, your doctoral committee or department faculty may function as the authority to give ethical approval for research projects. You must know the requirements set by your institution and meet them to get its approval. Ethical approval is a must before proceeding to execute your research project.

In addition to the above, as with all research and writing, research ethics requires you to avoid plagiarism, which is a breach of academic integrity.

Chapter Summary

This chapter defined, research as systematically searching for credible data and analyzing them to solve conceptual problems by answering research questions, and introduced you to social research that studies people and their world. Social research adopts approaches and methods that are accepted in social sciences to produce new knowledge concerning the social world to make life better.

You have learned the basic steps in choosing a topic that involves narrowing your research interest to a specific topic by using the funneling exercise, formulating research questions and hypotheses, defining a research problem, developing a research title, and assessing the feasibility of your research. In addition, this chapter introduced you to the importance of research ethics, ethical principles, and ethical parameters for collecting data.

Review Questions

1. What is research?
2. What is social research?
3. How do I start with my research interest?
4. How do I narrow down the interest to a topic?
5. How do I formulate research questions?
6. What is a hypothesis?
7. What is a research problem?
8. How do I develop a title for my research?
9. How do I determine the feasibility of my research?
10. What are the ethical concerns in social research?

Further Help

Booth, Wayne C., Gregory G. Colomb, Joseph M. Williams, Joseph Bizup, and William T. FitzGerald. 2016. *The Craft of Research*. 4th ed. Chicago: University of Chicago Press.

Kumar, Ranjit. 2011. *Research Methodology: A Step-by-Step Guide for Beginners*. 3rd ed. London: Sage.

Polit, Denise F., and Cheryl Tatano Beck. 2018. *Essentials of Nursing Research: Appraising Evidence for Nursing Practice*. 9th ed. Philadelphia: Wolters Kluwer.

Chapter 2

REVIEWING THE LITERATURE

Academic research aims to produce or advance knowledge, which requires researchers to review, analyze, and synthesize the existing literature on the topic being studied to assess the current knowledge. This process is the key factor in differentiating academic research from other research projects. As a researcher, you build your arguments on evidence from research-based publications or from field work. In social research, information from field work is the primary source while scholarly literature is the secondary source. Literature plays a vital role in writing your research proposal and dissertation/thesis or scholarly article or monograph.

Literature in Academic Research

A literature review serves various purposes for writing a thesis or dissertation or a scholarly article or monograph. In academic research, the term "literature" refers to research-based scholarly publications such as journal articles and monographs. As a researcher, you build your arguments on research-based publications because they go through a rigorous process to ensure they provide credible evidence from the field or from literature to support the claim being made. Specialists peer review and vet the articles before they are accepted for publication in a journal. Scholars and students of a discipline are the audience for journals and research-based books; contrarily, periodicals and popular books publish material to enlighten and entertain the public.

The literature plays a vital role at every stage of the research process and sets the stage for you to present your contributions in a dissertation/thesis. In your research proposal, the literature provides the background for your study by indicating the current trends in the area. You will define research questions or hypotheses and research problems based on the literature. The methodology section relies on the specialized literature on social research methods.

In your dissertation/thesis, the introduction chapter presents the background, research question or hypothesis, and research problem, which are based on literature. The literature review chapter locates your study against the bigger picture of the current state of knowledge. As with the research proposal, you will write the methodology chapter drawing on specialized literature on social research methods. In the discussion chapter you will interpret the findings or results of your study in light of the literature.

Definition of Literature Review

A literature review gives an overview of your topic, surveys the current knowledge to locate your research, and justifies the need for your study. Researchers do two types of literature reviews: systematic literature reviews and narrative literature reviews. Established scholars do a systematic literature review as stand-alone projects to find solutions through rigorous analysis and synthesis of many studies. This is not done as the background for a research project. But a narrative literature review is a discussion of related studies on the topic that is done as a background for a research project. It is "an examination of theory and research relating to your field of interest that outlines what is already known and that frames and justifies your research question(s)" (Bryman 2016, 91). You will do a narrative literature review for your project based on social research.

Before discussing what a literature review is, let us be clear about what a literature review is not. A literature review is not a series of brief descriptions of each study on a topic: this is known as an annotated bibliography. It is not a collection of studies that support your point of view (Efron and Ravid 2019) or a compilation of all studies related to the topic.

A literature review does identify relevant theories, models, concepts, and themes from the literature and engage them critically to set the stage for research. By reviewing the literature "you identify the theories and previous research which have influenced your choice of the research topic and the methodology you are choosing to adopt" (Ridley 2012, 3). A literature review for Sara Efrat Efron and Ruth Ravid (2019, 2) is "a systematic examination of the scholarly literature about one's topic. It critically analyzes, evaluates, and synthesizes research findings, theories, and practices by scholars and researchers that are related to an area of focus." A literature review, according to Helen Aveyard (2014, 2), is "the comprehensive study and interpretation of literature that relates to a particular topic." The essence of a literature review is "to synthesise sources into a coherent, integrated whole: a meaningful picture that gives the reader a broad and deep understanding of the issues that dominate the topic. It should reveal where the picture is unclear, where parts are missing and where there are gaps that need to be filled" (Greetham 2021, 123). Thus, the literature you assess, and the literature review you write are vital to show the contribution of your study.

Purposes of Literature Review

The main purpose of your literature review is to help you understand what research has been done on your topic, what needs to be done, how to extend the work of others, and how future research could answer the unanswered questions (Ridley 2012). It provides a historical background and a contemporary setting for your research because the review discusses current debates, questions, and controversies. It will also help you avoid repeating the work done by others. It helps you offer a rationale for your study by establishing the gaps in the literature and offers a basis for you to revise or modify or reinterpret or advance the existing knowledge.

One of the purposes of doing a literature review is to conceptualize your research topic. Your research interest may be a human or social problem in a religious community or society. Surveying the related studies will help you identify the concepts and theories related to the problem, which you would use for developing a theoretical framework for your research.

A concept is an abstract idea used to understand the world. It is a "representation of an idea in a word or phrase. The use of concepts gives us a means of making sense of the world" (Ridley 2012, 30). For example, Bible reading, prayer, and meditation are tangible acts and can be grouped as religious practices, which is an abstract idea denoting the activities based on a set of religious beliefs. An abstract idea denoting a tangible factor or act is called a concept.

A literature review aids you in defining the key terms. Reviewing the literature helps you understand how different scholars in different studies have defined the concepts related to your topic. Bearing in mind the definitions available in the literature, you define the key concepts to help readers understand the use of a concept in your study.

Concepts are also known as "variables" or "constructs" and are the building blocks of a theory, which explains how concepts are related and affect one another. A theory is an "explanation of why variables work together, how they are related to each other, and especially how they influence each other" based on research (Galvan and Galvan 2017, 6). Identifying various concepts and theories related to your topic by reviewing the literature helps you conceptualize the human or social problem that you propose to investigate. Unless you consider your topic at the conceptual level, you will not be thinking like a researcher. Thus, a review of literature plays a key role during the early stage of your research in conceptualizing your topic and building a theoretical framework.

Conceptualizing your topic shapes your research focus and helps you identify and formulate your research questions. As you progress in reviewing the literature, you may have to redefine the focal point of the study and modify your research questions.

A literature review enables you to understand the strengths and weaknesses of methodologies used in other studies, which will help you design your research. Exposure to several methodological approaches and perspectives helps you choose a suitable approach or a perspective for your research. You gain methodological insights about sample size, kind of samples, types of data, methods of data collection, and analysis from the literature. Reviewing the literature also prevents you from repeating the mistakes made by other scholars in their studies.

In addition, a literature review helps you identify the components of your research topic. After reading several studies, you can narrow down the focus of your investigation by limiting the scope to examine a few aspects or components or variables. No research investigates every aspect of a problem; that is not feasible. You can make an informed choice of the areas or aspects to investigate in your research.

At a later stage of your research, the literature review helps you interpret the findings of your research. By comparing your findings with the results of related studies, you establish the originality of your contribution to knowledge on a topic. The literature review is the context in which you present the significant contribution of your research. The advancement of knowledge by your research is established in the context of the existing knowledge.

Steps in Reviewing Literature

The process of reviewing literature includes the following steps: searching the literature, using SQ4R methods for reading, analyzing the literature, taking notes for research, and synthesizing the literature. This section discusses these steps and shows you how each step is guided by your research focus.

Searching the Literature

The first step you take in reviewing the literature is searching for relevant literature. When you have identified your topic based on your research interest, break the topic into several key terms or phrases for a literature search.

The goal of the initial search is to build your working bibliography. To begin with, it is worth searching tertiary sources such as encyclopedias, subject dictionaries, handbooks, and textbooks for summaries and reviews of the secondary sources. This will provide you with the names of key authors and texts. Make a list of them to be consulted later.

Search key terms and phrases of your topic on the internet, your library, and online databases to build your working bibliography. A comprehensive search for theological research includes field-based theological studies, theological and biblical perspectives of the topic, and studies from social sciences. In your search, look for closely related studies, remotely related studies, classical studies, and current studies.

While the internet makes research much easier than it once was, it is not easy to identify credible sources on the internet. You must sift through the junk of entries in a Google search to identify scholarly sources because Google searches throws up both scholarly and popular sources. Google Scholar (https://scholar.google.com/) is much more useful because it restricts the search results to scholarly books and articles. WorldCat (https://www.worldcat.org/) is another good source to find books and articles and it also lists the libraries where an item is available. Look at authors' website or those of their institution for lists of their publications.

To identify more sources, you can also search your institution's library and online databases such as ATLA, JSTOR, EBSCO, and ProQuest with key phrases. Many institutions give their students access to these subscription-based online databases.

Begin your literature search by identifying closely related studies and then look at loosely related studies. It is not possible to include all the related studies in an extensively researched area. Therefore, try to include only the studies directly related to your topic. For example, religious conversion is an extensively researched area. If the focus of your investigation is the psychology of religious conversion, you do not have to include studies from disciplines such as sociology, anthropology, and missiology. You can confine your search for studies to religious conversion and psychology. But for a less researched area, search widely to find any studies remotely related to your research topic. In theological research, for example, you may not find many field-based studies related to your topic. Therefore, search for related studies from social sciences.

A literature search involves identifying appropriate studies for your literature review. These include classical or landmark studies, studies by authoritative scholars, and current studies. Your literature review must be balanced with comprehensiveness and relevance.

A comprehensive review of the literature for theological research includes theological and biblical perspectives of your topic, field-based theological studies, and studies from social sciences. Although current theological research is interested in field-based studies, you may not find many field-based studies in theology; but you are likely to find many theoretical papers or theological reflections produced by theologians. Therefore, in addition to them, your literature search must include studies from social sciences.

Evaluating the quality of the sources includes assessing the credentials of the author and the publication. Many reputed journals publish in print as well as online and many open-source journals are published only online; besides, they are usually credible. You can include an article published in a reputed peer-reviewed journal without hesitation.

However, you want to be more cautious with other material. With bourgeoning number of new journals, some journals that claim to be peer-reviewed are of dubious credibility. With new journals, look at the editorial board for authoritative scholars and consider the credentials of the authors who have published in those journals, and read the peer review policy to determine the credibility of the publication.

For books, assess the credentials of the author and the scholars who gave the blurbs for the back cover. Sometimes, the author may be an emerging scholar and the credentials of the endorser may speak for the scholarly contribution of the author. You may come across several eBooks; look at the credentials of the author and decide if you should use them. Check dissertations or theses on the websites of reputable institutions for those worth considering.

The blogs and websites of scholars that summarize studies for the public can point to their scholarly publications. You can note their publications and access them in your library or on the internet. If you are citing a blog or webpage of a scholar, it carries only the value of a scholarly opinion, which may enlighten you, but they do not carry any evidential value to support your argument in research writing.

Reputable reference volumes like Encyclopedia Britannica, other subject-specific encyclopedias, and subject dictionaries are other sources of information available on the internet. Scholars contribute articles to these reference volumes, which are summaries of other studies and are not based on direct research. Therefore, you may cite them as background material but not as the basis of your arguments in your dissertation or thesis. Wikipedia is a popular encyclopedia on the internet. But it differs from scholarly encyclopedias because anyone may write or edit articles; therefore, you may consult Wikipedia articles only at an early stage of your research to get an overview of your topic.

Building your working bibliography and reading the literature is a cyclical process, which you will keep doing until you submit your research report. Shortly before the submission, it is good to look for the latest studies related to your topic and to incorporate them into your literature review, to bring your research report up to date.

Reading for Research: the SQ4R Method

Reading for research is not for pleasure or passive reading guided by the author. Your goal is to find material that is relevant to your study, rather than to grasp every detail about the study. The connection between a study and your research could be supportive or unsupportive of your perspective. You must look for how the text would fit into your scheme of argument. Interactive reading makes this possible because it helps you dialogue with the text.

A proven method of interactive reading for comprehension is SQ3R (survey, question, read, recall, review). Francis P. Robinson, (1946) an educational psychologist, developed this method for reading comprehension and it is used widely by college students across the world. For research reading, I have added one more R to make it SQ4R. In this method, the "S" stands for "survey," "Q" stands for "question," "R1" stands for "read," "R2" stands for "recall," "R3" stands for "relate," and "R4" stands for "review." This method of reading helps you actively engage the content instead of passively reading.

S: Survey

Surveying a text is the first step in reading for research. For a book, you read the title, publication date, author's biography, blurbs on the back cover, table of contents, introduction, and conclusion, and look for key terms related to your research in the index. The title and table of contents inform you about the book's relevance to your research. From the author's bio, you learn the credentials of the author and the institutional affiliation and something of the credibility of the study. The blurbs tell you who has endorsed the book and what they regard as valuable about the title. The introduction presents the thesis statement and the main arguments, which are expanded upon in the chapters. The conclusion restates the main claim, the significance, and the limitations of the study. The index reveals how frequently the keywords of your study are found in this book.

To survey a journal article, look at the title, the publication date, the author's biography, the abstract to get an overview of the article, the key terms and the introduction, and conclusion. In addition, read the headings and subheadings under each section to understand the structure of the argument.

Through the survey, you will come to know the main claim and the significance of the study. A survey of a text helps you determine its value, which is about the worth of the study as related to your proposed research, not about its general value. If you cannot find a valuable connection to your research, you can avoid reading the entire text. When you find the text is worth reading, the next step in the SQ4R method is raising questions.

Q: Question

To read interactively, turn the title of the book or article into a question. For a book, turn the chapter headings into questions before reading the chapters. Similarly, turn the subheadings in a chapter or journal article into questions before reading a chapter or section. By doing this, you are tuning your mind to look for answers to the questions. When you read with questions at the back of your mind, your brain actively looks for answers, instead of reading passively. Reading with questions improves your concentration and helps you focus on finding the answers.

R1: Read

The third step is to read selectively. In your reading, you aim to find answers to the questions that you have raised. Reading the introduction and conclusion of a chapter gives you the essence of the chapter and may give you answers to your questions. To get the details of the author's arguments and reasoning, you may read the chapter in-depth.

Read the first and last paragraph of each section in a book chapter or an article. From this, you are likely to understand each section. A topic sentence at the beginning of a paragraph introduces the subject and a concluding sentence at the end of a paragraph restates the topic. Generally, you do not need to read every detail and look at every illustration in a paragraph to understand the discussion. However, if you cannot understand the paragraph by reading the topic sentence, read the explanation and illustrations.

Sometimes, you may quickly identify the answers to the questions, but may not understand the basis for the answer. In this case, you can read in-depth to understand the author's argument and the evidence to support the answer or claim. Read selectively; if you do not understand the key points, read in-depth.

R2: Recall

The fourth step is "recall," some prefer to call this step "recite." After reading a chapter or an article, try to recall the answers that you have found to the questions you raised before reading. This is the stage in which you let your mind process the contents of the reading. Try to recollect the answers, the main arguments, and evidence of the arguments. Also, most important, summarize them in your own words and record them in your reading notes. Paraphrase and summarize the entire study. If you cannot do this, it is a sign that you have not fully comprehended the contents. In that case, repeat the previous step.

R3: Relate

The fifth step in the SQ4R method is "relate." In this step, you look for possible ways of relating the reading to your proposed research and discover how various studies relate to one another.

After reading a book or an article, reflect on the contents to understand how it relates to your study. Reflect on the main claim, key findings, main arguments, methodology, significance, and limitations in the light of your study. When you reflect on the contents, you may learn something new, find the definitions relevant to your research, come across a perspective that aligns with your thinking or contradicts your point of view, and steps and procedures for executing your research. Look at the study from the vantage of your proposed research and look for issues, definitions, background information, philosophical assumptions, theories, methods, significant findings, and statistical information that are relevant to your research (Efron and Ravid 2019). This helps you to design a robust study and avoid pitfalls.

As you read more studies, you can relate them to other studies and will find similarities among some of them. You are looking for how one study advances another one; which studies are closely related; how some studies are similar and how some differ; how a group of studies share a common philosophical assumption or methodological approach, and so on. When you read, identify the authors who support or disagree with your point of view and determine whether the author could be your ally or a challenger. This will help you to group the studies for analysis and synthesis.

R4: Review

The final step in SQ4R is "review." Review is skimming through the headings and questions in your reading notes and recollecting the answers. Review is not reading the reading notes. Review triggers your memory to recall.

If the questions or headings do not trigger a memory, then read your notes for that section and move on to the next heading. This exercise helps your brain to retrace the information stored in your memory. Do this periodically to keep your memory about the studies fresh.

You will read a lot at the early stage of your research, but you may not write your dissertation/thesis after months or years. Therefore, doing a periodic review of your reading notes, weekly and monthly, will help you remember the studies. The next step is analyzing the literature.

Analyzing Literature

The goal of analyzing literature is to evaluate the quality of the study and whether the literature is a suitable resource for your study. As a researcher, you must engage the literature critically; you cannot accept a study at face value and should not assume that everything that is published is quality literature.

Analyzing literature involves getting an overview of an article or a book and identifying the main claim or thesis statement of the study, findings, main arguments, and conclusions. It involves examining the evidence and arguments, looking for logical fallacy in the author's assumptions and arguments, and evaluating whether the conclusions are directly drawn from the evidence or overstated.

Jose L. Galvan and Melisa C. Galvan (2017) suggested several guidelines for analyzing literature, which include the following:

- Make note of the definitions of key terms in a study and how they vary from other authors.
- Note the key statistics presented in the study.
- Assess the strengths and weaknesses of the methodology of the study.
- Carefully differentiate the author's assertions from the findings based on evidence.
- Look for relationships among the studies.
- Identify the major trends and patterns emerging in researching your topic.
- Find gaps in the literature so that you can justify the need for your study.
- Identify whether this is a current or landmark or classic study related to your topic.
- Your analysis should be from the perspective of your research topic and take note of how each study is related to your research.

Deep reading is a way of analyzing literature. Dave Harris (2020) in his book *Literature Review and Research Design* suggests that you analyze whether you could do a similar study; identify the motives for the study and the people who would be interested in this study; assess the kind of literature used and the credentials of the authors cited; examine the researcher's ability to be self-critical, and writing skills. These components will help you interact with the text deeply and avoid passive reading.

Taking Notes

Note-taking for literature review is about capturing how a specific section or aspect of a study is related to your research. Record your analytical comments on how a study relates to your research and other studies. As you read, record the key information from each study. Note-taking begins when you read the first study to review the literature. Now, everyone takes notes electronically. Create a folder on your computer for literature review and store all the documents and sources that you collect for your literature review. Create a separate folder for reading notes to save all of them. As you progress in reviewing the literature, develop a tentative outline for your review. It could be thematic or based on discipline for an interdisciplinary review. Then, within the main folder for reading notes, create sub-folders for each theme or section in your outline and store your notes accordingly.

Reference management software programs have features to organize your notes and link them to the sources. EndNote (https://endnote.com), is a paid program, which many institutions have the institutional license for their students to access; Zotero (https://zotero.org) and Mendeley (https://mendeley.com) are free programs. These programs can store all your sources as a library, which is synched with their cloud server under your account. They can link your reading notes to sources, cite the sources directly into a Word document, and generate a bibliography of the cited sources automatically. They have several options for citation styles. NVIVO (https://www.qsrinternational.com/) is primarily a software program for analyzing qualitative data, which is also good for storing and sorting reading notes. If you are unaccustomed to any of these programs, you will find the tutorial videos on YouTube very useful.

Recording notes takes place for each source during the fourth and fifth steps of the SQ4R method: recalling and relating. Record the notes in a consistent format for ease of comparison in the synthesis stage; you can develop your own method or follow the format given in Table 1. Recording the following aspects will be handy in synthesizing and writing your review:

1. Bibliographic information: Note bibliographic information when you find the study valuable to your research.
2. Thesis statement or the main claim of the study: A thesis statement is the main claim of the study or the purpose or a summary statement of the entire study.
3. Definitions of key terms or concepts: Note the definitions of the key terms and how this is similar or different from other studies.
4. Main findings or results and the main arguments:For an empirical study, note the key findings or results. For a theoretical paper, which is common in theology, make a note of the main arguments.
5. Any new insights or new direction from the study: Identify how this study has advanced the knowledge or broken new ground or set a new direction for researching your topic.

Table 1: Format for Taking Notes

Bibliographic Information Author/s: Year of Publication: Title: For a book—Place and Name of the Publisher: For an article—Journal Name, Issue No, Volume No and Page Numbers of the Article:	
Thesis statement	
Definitions of key terms or concepts	
Key findings or results or main arguments	
New insights or new direction	
Methodology, approaches, and methods	
Strengths of the study	
Weakness or limitations of the study	
Direct quotes to be used (Record with page number/s)	
Statistics or graphs to be used (Record with page number/s)	
Your plans for using this study	
Your analytical comments	

6. Methodology, paradigms, and methods: Note the useful aspects and tips for designing your study. It could be the lens through which you could view your topic or sampling or kinds of data, or methods of data collection and analysis.

7. Strengths of the study: Identify the strengths of the study in terms of the design and execution.

8. Weaknesses/limitations of the study: Identify the limitations or weaknesses of the study in terms of the design and execution.
9. Direct quotes you plan to use: When you want to use a direct quote, record the quote accurately with the page number. Double-check the quote for accuracy.
10. Statistics or graphs that you plan to use: If you find some statistics or graphs or images that could be useful, note them down with the page number.
11. Your plan for using this study: Note the place of this study in your research proposal, literature review, and methodology chapter.
12. Your analytical comments: Write down your analytical comments in the light of your research. Describe how this study is related to your research and other studies. You could easily incorporate the analytical comments while writing the literature review chapter later.

Record the notes in a consistent format for ease of comparison in the synthesis stage; you can develop your own method or follow the format given in Table 1.

As you progress in your reading, develop a tentative outline for your review, a thematic outline covering the major themes related to the topic. The outline can be modified later.

Synthesizing Literature

Synthesizing is the work of bringing the analysis of the individual studies together to create a holistic understanding of current knowledge. When you synthesize, "individual studies or pieces of evidence are somehow combined to produce a coherent whole, in the form of an argument, theory or conclusions" (Pope, Mays, and Popay 2007, 15). You do this to locate the study in the bigger picture and to identify the gaps in the literature.

The process involves arranging your reading notes according to the revised outline in preparation for writing. Efron and Ravid (2019, 178) suggest "grouping the sources, comparing and contrasting the sources, exploring conflicting or contradicting findings, and adopting critical dispositions" for synthesizing literature. Based on the analysis of the individual studies, you identify how the studies relate in dealing with the concepts, perspectives, methods, and findings. Group them to build your argument.

Look for contrasting approaches, methods, and data to identify the differences and similarities among studies. You may create subgroups within a larger group of similar studies or regroup them. When studies contradict or conflict with your perspective or argument, do not exclude them because they may give you new insights. Those studies require further analysis to deal with them in your review. Your literature review cannot be homogenous, where all studies support your point of view. A quality review deals with all perspectives.

When you synthesize literature, you "critique the different sources together when you identify patterns of strengths and weaknesses that are common across these studies" (Efron and Ravid 2019, 183). You discuss the strengths and limitations of the studies so you can articulate your understanding of the body of literature related to your research. As we have seen, the literature review must be a coherent essay based on a critical analysis of the literature.

See Chapter 8 for writing a literature review for a dissertation/thesis.

Chapter Summary

This chapter taught you the role of literature in academic research and the importance of consulting research-based literature. You have understood that a literature review provides the setting for your study, surveys the current knowledge to locate gaps in the literature, and justifies the need for your study. The process of reviewing literature includes the following steps: searching for credible literature, using SQ4R methods for reading, analyzing the literature, taking notes for research, and synthesizing the literature.

You have learned that the SQ4R method involves surveying the text, raising questions on the headings, reading selectively to grasp the essence of the study, recalling the contents, relating the study to your research, and reviewing the reading notes. Analyzing literature, involves critically evaluating the strengths and weaknesses of each study and finding its relevance to your study, while synthesizing literature involves grouping the studies and analyzing them in groups.

Having read this chapter, you have gained the skills to critically engage the literature for your research.

Review Questions

1.   What is the role of literature in academic research?
2.   What is a literature review?
3.   What are the purposes of the literature review?
4.   How is a literature search conducted?
5.   What is the SQ4R method of reading for research?
6.   How do I analyze literature?
7.   How would I take notes for research?
8.   How would I synthesize literature?

Further Help

Efron, Efrat Sara, and Ruth Ravid. 2019. *Writing the Literature Review: A Practical Guide.* New York: Guilford.

Galvan, L. Jose, and Melisa C. Galvan. 2017. *Writing Literature Reviews: A Guide for Students of the Social and Behavioral Sciences.* 7th ed. New York: Routledge.

Ridley, Diana. 2012. *The Literature Review: A Step-by-Step Guide for Students.* 2nd ed. London: Sage.

Chapter 3

RESEARCH STRATEGIES AND PARADIGMS OF SOCIAL RESEARCH

This chapter provides an interdisciplinary perspective on social research and discusses the paradigms that shape research strategies. The three strategies in social research are: qualitative, quantitative, and mixed methods research. The four major paradigms of social research are postpositivist, constructivist, transformative, and pragmatic.

Social Research—Interdisciplinary Perspective

Social research facilitates interdisciplinary scientific investigations that analyze evidence based on different kinds of data collected from people and about people to find answers to questions concerning the social world. Social research is "carefully studying experiences, events, and facts in social reality. . . . It relies on the process and evidence of science as such, and it can differ from casual observation, common sense reasoning, and other ways to evaluate evidence" (Neuman 2014, 8). The primary data for social research comes from the field, and secondary data from the published literature. When doing social research, the researcher collects data from the field. As a result, the researcher can bring some unique and original data to the academic world. When a researcher deploys social research methods, they are venturing into making an original contribution. Thus, it enables theological/religious scholars to engage people and produce knowledge relevant to people and their cultural contexts.

Social research engages theories from the social sciences. Since social research deals with real-life issues and human problems or unresolved questions, it creates a channel of dialogue between scholars of religious studies and social scientists. Social sciences have established scientific methodology and methods to investigate human problems and real-life issues, and theological research deploys them. In this process, the researcher engages social scientific theories to understand a problem from an interdisciplinary perspective to gain a holistic understanding. "The social sciences can offer complementary knowledge that will enhance and sharpen our theological understandings. Similarly, theology will offer perspectives that will challenge and shape the perspectives offered by the social sciences" (Swinton and Mowat 2016, 81). Often, social sciences tend to be reductionistic in explaining a religious phenomenon. However, theological scholars can critique them and offer a holistic understanding by incorporating the religious or spiritual aspects associated with the phenomenon. Social research "transforms our ideas, theories, guesses, or questions" (Neuman 2014, 16) in producing new knowledge. Thus, scholars of theology and religious studies can produce new theologies/theories by incorporating religious dimensions with current theories of social sciences. Such theories have the potential to transform the participants' world.

Some theological scholars and students question the need to meticulously adhere to the scientific techniques and procedures of social research for doing field-based research, claiming they are not doing a social scientific study. But every researcher studying the social world must follow the scientific methodologies and methods, which are universally accepted. Just as theologians cannot have a different set of rules for accounting but must follow the universal pattern of accounting, they must follow the methodologies and methods developed by social scientists to study the social world. Research is a scientific endeavor, and theology cannot claim an exception to upholding scientific rigor. Following the scientific approaches and methods of social research will establish the credibility and authenticity of the findings in reflecting the real world.

Research Strategies

A research strategy is the overall research approach for executing a research project. Alan Bryman (2016, 32) describes it as "a general orientation to the conduct of social research." In social research, scholars use three basic strategies, qualitative, quantitative, and mixed methods. John Creswell and David Creswell (2018) call these strategies "approaches" and others call them "research designs" or "methodologies." In methodology texts, different authors may also use different terms to refer to qualitative, quantitative, and mixed methods strategies. I prefer to use Bryman's term "research strategies" when referring to qualitative, quantitative, and mixed methods. The choice of research strategy depends on the type of research problem, research questions, and the philosophical assumptions (research paradigms) adopted (Creswell and Creswell 2018).

Qualitative Research

Qualitative research collects narrative data from participants about their experiences and the meanings associated with them. It is an investigation to understand the world of the participants from their own perspectives in their natural settings and carried out by collecting data that are descriptive or in other forms and analyzes them thematically. It uses interpretive frameworks to advance or modify existing knowledge and aims at transforming the world of participants.

Quantitative Research

Quantitative research measures variables to offer a causal explanation for a relationship between variables, based on a theory or it may present a descriptive explanation of a population. It uses different methods to collect numerical data from predetermined samples and to analyze them statistically to answer the research question.

Qualitative and quantitative research have common topographies. The distinctions between the two are shown in Table 2; however, these distinctions are not always rigid.

Mixed Methods Research

Mixed methods research combines qualitative and quantitative strategies to minimize the limitations of each strategy and to augment the strengths of both. By systematically collecting and rigorously analyzing different kinds of data in a single study, the researcher integrates the findings to answer the research questions.

Table 2: Comparison of Qualitative and Quantitative Strategies

Elements of Comparison	Qualitative Research	Quantitative Research
Focus of investigation	Meanings of the participants	Relationship between variables
Goal	To understand and describe	To generalize or explain
Logic	Inductive	Deductive
Strategy	Flexible	Structured and rigid
Researcher's role	Reflective and subjective	Objective
Nature of data	Narratives, documents, photographs, audios, videos, online data, etc.	Numerical
Sampling	Purposive	Probability (Random)/ non-probability
Methods of data collection	In-depth interviews, focus group interviews, participant observation, and other suitable methods of collecting different kinds of data	Survey or observation or experiments
Data analysis	Thematic analysis	Statistical analysis
Findings/results	Hypotheses generated	Hypotheses tested or descriptive explanation given
Presentation of the findings/results	Themes with thick descriptions	Results with tables and graphs

Research Designs

Research design is a framework to collect and analyze data, a "logical structure of the inquiry" (D. de Vaus 2001, 9). For Ranjit Kumar (2011, 94), a research design is "a procedural plan that is adopted by the researcher to answer questions validly, objectively, accurately and economically." Research designs incorporate the type of data needed, sampling logic, procedures or methods of data collection and analysis, and they vary for qualitative, quantitative, and mixed methods research strategies.

Qualitative research adopts one or more of the following designs or approaches: phenomenological, ethnography, grounded theory, narrative, and case study. Quantitative research uses survey or quasi-experimental or experimental design. Mixed methods research uses convergent design or explanatory sequential design or exploratory sequential design (Creswell and Creswell 2018). See Chapter 4 for more on qualitative research, Chapter 5 for quantitative research, and Chapter 6 for mixed methods research.

Paradigms of Social Research

A paradigm is a worldview through which one sees the world; it is based on a set of beliefs, which may be philosophical or ideological or religious. Depending on their worldview, people can view a social problem or an issue differently. For example, abortion could be viewed as a medical procedure or as murder, depending on the lens one adopts. The feminist philosophy assumes an embryo is not a human person and considers abortion as a medical procedure to terminate a pregnancy, which is the right a woman has over her body. Contrarily, a view that an embryo has life and terminating a pregnancy is killing a life is based on a religious belief. A researcher's key concerns determine the philosophical assumptions or paradigms for a study.

Research paradigms combine ontological, epistemological, axiological, and methodological components to constitute a worldview. Ontology is about the nature of reality, whether the reality is single, or constructed, or multiple. Epistemology is a theory of knowledge that concerns the relationship between the researcher and the researched; how knowledge is generated; and the nature of knowledge. Axiology deals with the ethics or values that are underscored in a research project. The methodology is concerned with the choice of a research strategy, whether it is qualitative or quantitative or mixed methods (Mertens 2015). Researchers choose a paradigm based on their key concerns for doing their research.

Scholars have grouped worldviews into four major paradigms: postpositivist, constructivist, transformative, and pragmatic (Creswell and Creswell 2018; Mertens 2015). I rely on these authors in presenting these paradigms. See Table 3 for a comparison of the four.

Table 3: Major Paradigms of Social Research

Basic Tenets	Postpositivist Paradigm	Constructivist Paradigm	Transformative Paradigm	Pragmatic Paradigm
Key Concerns	Observation and measurement Theory testing Generalization Prediction Explanation	Exploring Understanding participants' perspectives Multiple meanings Theory generation	Transforming Multiple versions of meaning Oppression and human rights Power and justice Politics	Problem-solving Individual interpretations Social justice and politics
Methodology (Research Strategy)	Quantitative	Qualitative	Primarily qualitative Also, quantitative and mixed methods	Mixed methods Depends on the research question
Research Design	Cross-sectional surveys Longitudinal surveys Correlational Quasi-experimental Experimental Causal comparative Randomized control trials	Phenomenological Ethnographic Grounded Theory Case Study Narrative	Depends on the choice of research strategy Mixed methods	Mixed methods
Ontology (Nature of Reality)	One reality	Multiple realities	Multiple versions of reality	Single reality

Table 3 continued

Basic Tenets	Postpositivist Paradigm	Constructivist Paradigm	Transformative Paradigm	Pragmatic Paradigm
	Discoverable with a level of probability	Socially constructed	Socially positioned The privileged version has consequences	Individual interpretations
Epistemology (Theory of Knowledge)	Through observation and measurement Objective Neutral	Interactional Researcher and participants equal partners Explicit values Contextual factors Constructed findings	Interactional Deconstruction of socially and historically positioned knowledge Knowledge deals with power and trust	Level of relationship between the researcher and participants determined by the researcher
Axiology (Theory of ethics/values)	Respect for privacy Informed consent Minimal impairment	Balanced views Trustworthiness Illuminating participants Rapport and reciprocity	Trust Promotion of human rights, social justice Cultural norms respected	Researcher's values and politics Knowledge for targeted end
Theories	Testable theories	Theory generation	Critical theory Feminism Neo-Marxist Postcolonial Indigenous Critical race theory Queer theory	Testable theories Theory generation Emancipatory theories (Based on the choice of research strategy)

Sources: Adapted from Donna M. Mertens (2015) and John W. Creswell and J. David Creswell (2018).

Postpositivist Paradigm

Postpositivist paradigm is a worldview that is based on the philosophy of postpositivism, which emerged from positivism. The postpositivist paradigm rejected the claim of positivism that knowledge is discovered with certainty but introduced the concept of the probability of knowledge.

Positivism relies on empiricism, which claims that knowledge is based on observable and verifiable facts through senses. Some of the key philosophers of empiricism are Aristotle, Francis Bacon, John Locke, Auguste Comte, and Immanuel Kant (Mertens 2015). The basic assumption of positivism is that the social world can be studied similarly to how natural science studies the natural world. In this view, reality is discovered by observation and measurement of variables through experiments. Both positivism and postpositivism believed in objectivity; on the other hand, positivism believed in certainty of knowledge while postpositivism believed in probability of knowledge.

Some wrongly associate postpositivism with postmodernism and constructivism. But when postpositivism rejected the claim that knowledge can be discovered with certainty but introduced the probability of knowledge, it held onto objectivity and generalizability of results (Mertens 2015). Therefore, postpositivism is not anti-positivism but is a modified version of positivism that opted for probability of knowledge rather than certainty of knowledge.

The ontology of postpositivism believes that reality is single and can be discovered. The epistemology of postpositivism relies on the observation and measurements of variables, while the researcher maintains objectivity and is dispassionate about what is researched. The axiology or ethics for postpositivism demands respect for the privacy of the participants and informed consent from participants. The researcher must explain the purpose and nature of the research in simple terms to participants before obtaining their consent.

Quantitative research is suitable for the postpositivist paradigm, because it deals with the observable and measurable in the social world (Mertens 2015). Therefore, quantitative research is not popular among scholars of religious studies (Stausberg and Engler 2011), because religious studies are mainly concerned with unobservable beliefs and meanings. Moreover, "postpositivism has the elements of being reductionistic, logical, empirical, cause-and-effect oriented, and deterministic based on a priori theories" (Creswell and Poth 2018,

59). However, the postpositivist paradigm can be valuable in studying observable and measurable variables related to religions. Researchers concerned with testing a theory or generalizing the results to the target population or predicting or providing a numerical description of the sample, would choose postpositivist paradigm and adopt quantitative research as their strategy for their research in theology/religious studies.

Constructivist Paradigm

Constructivism believes that knowledge is constructed in a social context by the process of interpreting and reinterpreting. This paradigm is based on the philosophy of phenomenology advocated by Edmund Husserl, Wilhelm Dilthey, and Martin Heidegger that knowledge is interpretive (Mertens 2015). Therefore, the ontology for the constructivist paradigm is that realities are multiple and are socially constructed. The epistemology for the constructivist paradigm believes that knowledge is created by the interaction between the researcher and participants. Researchers construct the findings through an interpretive process. Constructivist axiology encompasses values and contextual factors and are made explicit in the process. Researchers do not claim objectivity, rather, subjectivity is considered as resource in the interpretive process. The trustworthiness and credibility of the research are established through various steps.

The constructivist paradigm is suitable for the researcher who wants to understand the participants' perspectives and meanings instead of explaining a phenomenon through existing theories. Qualitative research is used for the constructivist paradigm as a strategy to generate theories/hypotheses from the data by taking into consideration multiple realities.

The constructivist paradigm is suitable for studying lived experiences, beliefs, meanings, and unobservable dimensions of life. This paradigm is typically associated with using qualitative research, which is a popular strategy among scholars of religion and theology. John Swinton and Harriet Mowat (2016, 72) claim that practical theology is "deeply embedded within the hermeneutical/interpretative paradigm." Therefore, the constructivist paradigm is a lens for use in practical theology to interpret Christian beliefs and practices. In addition, with this paradigm, researchers can bring their theological/religious positions, religious traditions, and the scripture into reflection to interpret the data and vice versa.

Transformative Paradigm

The transformative paradigm draws its philosophical foundations from theories and philosophies that address oppression, marginalization, power, and social justice. There is no single philosophical foundation for the transformative paradigm: however, it has its roots in the emancipatory theories that are concerned with the marginalized. It emerges from the broad perspectives of Paulo Freire's Pedagogy of the Oppressed and Habermas's theory of communicative action (Mertens 2015), which speak for social transformation.

The ontology of the transformative paradigm is concerned with multiple versions of reality that are socially positioned and historically situated. It takes stock of the consequences of the privileged version of a reality for the socially oppressed or marginalized. The epistemology for this paradigm aims at deconstructing the socially and historically positioned knowledge by jointly working with participants. It exposes the consequences of the privileged version of reality. The axiology is concerned with human rights and social justice and creates space for the participants to shape the research. Here, the participants may contribute to shaping the nature and focus of the investigation and could help the researcher ask the right questions. Knowledge in this paradigm deals with power, trust, and social transformation. Trust, transparency, and reciprocity are important ethical values; the transformative paradigm promotes human rights and social justice.

The transformative paradigm is typically associated with using a qualitative research strategy; however, when it adopts quantitative or mixed methods research, they are located under the transformative paradigm. A researcher using a transformative paradigm adopts an appropriate theory to suit the nature of the research from among the following: critical, postcolonial, indigenous, feminist, critical race, neo-Marxist, participatory action research, and emerging theories dealing with the transformation of the oppressed. The transformative paradigm is suitable for researching victims of oppression based on gender, race, caste, and other categories.

The transformative paradigm does not confine researchers to generating knowledge but enables the researcher to reach out to transform the world of the participants. Nancy Ramsay, Emerita Professor of Pastoral Theology and Pastoral Care at Brite Divinity School, presented the results of a survey of practical theology's concern for emancipation and liberation. Ramsay (2012, 190–91) acknowledged

Paulo Freire's contribution to liberation theology and concluded, "emancipatory theory urges attention to research and the construction of methods for such research that insist on attention to issues of justice that disclose structural, political, relational, and personal possibilities with constructive and transformative proposals for redemptive and restorative change." Practical theologians and liberation theologians have argued for the use of innovative methods to achieve social transformation. The transformative paradigm is well suited for achieving this purpose and a good choice for researchers concerned about oppression, human rights violations, justice, and power and politics. Transformative paradigm uses qualitative strategy, but it allows for the use of quantitative strategy or mixed methods if the research question requires it.

Pragmatic Paradigm

The pragmatic paradigm is not concerned whether the reality is single or multiple but believes individuals interpret reality differently. The goal of the research is to find a workable solution.

The pragmatic paradigm is based on the philosophy of pragmatism, which ascribes importance to common sense, practical wisdom, workability, and solutions. Some of the early pragmatic philosophers are Charles Sanders Peirce, William James, Josiah Royce, John Dewey, and Jane Addams. Richard Rorty introduced neo-pragmatism by rejecting any external authority and appealing for alternative descriptions (Legg and Hookway 2021).

Intersubjectivity is an important component in the pragmatic paradigm. How one's interpretation differs from another's is the key to this paradigm. Epistemology in the pragmatic paradigm provides freedom to the researcher to use multiple ways of knowing that are part of the researcher's value system, but ultimately, the knowledge generated is weighed against the outcome of the research. In this paradigm, the researcher chooses the level of relationship with the participants best suited to achieve the purpose of the research. Ethically, researchers' values and politics are key factors in finding a solution to a problem. This paradigm is suitable for activists using participatory actions research because the goal of research for the pragmatic paradigm is to find a workable solution for a real-world problem.

Researchers adopting a pragmatic paradigm generally prefer mixed methods research; however, they can determine whether to adopt qualitative or quantitative or mixed methods, based on what is best for the community.

How can theology and religious studies that are preoccupied with belief in God and with reality beyond the physical world engage pragmatism, which rejects metaphysics altogether? There may not be a common ground between theology and pragmatism regarding metaphysical realities but the outcome of research for pragmatism and the primary concern of theology and religious studies is human welfare. Pragmatism provides an "experience-based, action-oriented framework" for understanding human problems and finding practical solutions (Kaushik and Walsh 2019, 9). Theology can find both theoretical and practical insights by adopting the pragmatic paradigm. Moreover, pragmatism as a research paradigm involves working with "marginalized and oppressed communities and provides hard evidence for micro-to macro-level discourse" for empowering them (Kaushik and Walsh 2019, 12). Public theologies and contextual theologies share the same vision, and a pragmatic paradigm has the potential to make the vision into reality through social research.

In the research proposal and in the methodology chapter of the dissertation/thesis, the writer must discuss the chosen research paradigm in terms of their key concerns. In the methodology section, they must offer a definition of the paradigm and of the key features to inform the readers about how the research paradigm shaped their research (Creswell and Creswell 2018). This information will help readers understand the rationale behind the choice of research strategy and research designs.

Chapter Summary

This chapter discussed social research for an interdisciplinary approach in theology/religious studies research. You have learned the definitions of qualitative, quantitative, and mixed methods research strategies. You have understood the four major paradigms of social research, postpositivist, constructivist, transformative, and pragmatic as well as the key concerns and elements associated with each of them. The postpositivist paradigm views social reality as objective and measurable, whereas the constructivist paradigm stressed on subjective experiences and the role of context in shaping social reality. The transformative paradigm focused on social justice while the pragmatic paradigm emphasized on transforming the world of the participants. You have also understood the relevance of each paradigm for theology/religious studies.

Review Questions

1. What is social research?
2. What is qualitative research?
3. What is quantitative research?
4. What is mixed methods research?
5. What is a research design?
6. What is the postpositivist paradigm?
7. What is the constructivist paradigm?
8. What is the transformative paradigm?
9. What is the pragmatic paradigm?

Further Help

Creswell, John W., and J. David Creswell. 2018. *Research Design: Qualitative, Quantitative, and Mixed Methods Approaches.* 5th ed. London: Sage.

Mertens, Donna M. 2015. *Research and Evaluation in Education and Psychology.* 4th ed. London: Sage.

Chapter 4

QUALITATIVE RESEARCH

Qualitative research is context specific and explores the world of the participants in their natural settings. The goal of qualitative research is to gain an in-depth understanding of participants' meanings and the meaning-making processes based on their beliefs, attitudes, perceptions, feelings, and experiences. Therefore, qualitative research examines how participants interpret their experiences in their natural settings by collecting non-numerical data from the field to construct knowledge. This chapter will help you in choosing an approach or approaches suitable for the purpose and nature of your research, in identifying the type of data needed to answer the research questions and the methods to collect them, and in analyzing qualitative data.

Generally, qualitative research is defined in terms of its differences from quantitative research. However, scholars do not regard this as a proper way of defining qualitative research. Norman Denzin and Yovanna Lincoln (2018, 43) say that qualitative research studies "things in their natural settings, attempting to make sense of, or interpret phenomena in terms of the meanings people bring to them." Denzin and Lincoln emphasize the significance of the natural settings of the research and the meanings of the participants. In qualitative research, a phenomenon is an aspect of human experience. This definition emphasizes that qualitative research is interpretive and is done in the natural settings of the participants.

By incorporating the elements from the above definition, qualitative research can be defined as an investigation for understanding the world of the participants from their own perspectives in their natural settings, and carried out by collecting data that are narrative or in other forms, and analyzing them thematically. It uses interpretive frameworks to advance or modify the existing knowledge and aims at transforming the world of participants.

Qualitative research demands the systematic gathering of evidence based on the experience of people. As explained in Chapter 1, the differences between a journalist reporting and an investigating officer reporting is that the researcher assumes the role of an investigator to resolve the "unknown" by collecting evidence that are grounded in the experiences of the participants.

In qualitative research, the researcher does not use a theory or a perspective to explain the phenomenon but makes every effort to understand the perspectives of the participants. The researcher acts as a learner, not as an expert. However, the researcher must know the relevant theories to advance the existing knowledge or modify the existing theories in light of the findings. As a contribution to the field of study, qualitative research produces new insights, challenges perspectives, offers new perspectives, or modifies existing theories.

In addition, qualitative research contributes to the transformation of the participants' world. Patricia Leavy (2014, 2) observed, "There is a social justice undercurrent to qualitative practice, one that may be implicit or explicit depending on the positioning and goals of the practitioner and the project at hand." Along similar lines, Denzin and Lincoln (2018) hold the view that the transformation of the world of the participants can be an outcome of qualitative research. These days, social scientists are more concerned about transforming the world of the participants as part of the academic pursuit, rather than doing research for the sake of research. Thus, qualitative research can be a tool for social or community transformation when used by scholars of theology/religious studies.

Qualitative Research for Theology and Religious Studies

Living religions exist in the lives of people. Currently, lived religion is the focus of investigation among religious scholars. A study of lived religion investigates how religion is practiced by individuals or a community in their everyday lives, rather than examining the institutionalized form of a religion. Qualitative research is the appropriate strategy for studying lived religion to understand the role of religion in the meaning-making process.

Qualitative research is suitable for understanding meanings, beliefs, and practices in general and more particularly, religious meanings, beliefs, and practices; it will enable researchers to understand the meaning-making processes that people adopt. Qualitative research can help researchers understand religious phenomenon holistically because it concerns process. For example, qualitative research could be used to study the process by which teens move away from their parents' faith. In a study of domestic violence, qualitative research is suitable for understanding the role of religion or culture in preserving marriage for women who are physically abused by their husbands, in some cultures. In the case of religious pilgrimages, especially of those who walk for several kilometers to reach a shrine and walk back home, qualitative research is suitable for exploring the pilgrims' thoughts and feelings during the journey, at the shrine, and on their return. The focus of the study could be the spiritual aspect, the psychological effects, the physical state during the journey, or all of these. Thus, qualitative research helps in researching the lived experiences of people and lived religion.

All sub-disciplines of theology can use qualitative strategy to break new grounds. Seminary students and scholars from the departments of theology, biblical studies, and history have often considered qualitative research and in general field-based studies as irrelevant for their disciplines. If you look at the contours of theological research, theology moved from systematic to contextual, then to empirical, and now to ordinary theology, in which people's perceptions are gathered to construct a theology. We need more such studies in this direction to generate grounded theologies for which qualitative research is the appropriate strategy. The future of theological research lies with constructing grounded theologies in partnership with people.

Biblical studies, which have stayed behind the text for centuries, are now dealing with liberative perspectives by offering feminist readings, liberationist readings, ecological readings, and so on. Offering a perspectival reading by scholars does not reflect the reality of the community or group they claim to represent. However, it must move forward to engage people's experiences of reading the biblical text. By adopting qualitative strategy, biblical scholars can explore how a marginalized group or a community reads a biblical passage or how a text is understood by different persons from different cultures. Studying this can shed light on how God makes himself known differently to different people through the text. Such studies would highlight the experience of reading the text, besides bringing out rich meanings of the text. A paradigm shift is required among biblical scholars to move before the text and engage people for biblical research by adopting qualitative research.

Historians can employ qualitative strategy to write the history of world Christianity and history of indigenous mission by collecting oral histories, narratives, documents, and other forms that exist locally. Church or mission history is largely written by historians from the West, which is laden with colonial hangovers. Adopting qualitative research for history writing will highlight the contributions made by the locals.

Students and scholars of practical theology and mission studies/ missiology are familiar with qualitative research. Qualitative research is the appropriate method for researching areas of human life that cannot be measured. It can be used to study feelings, perceptions, attitudes, meanings, religious and cultural beliefs, religious experiences, religious practices, lived experiences of suffering, pleasure, and happiness; the victims of exploitation and abuse, and so on. A lot can be achieved in solving human problems and issues in Christian ministry by adopting qualitative research strategy.

Contextual theologies emerged with an emancipatory paradigm but fell short of achieving the liberative vision. Although the approach for contextual theologies has been "from below," the methods were guided by reflection and speculation. Contrarily, qualitative research could be an effective tool in the hands of contextual theologians to bring about transformation by engaging the lived experiences of the community they intended to liberate. Research-based facts/findings could be used for appealing for policy changes, helping NGOs to deal with an issue, creating awareness among churches/religious communities to address the issue, and drawing public attention to bring a change based on the findings. Theology/religious studies students and scholars can use qualitative research in making the world a better place for people.

Approaches in Qualitative Research

Qualitative research is inductive. It adopts one or more of five approaches for understanding the phenomenon under investigation. These are, the phenomenological approach, grounded theory approach, ethnographic approach, case study approach, and narrative approach. Based on the purpose of their study, researchers choose one or more of these approaches.

Phenomenological Approach

The phenomenological approach is suitable for studying the lived experiences of people. Phenomenology studies how individuals interpret a particular phenomenon and how they perceive their experience. "Phenomenology is the study of human experience and the way in which things are perceived as they appear to consciousness. . . So, the focus is on people's perceptions of the world . . . 'things in their appearing'" (Langdridge 2007, 10–11). Phenomenology is concerned with a particular phenomenon, like a conversion experience, the experience of glossolalia, racial/caste discrimination, domestic violence, motherhood, bereavement, divorce, learning experience in the classroom, and so on.

Phenomenology emerged from the philosophy of consciousness aired mainly by the following philosophers. Edmund Husserl (1859-1938) was concerned with the experience at the conscious level. Martin Heidegger (1889-1976) emphasized the relational nature of our existence to objects in the world, while Jean-Paul Sartre (1905-1980) extended the relational dimension to the absence or presence of social relationships in perceiving one's experience.

Religious studies scholars like Rudolf Otto (1970) and Ninian Smart (1971), who were concerned about the objectivity and universality of a religious phenomenon, used the transcendental phenomenology to study religious experience at the conscious level. However, Gavin Flood (1999), a scholar in the comparative study of religion, argued in *Beyond Phenomenology* that in order to understand a religious phenomenon, theology must dialogue with social sciences because a religious phenomenon is experienced in a socio-cultural context. How an individual perceives an experience is contextual. Therefore, phenomenological researchers "reject the notion that the detached scientific empirical tradition is the superior method of research" (Eddles-Hirsch 2015, 251). Phenomenological approach in social sciences factors in subjectivity, temporality, and particularity in understanding lived experience. In adopting this approach, researchers can better understand the meanings the individuals attribute to their experiences and the role of religion in the meaning-making process.

The phenomenological approach enables researchers to see a phenomenon as "it appears" in natural settings and assumes that there is a "shared essence" in the experiences of individuals. The aim of this approach is not to measure but to understand the world of the participants.

The common features of phenomenological research include thick description, shared essence, and participants' meaning. The researcher aims for a detailed description of the lived experiences of the participants that come with layers of complexity, messiness with everyday life, and richness. The researcher finds common features or shared essence in the lived experiences of the participants from thick descriptions of narrative data. Essence, in other words, is the nature of the lived experience which is common to the participants. Phenomenological research aims at capturing participants' meanings of their lived experiences.

In using the phenomenological approach, researchers must free themselves from theoretical biases and give significance to participants' meanings. Therefore, researchers recognize their ideological, philosophical, religious, or theological position about the phenomenon under study and explicitly state them to contain their biases and feelings. This is called *epoche* or bracketing and is done to establish the credibility and trustworthiness of the study.

There are two types of phenomenological approaches: descriptive phenomenology and interpretive phenomenological analysis (IPA).

Descriptive phenomenology describes a phenomenon as it appears instead of offering a theoretical explanation for it. Descriptive phenomenology explores individuals' experiences as narrated by the participants and analyses the narrative to find the essence of the experience and individuals' meanings. The focus is on the first-hand experience as narrated by the individual, either through in-depth interviews or in written form. The researcher then analyses the units of meaning to find the layers of experience and the essence of the experience or the commonalities among the individuals. Descriptive phenomenology ensures that the "knowledge generated reflects the phenomenon as experienced by participants first-hand" (Matua and Van Der Wal 2015, 25). Therefore, the goal is to find the common essence of the experience among the participants and the individual meanings for everyone.

Descriptive phenomenology demands that researchers bracket their prior understanding of the phenomenon. Some scholars suggest that, at the early stage of descriptive phenomenological research, the researcher should avoid consulting of the literature; some suggest doing a partial literature review (Vagle 2018). However, because the ultimate aim of academic research is to produce knowledge, if the researcher does not know the existing body of knowledge, the study could be redundant or irrelevant. Moreover, one can never completely shed preunderstanding of a phenomenon. Therefore, "it is better to make explicit our understandings, beliefs, biases, assumptions, presuppositions, and theories . . . to hold them deliberately at bay" (Manen 1990, 47). With the bracketing of prior knowledge, personal values, preconceived notions, and ideological positions, the researcher makes a conscious effort to give significance to the participants' meanings and perceptions.

Interpretive Phenomenological Analysis (IPA) is adopted to explore a major experience that altered a person's life. "When people are engaged with 'an experience' of something major in their lives, they begin to reflect on the significance of what is happening" (Smith, Flowers, and Larkin 2009, 3). For example, when a person experiences religious conversion, their everyday experience of going to work is changed and they begin to see their work as a God-given opportunity to contribute to the world. IPA explores such reflections on their experience from the participant's point of view and tries to make sense of their world as much as possible. IPA examines, "what happens when the everyday flow of lived experience takes on a particular significance for people" (Smith, Flowers, and Larkin 2009, 1). IPA tries to capture the reflection to understand the participants' meaning of that experience. In other words, IPA is suitable to explore how people make meaning of the experience that brought major changes in their lives.

Using this approach, a researcher can study several experiences of people in the fields of theology or religious studies. They could, for example, study the experience of pain and suffering of the religiously persecuted. They could develop a theology of suffering or persecution based on the lived experiences of the persecuted. Some theological scholars and students are more comfortable in writing a theology of suffering or theology of persecution by reading a few theological works than studying the reality of persecution in the lives of the victims of violence. In a phenomenological study of the pain and suffering of the persecuted, the researcher does not seek to measure the pain, but to understand it and how the participants make sense of their suffering through their faith.

The phenomenological approach uses qualitative interviews or semi-structured interviews as the method of data collection; if required, multiple sessions of interviews can be conducted to collect thick descriptions of the participants' experiences. Other forms of data include poems, art, photos, personal diaries, blogs, and social media postings related to the participants' lived experiences.

Grounded Theory Approach

The grounded theory approach, which generates theories from data, is suitable for studying a process or action. In our broad area of theology and religious studies, the grounded theory approach is suitable for investigations in the fields of mission studies, intercultural studies, practical theology, pastoral theology, church history, sociology of religion, psychology of religion, and anthropology of religion.

Two sociologists, Barney Glaser and Anselm Strauss (1967), developed grounded theory. They found that the existing theories related to patient care were not reflecting the reality. Therefore, in a study on awareness of dying among terminally ill patients, they generated a theory based on their data and argued their theory could be useful to patient care because it reflected reality. They developed a method to discover theories based on data to explain a phenomenon under study, which they called "grounded theory" (Glaser and Strauss 1967). Since then, this approach has been widely adopted because laypersons or practitioners and social scientists could understand grounded theories generated from data and apply them to benefit people.

However, the founders of grounded theory parted ways over a period due to epistemological differences. Other scholars further developed the grounded theory approach to be relevant to the twenty-first century. Adele Clark (2005) developed situational analysis grounded theory to accommodate postmodern features. Kathy Charmaz (2006), who felt the need to remove the positivist tendency of discovering a theory that exists—"out there," developed a constructivist grounded theory in which the researcher plays an active role in constructing a grounded theory in dialogue with the participants. Despite the differences among the variances of grounded theory, it has many common features. If you are adopting grounded theory approach for your study, you must explain and justify the chosen type of grounded theory.

The grounded theory approach is suitable for studying any social process or action like a religious or social movement, church growth, effects of education (theological or religious), school or college dropouts, learning experience in classrooms or Sunday schools, married life, parenting, the effects of addiction on individuals or families or children, addiction recovery, religious or spiritual experience, leadership, and so on. By using grounded theory, researchers can generate theologies/theories that reflect realities.

The grounded theory approach largely depends on interview data of individuals who have experienced being part of the process or action. In addition, the researcher can collect data through observations, documents, photographs, audio, and other digital forms related to the phenomenon under study.

Ethnographic Approach

The ethnographic approach is a method for studying the social behavior of a group that shares a common culture. Ethnography aims to describe the complexity of a group's culture by studying their beliefs, language, and behaviors to find patterns, social organization, and worldviews. The ethnographic approach is widely used in the fields of anthropology, sociology, education, and organizational studies. For theological scholars, ethnography is useful not only for understanding the culture in general but also in understanding the religious reality expressed in a particular culture. In the hands of theological scholars, the ethnographic approach could be a tool for transformation.

Ethnography is about a story of a group. "Ethnography is about telling a credible, rigorous, and authentic story. . . . The story is told through the eyes of local people as they pursue their daily lives in their own communities" (Fetterman 2010, 1). Anthropologists used ethnography to study primitive cultures and now this approach has been used to study any group that shares a common culture. Ethnography uses fieldwork to collect data. "The most important element of fieldwork is *being there*—to observe, to ask seemingly stupid but insightful questions, and to write down what is seen and heard" (Fetterman 2010, 9; emphasis added). LeCompte and Schensul (2010, 12) identify seven characteristics of ethnography:

- It is carried out in a natural setting, not in a laboratory.
- It involves intimate, face-to-face interactions with participants.
- It presents an accurate reflection of participant's perspectives and behaviors.
- It uses inductive, interactive, and recursive data collection and analytic strategies to build local cultural theories.
- It uses multiple data sources, including quantitative and qualitative data.
- It frames all human behavior and belief within a socio-political and historical context.
- It uses the concept of culture as a lens through which to interpret results.

To capture the bigger picture of a culture with minute details, ethnography requires the researcher to live with the community for a long period. The period of fieldwork varies from six months to eighteen months based on the nature of research and institutional requirements.

Ethnography aims to describe the complexity of a group's culture by studying their beliefs, language, and behaviors to find patterns, social organization, and worldviews. Take, the cultural concept of kinship and marriage; it varies from culture to culture; each culture has norms on whom to marry and whom not to marry. The members of a group uphold relationship structures and networks that have been practiced for a long period. The researcher explores the beliefs and practices associated with kinship and marriage to understand a group's social behavior and finds how shared knowledge is being passed on. The outcome of ethnographic research is a "theoretically informed interpretation of the culture of the community, group, or setting" (LeCompte and Schensul 2010, 11). Ethnography examines cultural behaviors and the beliefs behind such behaviors and interprets them theoretically.

For theological/religious scholars, ethnography is not only understanding the culture but also understanding the religious reality expressed in a particular culture. Christian Scharen and Aana Marie Vigen, (2011, 16) define ethnography for theology and ethics as:

> a process of attentive study of, and learning from, people— their words, practices, traditions, experiences, memories, insights—in particular times and places in order to understand how they make meaning (cultural, religious, ethical) and what they can teach us about reality, truth, beauty, moral responsibility, relationships and the divine, etc. The aim is to understand what God, human relationships, and the world look like from their perspective—to take them seriously as a source of wisdom and to de-center our own assumptions and evaluations.

Here, Scharen and Vigen have broadened the scope of ethnography in theological research to include truth, beauty, morality, and God.

The ethnographic approach could be a tool for transformation in the hands of theological/religious scholars. Margret Crain and Jack Seymour (1996) argue that ethnographers must assume the role of ministers to aim for the transformation of the community. While doing an ethnographic study, theological scholars are concerned about both understanding the culture of the people and the group's welfare. The ethnographic approach is suitable for studying various group behaviors such as cultural changes, church growth, worship patterns of congregations, behaviors of employees or theological students or trainees, and so on. Ethnography is suitable for the fields of practical theology and mission studies, while other subdisciplines of theology or religious studies could use ethnographic approach when the focus of study is a group.

Qualitative Case Study Approach

By adopting the qualitative case study approach, a researcher investigates a particular case or multiple cases, which could be an individual, institution, event, program, or process. The qualitative case study is suitable for studying the complexity of a problem and uses multiple sources of data and analyzes the phenomenon or examines the issue from different angles. The qualitative case study provides a thick description of the case and the phenomenon.

As Robert Stake (1995, xi) says, the qualitative case study is about the "particularity and complexity of a single case, coming to understand its activity within important circumstances." Qualitative case study is suitable to explore particularity and complexity of a phenomenon. For Robert Yin (2003, 13), "case study is an empirical inquiry that investigates a contemporary phenomenon within its real-life context, especially when the boundaries between phenomenon and context are not clearly evident." In Yin's definition, the keywords are "contemporary phenomenon" and "real-life context." The case study approach examines something that is a current or ongoing process and studies it in its natural context, where the phenomenon is closely linked to the context.

The aim of qualitative case study is to understand the case and its uniqueness. Robert Stake (1995, 8) explains that the purpose of the case study approach is "to know it well, not primarily as to how it is different from others but what it is, what it does. There is emphasis on uniqueness, and that implies knowledge of others that the case is different from, but the first emphasis is on understanding the case itself." Thus, the purpose of a qualitative case study is to understand the case compared to other cases.

The qualitative case study uses multiple sources of data. For example, in a study of religious violence, the focus is a case of an attack on a church. The researcher will collect data from the victims of violence, eyewitnesses, pastors, leaders of the church or community, police, government authorities, hospital staff who treated the victims, and so on. The nature of the data will vary—narrative data from interviews, documents from the church, police, hospital staff, and government authorities, audio-visuals, videos, and observation notes. In this imaginative study, different kinds of data are collected from different sources. The researcher is likely to come up with findings like fear, safety, divine protection, the meaning of suffering, pain, shaken beliefs, loss of faith, religious freedom, citizen's rights, the role of church authorities, preceding events, triggering instances, attackers' motives, and responses of the police and government officials. All these findings could be grouped under a few major themes: spiritual factors, role of the church authorities, role of the state authorities, and protective measures. Based on these findings, the researcher could offer recommendations to ensure the religious freedom and safety of the churchgoers. A theology researcher must locate their study in the field of theology with a theological framework and must draw practical implications. In this case, the researcher could draw practical implications for churches, NGOs, and authorities to take suitable measures to prevent religious violence in the future.

There are two types of case studies: intrinsic and instrumental (Stake 1995). An intrinsic case study is one that arouses interest in itself because of some unique features associated with it; the case is studied to understand and explain its unique features. An instrumental case study is one in which a case is used as an instrument to describe an event or problem.

An example of an intrinsic case could be a study of a particular seminary in which most graduates go out as intercultural missionaries, which is contrary to the general perception that seminary graduates do not do this. The researcher could choose to study this seminary as an intrinsic case study because it is unique. The focus would be to study the theological training provided at this seminary to understand and explore the unique features that motivate graduates to serve as intercultural missionaries.

An example of an instrumental case is a study of seminaries to investigate the learning experience of theological students. The researcher would select one or two seminaries as cases for conducting their research; these cases would be instrumental in understanding the learning styles of theological students in seminaries.

Qualitative case studies can be used in theology and religious studies to investigate several programs, problems, events, institutions, processes, and so on. The difference between this and other qualitative approaches discussed earlier is that the researcher would use multiple data sources to study the case from multiple angles. In a qualitative case study, the researcher uses several data sources as the primary source to understand the complexity of the phenomena.

Narrative Approach

The narrative approach studies the "experiences as experienced in lived and told stories of individuals" (Creswell 2013, 70). It is suitable for studying the experience of an individual or a small group as narrated by an individual or a group. For example, the contribution of a missionary or a leader of an institution, or a pastor of a church to a community and culture could be studied by using a narrative approach. John Creswell (2013) identifies four types of narratives: biographical, autoethnography, life history, and oral history.

Biographical Type

For the biographical type, the researcher constructs a biography of the participant by collecting experiences of the participant through interviews with the participant and with others. The researcher could also use documents, diaries, letters, photographs, speeches, and so on. A researcher could use a biographical approach to study the life stories of leaders of a local culture or community to explore their contribution to the advancement of a religion, Christian mission, a religious organization, or human rights.

Autoethnography

Autoethnography is the writing of a story about oneself. In this approach, the researcher is the subject and their deep reflections on the experience are the data. Autoethnography "allows researchers to draw on their own experiences to understand a particular phenomenon or culture" (Mendez 2013, 280). For example, the autoethnography method is suitable for a cross-cultural missionary writing about their experience of engaging in a foreign culture. Another example is a theological teacher writing about her experience of being a woman in a male-dominated arena of theological education. In autoethnography, the researcher presents the personal story to highlight larger issues or meanings in a cultural context. Reports based on autoethnography have received unfavorable reviews because of the author's focus on their self. Therefore, it is recommended to engage literature in narrating one's story (Hayes and Fulton 2015; Wall 2008), and interpreting it in light of other studies.

Life History

Life history is an approach to study an individual's life and is especially suitable for studying known leaders or marginalized leaders and voiceless people. Researchers can use life history approach for studying both known heroes and unsung heroes. This approach is suitable for studying the stories of the marginalized and oppressed. By using the life history approach, the researcher could make known the voice and meanings of the oppressed or exploited.

Oral History

Oral history collects information from people regarding events in the past. These data are a reflective interpretation of the events. The histories of Christian missions are constructed primarily from archival materials of missionaries' reports and letters housed in their home countries. However, for indigenous history, archival documents may not be available, but using the oral history approach a researcher could collect stories preserved by indigenous people. Such a history could disrupt the dominant discourse of Western mission history and offer a different picture, by highlighting the contribution of indigenous people to the study of world Christianity.

Data for the narrative approach are in the form of stories told by individuals about their lived experiences and stories told by others. The approach also uses interviews, documents, pictures, and diaries to collect stories. The researcher analyzes the data to find themes, structures, turning points, and performance in constructing the story chronologically. Context is a significant factor in narrative research. When this approach is adopted, researchers must make sure they collect all the available information to tell the story. It requires a collaborative effort between the researcher and the participant.

Theories in Qualitative Research

All academic research must deal with the existing concepts, theories, models, and perspectives related to the topic. Some researchers have a misconception that qualitative study does not deal with theories and write whatever fits within their scheme, based on interviewing a few people. As discussed earlier if research does not deal with the existing knowledge, then it is not academic research. Bryman (2012, 20) argues, "Theory is important to the social researcher because it provides a backcloth and rationale for the research that is being conducted. It also provides a framework within which social phenomena can be understood and the research findings can be interpreted." Hence, theory is important for qualitative research.

Qualitative research may not start with one, but it will end with a theory or model or several hypotheses. However, qualitative researchers need to be aware of the existing theories or perspectives related to the phenomenon under study. Such awareness could enhance the design of a study. But the existing theories and models should not direct the researcher, which may limit the researcher in finding the participants' meanings and perspectives.

A theory is an explanation of how different variables relate and work together. Variables are attributes that are measurable or observable such as age, gender, caste, and income. In qualitative research, a theory is understood in a broader sense as *"patterns, theoretical lens, or naturalistic generalizations"* (emphasis in the original, Creswell 2014, 51). Alan Bryman (2012, 22) stretches the definition to include literature review: "the literature acts as a proxy for theory . . . theory is latent or implicit in the literature." Qualitative researchers can design good research if they are exposed to existing theories, perspectives, and models of the phenomenon that is under investigation. As we have seen, the literature review is an important step in designing your research. Although scholars differ in their opinions on the use of literature in qualitative research, I recommend engaging it because it enhances the study. Exposure to theories at the start will enhance the data collection and eventually will help the researcher make a valuable contribution to the field of knowledge.

Qualitative research engages theories differently from quantitative research. John Creswell (2014, 64) observes that theory is used in four different ways in qualitative research.

1. Qualitative researchers use theory as a "broad explanation." The researcher might choose a theme or an aspect of cultural behaviors or beliefs. For example, a researcher might adopt 'shame' as the frame to study the social behaviors of people in a culture or use sin and shame as a broad frame to examine the social behaviors of Christians in a particular culture.

2. Researchers use theory as a lens or perspective in qualitative research. Researchers can adopt gender, class, race, and caste as a lens to investigate a phenomenon from the perspectives of feminism, critical theory, liberation theology, Dalit theology, and

so on. Such a use of theory helps researchers identify:

what issues are important to examine (e.g., marginalization, empowerment, oppression, power) and the people who need to be studied (e.g., women, low economic social status, ethnic and racial groups, sexual orientation, disability). They also indicate how the researcher position himself or herself in the qualitative study (e.g., up front or biased from personal, cultural, and historical contexts) and how the final written accounts need to be written (e.g., without further marginalizing individuals, by collaborating with participants), and recommendations for changes to improve lives and society. (Creswell 2014, 64)

3. Theory becomes the end product of a qualitative study. Qualitative researchers generate theories or models or broader explanations inductively from the data. In this kind of research, categories are identified and grouped as themes to offer an explanation or create a model that is compared with the existing understanding in the literature. Even though the researcher is aware of the available explanations of the phenomenon from the literature review but consciously chooses not to be guided by those theories.

4. In a phenomenological study, some researchers do not use a theory but discover the essence of the phenomenon from participants' experience. However, in my opinion, the discovered essence needs to be brought into dialogue with the literature. In such research, theories are used toward the end of the research, if not at the beginning.

When you prepare a research proposal, first you need to identify the available theories in your field of study and then find theories and models from other disciplines. The literature review functions as a theory in designing qualitative research. Academic research must deal with theories or literature to produce knowledge.

Sampling in Qualitative Research

Sampling is a process of selecting data sources that answer the research questions. When the data source is people, then the sample is a small number of people out of the many who share an experience or were part of a process or action, or event. Qualitative research is about "depth, nuance and complexity, and understanding how these work" (J. Mason 2002, 121). Therefore, it requires non-probability sampling and a small sample size.

Purposive Sampling

Sampling logic is a principle for choosing a sample. In qualitative research, the purpose of the research serves as the sampling logic, an approach known as "purposive sampling," which is a form of non-probability sampling. Purposive sampling lets you determine the criteria for selecting participants based on the purpose of the research. Purposive sampling helps you identifying the people who have "access to data that will allow you to develop an empirically and theoretically grounded argument about . . . the focus of your research questions" (J. Mason 2002, 121). Therefore, purposive sampling is vital in identifying the right participants.

Qualitative research is flexible, and the researcher can change the sample as the research progresses. In qualitative research, data collection and analysis go together; therefore, based on the initial analysis, the researcher can look for different samples that could provide more information on a theme or category that emerged in the analysis. However, the researcher cannot start the research blindly but needs to plan in detail who the participants will be or what kinds of data will be suitable, or which research site will serve the purpose. The researcher needs to have a set of criteria based on research questions in selecting the samples. "Choices of participants, episodes, and interactions should be driven by a conceptual question, not by a concern for representativeness . . . we need to see different instances of it, at different moments, in different places, with different people" (M. B. Miles, Huberman, and Saldana 2014, 33). Purposive sampling is strategic and accommodates a variety of characteristics rather than being representative (Bryman 2012).

Purposive sampling determines the selection criteria based on the purpose of the research. It enables researchers to include only the participants who have experienced the phenomenon and eliminates those who do not share it. For example, for a study on spiritual experiences of the youth in a church, the researcher must specify the criteria for selection. The researcher must define what makes up a spiritual experience and the characteristics of the youth who could be part of the sample. The researcher cannot include pastors, parents, and elders saying that they know the youth closely. But they are not youth, and they can give only opinions, not evidence to construct the reality of the spiritual experience of the youth in the church. Therefore, they will be excluded from the sample. If the researcher wants to include pastors, parents, and elders, they must change the purpose of the study to examining the perception of different stakeholders on the spiritual experience of youth. Novice researchers tend to include in the sample a set of people who do not share the experience under examination; this goes against the logic of purposive sampling.

There are three types of purposive sampling: maximum variation sampling, theoretical sampling, and snowball sampling.

Maximum Variation Sampling

Maximum variation sampling helps the researcher maximize the differences among the samples in order to have variations in the findings. Such variations could result in identifying multiple perspectives of the phenomenon under study. Therefore, the researcher introduces variations for demographic categories like age, gender, education, race, caste, and income, as the criteria for sample selection. A variation could be introduced based on the types of cases like typical cases that are normal or widespread; deviant cases that are unusual; critical cases that are particularly significant regarding a specific aspect; intensive cases that are information-rich; and politically significant cases that are prominent or marginalized (M. B. Miles, Huberman, and Saldana 2014).

Theoretical Sampling

In theoretical sampling, the emerging theory guides the sampling. Glaser and Strauss (1967, 45) define theoretical sampling as "the process of data collection for generating theory whereby the analyst jointly collects, codes, and analyzes his data and decides what data to collect next and where to find them, in order to develop his theory as it emerges." Theoretical sampling helps the researcher to find categories and their interconnectedness. The analyzed data give shape to the emerging theory; as the research progresses, the emerging theory guides the researcher in what to look for next. "The emerging theory points to the next steps— the sociologist does not know them until he is guided by emerging gaps in his theory and by research questions suggested by previous answers" (Glaser and Strauss 1967, 47). As the study progresses, the researcher may find missing categories in the emerging theory; then they select cases that would provide data for the missing gaps in the emerging theory.

For example, in my study of religious conversion (Iyadurai 2015), many participants had a personal crisis prior to their conversion experience. To explore conversion experience that was not preceded by a crisis, I looked for converts who faced no crisis before conversion. Thus, the emerging theory guided me on what to look for next in data collection.

Snowball Sampling

Snowball sampling is a non-probability sampling technique, a type of purposive sampling, used in qualitative research. Why "snowball"? When a snowball is rolled in snow, it becomes bigger and bigger as it picks up more snow. In snowball sampling, a research participant introduces future participants to the researcher and the sample grows. This technique might be used when, at the start of the research, the researcher does not know enough potential participants to provide data to answer the research questions. Hendriks and others (1992, 21) observe, "snowball sampling offers clear practical advantages in obtaining information on difficult-to-observe phenomena, in particular in areas that involve sensitive, illegal or deviant issues. It provides an efficient and economical way of finding cases that may otherwise be difficult or even impossible to locate or to contact." Snowball sampling is suitable for studying sensitive issues or hidden cases or marginalized people, like commercial sex workers, drug misusers, HIV patients or their families, women victims of abuse, bonded laborers, and victims of racial/caste discrimination. In a religious context, it is suitable for studying secret followers of another faith, people who have had a religious experience, recovered from addiction, and so on.

Determining Sample Size

The sample size is significant in all research. However, there is no fixed formula for arriving at a sample size for a qualitative study. Although scholars have varied opinions on sample size, the principle of saturation is generally accepted as a parameter for determining it in qualitative research.

Glasser and Strauss (1967, 61) introduced the principle of saturation in their grounded theory method. "*Saturation* [emphasis in the original] means that no additional data are being found whereby the sociologist can develop properties of the category." Saturation is not about the same kinds of experience but reaching theoretical saturation. Theoretical saturation occurs when "fresh data no longer sparks new theoretical insights, nor reveals new properties of core theoretical categories" (Charmaz 2006, 113). When new categories are not coming forth, the researcher looks out for variations in samples to make sure that theoretical saturation is reached with diverse samples.

While it is possible to arrive at saturation of a few categories at an early stage of data collection, the researcher must not stop with that. As they maximize variations in their samples, they will find new categories emerging and continue to collect more data to saturate the new categories. When they find their emerging theory does not have any gaps that need new categories to fill them, they can be sure they have reached theoretical saturation. Scholars observe that researchers claim saturation, but do not explain the process of achieving saturation, so it would be prudent for them to justify the reach of saturation in their research.

The question of how many participants should make up a sample is unanswerable. John Creswell (2013, 157) finds phenomenological studies have been done with one to 325 participants. Mark Mason (2010), in a survey of 560 doctoral dissertations that used qualitative research, found that the sample size varied from ninety-five to one. He claims that researchers prefer "a quota that will allow them to call their research 'finished'" rather than looking for saturation (sec. 4, para, 10). Many practical considerations play a role in deciding sample size. University committees, ethics committees, and funding agencies, for whom "saturation" is an abstract concept, may demand a specific sample size because they are familiar with the quantitative approach in which the researcher provides a specific number for the sample size. Therefore, qualitative researchers are compelled to give a number to play it safe. However, when a small sample size is given, reviewers may still question the validity.

John Creswell (2014, 189) recommends a range of sample sizes for different approaches:

- Narrative research: One or two
- Phenomenological research: Three to ten
- Grounded theory: Twenty to thirty
- Ethnography: One culture
- Case studies: Four to five

Keeping these ranges in mind at the start of the research, you need to aim for theoretical saturation as you progress in your data analysis. Qualitative research aims for an in-depth understanding of the phenomenon under study; therefore, it relies on a small sample size suitable for the chosen approach. However, you must justify the choice of sampling procedures, methods, and size in your research proposal and report or dissertation by citing the methodology texts.

Methods of Data Collection in Qualitative Research

In qualitative research, data primarily deal with lived experiences, real-life stories, actions, events, and day-to-day happenings; the focus is on studying how people lived, experienced, and made meaning out of their experiences. The data are descriptive or narrative in nature. The experience under investigation could be one individual's experience or a few individuals' experiences or a group of people's experiences. Researchers collect data in different forms by using various methods to understand the experience holistically. Qualitative methods of data collection include qualitative or in-depth interview, participant observation, gathering documents, taking photographs, recording audio/video, capturing online data, and qualitative survey.

Data Sources and Types

Qualitative research uses people as the primary source for investigations to collect their experiences, real-life stories, actions, events, day-to-day happenings as data. Jennifer Mason (2002, 52) identifies broad categories of data sources for qualitative research:

- People (as individuals, groups, or collectivities)
- Organizations, institutions, and entities
- Texts (published and unpublished sources, including virtual ones)
- Settings and environments (material, visual/sensory and virtual)
- Objects, artifacts, media products (material, visual/sensory and virtual)
- Events and happenings (material, visual/sensory and virtual)

The individuals or sites selected are based on the approach chosen (Creswell 2013). The phenomenological approach seeks individuals who have experienced the phenomenon; they could be from a single location or multiple locations. Similar to the phenomenological approach, the grounded theory approach seeks individuals from diverse contexts who share the experience or are part of the process or event. The ethnographic approach looks for a cultural site where a group of people shares a set of beliefs, values, and behaviors; a cultural site could be a community, congregation, organization/institution, or any location where behaviors of a group could be studied. The case study approach selects a site or institution, church, program, event, or one individual. The narrative approach looks for individuals to obtain their stories, which could be personal or stories about other individuals.

Data in qualitative research may originate in the form of text from the transcription of interviews and field notes from participant observation, or documents, both informal and formal, related to individuals or groups or organizations. The data might also be photographs, and audio or video recordings of interviews, speeches, events, actions; and online data that capture virtual communities, or the online presence of individuals and communities, and online interactions among them. Qualitative researchers adopt multiple methods of data collection to find answers to their research questions. Qualitative interview is a common method to all approaches in qualitative research.

Qualitative Interview

A qualitative interview or in-depth interview collects narrative data from participants about their experiences and the meanings associated with them. Narrative data is vital because "telling stories is essentially a meaning-making process. When people tell stories, they select details of their experience from their stream of consciousness" (Seidman 2006, 7). Thus, a qualitative interview is a conversation between the researcher and the participants about the lived experience under study. Although the conversation may be centered around the daily life of the participant, it is neither a simple conversation nor a question-and-answer session; it is a meaning-making process. The description of the experience helps the researcher enter the world of the participant to understand the meaning.

Qualitative interview aims at capturing narratives of experiences which have evidential value for research. The researcher asks questions to elicit "descriptions of *how* interviewees experience the world, its episodes and events, rather than speculations about *why* they have certain experiences" (Brinkmann 2013, 22; emphasis added). Qualitative interview helps researchers capture the day-to-day life of participants. Steinar Kvale (2007, 11) says: "The interview is a uniquely sensitive and powerful method of capturing the experiences and lived meanings of the subjects' everyday world. Interviews allow the subjects to convey to others their situation from their own perspective and in their own words." For example, a researcher studying the lived experience of women pastors in an Episcopal church interviews women pastors because they have the necessary experience. Contrarily, if the researcher interviewed men in leadership positions, the men could only give their opinions about what it means to be a woman pastor, which has no evidential value for the research. As Seidman (2006, 18) says, "we do not ask for opinions but rather the details of their experience, upon which their opinions may be built." Therefore, a qualitative interview is not about seeking the opinions of the participants on a theme but enabling them to talk about their experiences of a theme.

In a qualitative interview, the researcher and the participant are in a conversational relationship to construct knowledge. The knowledge produced is "contextual, linguistic, narrative, and pragmatic. . . . the process of knowing through conversations is intersubjective and social, involving interviewer and interviewee as co-constructors of knowledge" (Kvale and Brinkmann 2009, 18). The researcher does not take the role of an expert but of a partner with the participant, in constructing knowledge. The key elements of the process include the relationship between the researcher and the participant and intersubjectivity in the conversation. The relational dimension is key because the researcher must gain the confidence of the participants so they will open up their personal life stories to make them public knowledge, although anonymity is maintained. The subjectivity of the participant and researcher is integral in constructing knowledge through qualitative interviews because the lived experiences are narrated retrospectively, which is laden with subjectivity. Qualitative research is not interested in producing abstract knowledge, but knowledge that is rooted in the real world and expressed through participants' language in narrative form, not as propositions but value-laden narratives.

The qualitative interview may take different forms: semi-structured, unstructured, and focus group. A qualitative interview seldom uses a structured interview, which is widely used in quantitative research. Contrary to the structured interview in which the researcher's point of view is pivotal, the qualitative interview gives significance to the participant's point of view. Therefore, the qualitative interview is "designed to ask participants to reconstruct their experience and to explore their meaning. The questions most used in an in-depth interview follow from what the participant has said" (Seidman 2006, 92). The qualitative interview takes a semi-structured or unstructured form, with open-ended questions to kindle the memories of the participants to narrate their experiences.

Semi-structured Interview

The semi-structured interview is partially structured by the research purpose and by the research sub-questions. The semi-structured in-depth interview is the primary method of data collection for qualitative research. In semi-structured interviews, the researcher asks only a few predetermined questions based on the research purpose and research sub-questions, with the rest depending on the flow of conversation in the interview. According to Brinkmann (2013, 25), semi-structured interviews are "structured by the interviewer's purpose of obtaining knowledge; they revolve around *descriptions* provided by the interviewee; such descriptions are commonly about *life world phenomena* as experienced; and understanding the meaning of the descriptions involves some kind of *interpretation*" [emphasis in the original]. The semi-structure broadly guides the conversation but never binds the conversation to preformulated questions.

The research sub-questions provide the semi-structure for the interview and guide the conversation. As we have seen, research questions are not interview questions. Therefore, they are not asked of the participants in the interviews. Rather, for the interview, the researcher frames a set of questions that are based on the research sub-questions to cover all aspects of the phenomenon. However, in an actual situation, the researcher may not ask all the questions, but ask one to trigger the participant's thoughts on their experience and narrate it. When the narration does not address a particular aspect of the research, the researcher asks a question to elicit their memories on that aspect of their experience. Thus, the research purpose and research sub-questions provide an underlying fluid structure for semi-structured interviews.

Unstructured Interview

The unstructured interview is a data collection method that is suitable for narrative or biographical research in which the purpose of the research is to capture the life story of an individual. No structure guides the interview because a life story interview is not based on a set of questions. The interviewer primarily takes the role of a facilitator to let the participant narrate their life story. "The main role of the interviewer is to remain a listener, withholding desires to interrupt and sporadically asking questions that may clarify the story" (Brinkmann 2013, 20). The goal is to elucidate the personal meaning, experiences, influences, and events in interviewee's life. "The life story interview is . . . not typically guided by specific theoretical or research questions, other than the questions that would be used to help elicit the story itself" (Atkinson 2012, 121). An unstructured life story interview captures both the life of the participant and its meaning.

The unstructured interview is also used for narrative interviews or oral history interviews. The goal of these interviews is to capture a narrative that addresses the research theme or purpose. However, the focus is on the individual's entire experience related to the research theme. For example, if you are researching on a leader who built an institution, the purpose is to capture the entire story of their experience in building the institution. In such an interview, the theme directs the flow of conversation. This type of interview is suitable for studying the contributions of individuals, bringing out the voices of the marginalized in history, and studying the contributions of indigenous peoples to the growth of their churches/religious communities.

Focus Group Interview

In a group interview, the focus of discussion is the research theme, and the researcher assumes the role of a moderator. The focus group interview is another form of a semi-structured interview. A group is normally composed of five to ten people who share similar experiences. The aim is not to get a consensus from them but to get multiple narratives and diverse perspectives. Interactive group dynamics play a vital role in letting the participants bring out rich data. Reserved people are likely to open up about their story when another member initiates the discussion with a personal experience.

A focus group gives the researcher access to "the ways in which individuals collectively make sense of a phenomenon and construct meanings around it" (Bryman 2016, 502). In this way, contrasting experiences and variance in the shared experiences come up in the discussion. Participants could also raise questions for clarification or offer counter perspectives. Monique Hennink (2014, 3) observes, "It is the group environment that brings out the variety of perspectives, but the interactive discussion that prompts rationalizations, explicit reasoning, and focused examples, thereby uncovering various facets and nuances of the issues that are simply not available by interviewing an individual participant." A focus group interview is suitable for studying new themes, sensitive issues, and vulnerable people.

Modes of Qualitative Interviews

Qualitative interviews are generally conducted face-to-face to capture what is said and how it is said. Face-to-face interviews create an ambience for relational conversation between the researcher and participants.

Qualitative researchers may also make use of telephones for interviews; it eliminates the barrier of distance. One drawback is not being able to observe body language; another is that the quality of data may sometimes fall under suspicion. However, Bryman (2016, 485) asserts, "concerns about data quality in the telephone mode are not as great as sometimes feared." Therefore, I recommend that you use telephones for interviews only if no other option exists.

The COVID-19 pandemic and the subsequent lockdowns threw up many challenges in conducting face-to-face interviews. Amidst this, institutions advised researchers to adopt the virtual mode of collecting data. Researchers use video conferencing apps for qualitative interviews, which has many advantages over the telephone or email/online interviews. Many options are available, like Zoom (https://zoom.us), Webex (www.webex.com), Google Meet (https://meet.google.com), and Skype (www.skype.com). All applications require a paid subscription to use the advanced features. Video calls can be recorded with software such as Debut Video Capture (https://www.nchsoftware.com/capture/index.html) for both audio and video or screen recording applications such as Camtasia (https://www.techsmith.com/store/camtasia). In addition, Audacity (https://www.audacityteam.org/), an open-source application, is good for recording audio. All these applications can be easily installed on PC or Mac laptops. These applications allow the interviewer and interviewee to see each other and observe facial expressions. Sometimes working together to resolving technological problems with the application may provide an opportunity for the interviewer and participants to build rapport (Archibald et al. 2019).

Email or online interviews are being used increasingly; in this method the researcher posts all the questions at the same time or in batches. The participants type their answers with thick descriptions. However, this mode involves minimum interaction between the researcher and the participant, because it is "more akin to answering open-ended questions in a self-administered questionnaire" than in an interview (Bryman 2016, 491). This could also be called a qualitative survey, which we will discuss later.

For focus group interview, researchers gather the participants in a group and moderate the discussion face-to-face. Qualitative researchers also make use the facilities like teleconferencing, videoconferencing, and online discussion groups to conduct focus group interviews. In using a teleconference facility, you can conduct focus group interviews in which participants exchange their thoughts and respond to one another over the telephone; however, they cannot see each other. With video conferencing facilities, you can organize group interviews in which participants can see each other during the discussions. Another online mode is the use of bulletin boards. The researcher posts a question, and the pre-selected participants answer the questions and respond to one another's posts. This can be conducted in a live session, where all are present and type their responses or in an asynchronous session in which each participant logs in at different times to post their responses. You can use Google Groups for this type of discussion.

Using technology for qualitative interviews has advantages and disadvantages. A major advantage is that it crosses barriers of distance and time. However, on the downside, maintaining anonymity could be challenging for researchers, when dealing with video data. Availability and accessibility of technology in remote places, and resolving technical interruptions could also pose challenges. Therefore, before selecting a particular mode, the researcher should weigh in the advantages and limitations of each by considering their and the participants' contexts (Oltmann 2016). You can use multiple modes to conduct qualitative interviews based on feasibility and contextual factors.

Art of Interviewing

Interviewing is both an art and a scientific exercise. Interviewing is an art because the researcher must use creativity and spontaneity in eliciting the stories of the participants. It is also a scientific exercise because it seeks to produce knowledge. The success of an interview largely depends on the rapport the researcher builds with the participant before the interview. "Rapport implies getting along with each other, a harmony with, a conformity to, an affinity for one another" (Seidman 2006, 96). However, Seidman warns that developing a close relationship with participants may hinder the interview. Therefore, you must build an appropriate level of rapport for the success of an interview. The researcher must be ready to answer all the questions the participant has about the researcher, the research, and the interview. The researcher must win the confidence of the participants so that they will share their personal experiences with a stranger.

Qualitative interviews must be conducted in natural settings of the participants where they feel secure and comfortable. The researcher must also check that the place is suitable for an uninterrupted conversation and for recording the interview.

Research ethics require the researcher to obtain participants' informed consent to take part in the research voluntarily. Informed consent involves informing the participants of the purpose of research and permission to record the interview. A consent form must state the purpose of the research, the identity of the researcher and supervisor and their institutional credentials, and the assurance of anonymity. The voluntary nature of the participation, the right of the participant to withdraw, and to refuse to answer any question are to be warranted in the form. Explain this information clearly before obtaining the signatures of participants. In some cultures, people may hesitate to sign the consent form; in such cases, record their oral consent as part of the interview in video/audio.

Researchers must maintain the anonymity of the participants by not disclosing their names or identifiable information; if needed, conceal or change the identifiable information in your research reports. In your write-up, you should use pseudonyms instead of a number or a code for each participant, which may depersonalize the narrative. You will also have to maintain anonymity throughout the research process. For example, if you hear a similar story in an interview, you cannot comment that so and so also had a similar experience. It is good to avoid commenting at all on other participants' experiences during an interview.

In life story interviews, you can decide about anonymity depending on the research purpose. If your study is about a leader's contribution to building an institution or starting a movement, you cannot maintain anonymity; in such cases, the identity of the person is vital for the research purpose. But if your research is about the life story of a vulnerable person, then you must take care to maintain anonymity. However, researchers using pragmatic paradigm prefer to use real identity because they aim at transforming the world of the participants.

Preparing an interview guide or protocol can be valuable for helping you think through the potential questions, which will help you prepare yourself to conduct the interview spontaneously. Translate your research sub-questions into interview questions, phrasing them in such a manner that the participants can understand the questions and answer from their experiences. Use conversational language, not academic jargon, to frame your interview questions.

Let us assume, you are studying the church growth principle of homogeneity. The homogeneity principle says that churches grow faster among the same caste or community in India because of the similarities found among the members. In your interview, you would not ask a church member, does your church grow based on the homogeneity principle? Contrarily, you would ask questions like: Who are the people attending your church? What kind of people are they? Where do they come from, a particular town or village? Which caste group accounts for the majority community in your church? Have you found any newcomers? Who brought them to your church? Are there any of your close or distant relatives who attend your church? How many of your relatives attend your church? Who introduced them to your church? Similarly, you could ask several questions to investigate the homogeneity of a congregation. It is always good to start with broad questions and then move on to specific questions.

You may not have to ask all the questions from the interview guide because the participants may cover a particular aspect of the experience without you asking a question. On the other hand, you may have to revise your interview guide by adding questions for new themes that emerged from previous interviews. This would allow you to further explore the topic in subsequent interviews.

Active listening is vital during the interview. The success of the interview does not only depend on how well you ask questions but also on attentive listening. Seidman (2006, 78) observes, "The hardest work for many interviewers is to keep quiet and to listen actively." Only if you listen attentively, can you come up with probing questions to clarify something or even ask follow-up questions to get more details.

You must be ready to ask probing and follow-up questions to clarify and get more details on a particular aspect; this is possible with careful listening. With probing questions, you can also let the participant move from a public posture into the real world. Initially, participants tend to present a narrative that suits the public. But their body language may contradict a positive picture. In such instances, you could ask a question to clarify or describe more in detail to get a clear picture of the real situation. Participants may then be comfortable in opening up with the real story.

Normally, "why" questions are not asked in qualitative interviews, because they might trigger the participant to speculate; instead, we ask "how" they reached this situation. For example, in a study of religious change, instead of asking, 'Why did you change your religion?' We can ask, 'In what situation did you change your religion?' Then the participants would come up with a life situation in which they changed their religion. By understanding the real-life context of the participant, you can infer the factors for changing religion.

Taking notes during an interview helps you in transcribing and analyzing the interview. Take down key terms or instances that you are interested in; the latter enables you to ask for more information later and not interrupt the narration. Make notes of the nonverbal communication. But avoid taking down every word because that might distract the participant; also, you may not be able to listen attentively.

Sometimes, participants appear to be digressing; but it is not advisable to interrupt immediately. Rather, wait for a pause and then ask a probing question to clarify what made them talk about an unconnected experience. Sometimes, your question would have triggered their memory to narrate a particular incident; they would have assumed a link. With a probing question, you could let the participant clarify the assumed link explicitly. If there is no connection, the probing question would bring them back on track to answer your question specifically.

Participants may sometimes invite you to comment on their experience; it is good to be silent and avoid making any comment, especially if it involves a moral judgment or taking a position on a public controversy. Do not indicate your surprise or shock or a condoning attitude at a particular behavior or response of the participant, something like: Oh, Pastor! You did that! or It's all right, everyone does this. Even if the participant does not expect a comment, as a researcher, you need to be alert about your reactions in handling such a situation. What your body language communicates could either put a person off or could trigger them to talk more about those things because you liked such narratives, or to seek your approval.

As an interviewer, you must learn to be comfortable with silence because participants need time to reconstruct their experiences. "It is important to give your participant space to think, reflect, and add to what he or she has said. This may take a second or two for some participants and 20 seconds for others" (Seidman 2006, 93). You need to be thoughtful and to allow the participants to take time to recollect and reconstruct their stories.

Qualitative interviewing is not a mechanical process, yet a researcher can easily acquire a set of skills to be a successful interviewer. Although interview skills are important, qualitative interviewing is fundamentally an informal conversation between two real people. The interaction is based on the relationship between the researcher and the participant and thus, the success of an interview depends on your genuine interest in their life. When the participants find you are genuinely interested in their life, they will offer you rich data from their life-world.

Ending the Interview

As you bring the interview to an end, debrief by asking the participants if they have anything else to say on the theme. Sometimes, they might feel more secure after the recorder is switched off to offer new insights into their experience, which might closely reflect their real-life world. In such instances, it is ethical to take their permission to use those insights as part of the interview. Bryman (2016) suggests not to switch off the recording at the formal end of the interview, but to keep it on while debriefing; however, the participant must know that the recording is on.

One way of ending the interview is to ask the participants about their experience of the interview. Participants in general feel positive about their interviews as "genuinely enriching, . . . enjoyed talking freely, . . . and obtained new insights into important themes of their life worlds" (Kvale and Brinkmann 2009, 129). Participants may express their gratitude to the researcher for listening to them and showing genuine interest in their life.

When the interview is over, write down your reflective comments, observations, feelings on the interview, the highlights, new themes that emerged, and anything that stands out from other interviews. If you cannot write your reflections immediately after the interview, do it as soon as you can.

Thank the participants and indicate that if needed, you will contact them for further discussion. If the participant wants one, you should be able to provide them with an audio file or transcription of the interview.

Sometimes, if the participants experience intense emotions while narrating their personal and private stories during the interview, they may expect the researcher to play the role of a therapist. Seidman (2006, 108) warns, "researchers must be very cautious about approaching areas of participants' private lives and personal complexities to which they are ill-equipped to respond and for which they can take no effective responsibility." Debriefing questions like, how do you feel about telling your story in the interview? could help participants come out of the emotional upheaval. Sometimes, being patient and silent, instead of abruptly finishing and leaving, could let the person regain their self.

In theological research, while you are acting as a theological or religious researcher, people may expect you to play the role of a religious leader or pastor, or priest. I do not see any harm in you playing such a role as long as the participants are comfortable with and are willing to receive a word of encouragement, some spiritual input, and a word of prayer. In the majority world, people regard religious leaders highly, and it would be a disappointment for them if you did not offer a prayer for them after listening to their life stories, especially if they are victims of some kind. However, you must take care not to offend them in any way with your religious role.

Students and scholars of theology tend to be judgmental because of their strong convictions rooted in their traditions. You must avoid being judgmental at all costs about participants' beliefs, practices, and experiences. If they seem contradictory to your tradition, do not attempt to teach the participants explicitly or subtly what is right according to your convictions either during or after the interview. Remind yourself, the purpose of the meeting is to collect data for your research.

I see qualitative interviews for theological scholars as not only an academic exercise but can be a transformative experience. When people narrate their story in the context of religious or theological inquiry, they bring in their experience of God, spirituality, and beliefs to shape their meanings. Their lived experiences could challenge your theological perspectives and let you see the reality of how people on the ground perceive theological ideas based on their life world. The qualitative interview can be a transformative experience for theological researchers who are preoccupied with speculative theological propositions. Therefore, be open minded.

Audio Recording

Audio recording is an essential feature of qualitative interviews. Participants may appear to be self-conscious when they see a recording device; however, as they talk, they get used to it. Before the start of the interview, speak into the recorder the name of the participant, date, time, and place of the interview for your reference. Because the audio recording captures every word spoken and makes it easier, than just notes would, for you to transcribe the interview for analysis. Audio data also preserves the original conversation for future reference if transcriptions or translations are not clear.

The audio recording also captures the tone, mood, hesitations, silence, fillers, laughter, cries, and sighs that are part of the conversation. They play a key role in the analysis of interview data. "If this aspect is to be fully woven into an analysis, it is necessary for a complete account of the series of exchanges in an interview to be available" (Bryman 2016, 479). These elements are to be noted down in the transcription. Audio recording of individual and focus group interviews is essential, for it gives the researcher access to everything that was part of the conversation.

Digital voice recorders are best suited for qualitative interviews because of their small size, the quality of recording, and compact storage. It is also prudent to have another device, such as a smart phone or laptop available as an alternative to a digital recorder. Audacity software program records audio in a laptop; it can convert the audio file into MP3 for easy playback, transfer, and storage. Before starting the interview, make sure that the device is working and have spare batteries or a power bank for backup.

Using a video recorder depends on the willingness of the participant and the mode of interview. Some participants may not agree with recording videos of face-to-face interviews; if those who agree become highly self-conscious, it is better to limit yourself to audio recording. However, participants may not object to recording a virtual interview because you are not using a separate recording device, which would otherwise make them self-conscious.

Participant Observation

The ethnographic approach uses participant observation as the main method of data collection through fieldwork. This requires the researcher to live with the community for a long period (six months to eighteen months) to collect information about specific behaviors, practices, and events, and to explore how they are placed in the larger picture of the culture. For an ethnographic study, researchers record fieldnotes based on their observations and informal interviews. Field notes are a form of data gathered through participant observation.

Participant observation involves "immersion in a culture" (Fetterman 2010, 37). Through immersion, the researcher can see from "the inside how people lead their lives, how they carry out their daily rounds of activities, what they find meaningful, and how they do so. In this way, immersion gives the fieldworker access to the fluidity of others' lives and enhances his sensitivity to interaction and process" (Emerson, Fretz, and Shaw 2011, 3). The researcher must look for both a bigger picture of the culture as well as the minute details of the culture. "It begins with a panoramic view of the community, closes into a microscopic focus on details, and then pans out to the larger picture again—but this time with new insight into minute details. The focus narrows and broadens repeatedly as the fieldworker searches for breadth and depth of observation" (Fetterman 2010, 39–40). Immersion in culture captures the bigger picture of a culture with its details.

Rapport

Establishing rapport is a key factor for entering the community and being accepted as one among them. In some places, you first need to approach the gatekeepers, the community leaders or institutional heads whose permission you need for carrying out the research. They will introduce you to the community; however, this has its advantages and limitations. You will have easy access to community members or the settings, but people may be suspicious about your affinity with the gatekeeper and may not give you a true picture.

To establish rapport, identify some key informants or key actors who could offer information on the bigger picture. Gatekeepers could also play the role of key actors. "Key actors can provide detailed historical data, knowledge about contemporary interpersonal relationships (including conflicts), and a wealth of information about the nuances of everyday life" (Fetterman 2010, 50). You will interact with many people, but the key actors can offer insights that are not commonly stated by others. However, you should not rely only on their perspective.

The community expects the researcher to respect their cultural values and norms and behave in a culturally acceptable manner. It requires "learning what constitutes good manners and practicing them to the best of your ability. It can include proper, polite speech; appropriate reciprocity; table manners; appropriate levels of eye contact: all the many niceties (as defined by each culture) that make up day-to-day interaction" (DeWalt and DeWalt 2011, 58). You can spend the initial days learning these things, so you can be one with the community.

Before they share about their cultural life, people like to know more about you, the researcher. It is good to tell the truth about yourself so that you can win the confidence of people. However, Kathleen DeWalt and Billie DeWalt (2011) suggest that for women researchers, it is acceptable to claim to be married or pretend to be in a relationship to deflect any sexual interest from the members. Other than this, you are expected to tell the truth about yourself, your beliefs, and your values. On matters related to religion or politics, you will have to be cautious and offer a neutral opinion, which are worded on the lines of, "I do not share the same view with you, but I value your point of view." Since you will live with the community for a long period, they will come to know whether you are truthful. Therefore, you must be consistent from the beginning in sharing your personal information.

The community has the right to know about your research, which you must explain to the community in a way they will understand. They would be interested in knowing the outcome of your research and how it might affect them. You need to know the concerns and goals of the community to be accurate in presenting your findings from their point of view. It is important that "both investigator and informants come to share common goals or move to develop joint goals for the research. The participants in the setting or events under study must come to agree to help the investigator" (DeWalt and DeWalt 2011, 52). The members of the community own your research and accept you as one among them when they are convinced about the outcome of the research and its benefits for the community.

Language is a key factor in participant observation. If your study is in a cross-cultural setting, you need to learn the local language to understand the culture on terms of the community. When you speak their language, they accept you as part of the community. It is also essential to understand meaning from a local perspective, because "understanding local meanings is critical to understanding what is going on" (DeWalt and DeWalt 2011, 58). You can understand local meanings only in the local language.

Observation

As you live with the community, you need to observe everyday activities like children going to school, cooking, eating, and taking care of children and the aged. You also need to observe various transactions, selling and buying, and regular activities like going to a worship place, community gatherings, and so on. Other areas of observation are activities associated with the roles of men, women, parents, children, elders, leaders, and religious leaders in the community. Other events like life-cycle rituals, celebrations, festivals, leisure, recreational activities, and so on are also important to observe.

Observation varies, based on the research purpose and research site of the study. If your study is about the culture of an organization, you will observe what goes on in the office every day. When and how people enter the office. How they dress to come to the office. What each one does. How each one plays their role. How disputes are triggered and resolved. If your study is about worship in a church, you will participate in the worship and observe all that goes on. You will observe most of the things mentioned above. Worship may be a weekly activity or, in some churches, a daily activity. In all research sites, the focus of the observation is on both routine and non-routine activities.

Observation involves capturing everything in detail including "the arrangement of physical space, the arrangement of people within that space, the specific activities and movement of people in a scene, the interaction among people in the scene (and with the researcher), the specific words spoken, and nonverbal interaction, including facial expressions" (DeWalt and DeWalt 2011, 81). It is not sufficient to note what people do and speak. As a participant-observer, you need to note the physical location, people's position and movements in the physical space; and their activities, conversations, body language, and so on.

Researchers can lose their interest in mundane activities and become keen on unrepeated events. However, observing mundane activities is very important because in them lie "patterned behaviors, embodying and exemplifying culturally significant knowledge and attitudes" (DeWalt and DeWalt 2011, 90). Daily activities carry shared values and meanings in a culture. Repeated participation in an event or activity helps the researcher to compare with previous occasions which would throw some light on the variations.

Non-participant Observation

Some research requires non-participant observation, in which the researcher does not take part in the activity but acts as a passive observer. In this method, observation is done in a "completely unobtrusive manner, without any interaction with the research participants" (Roller and Lavrakas 2015, 173). Some research requires offsite non-participant observation and other studies require onsite non-participation.

In a study of offsite non-participation, the researcher observes remotely. This is the case, for example, in studies on a program or an activity or virtual communities or social media groups where the presence of the researcher could make people conscious of being observed. Such offsite non-participant observation is done through remote access via live stream, a remote monitor, or some other channel.

Some studies require researchers to do on-site non-participant observation. The researcher cannot take part in the activity and has only the option to observe as a non-participant. This might be the case if a researcher is studying the culture of an organization and wanting to observe the discussion in a stakeholders meeting, in which the researcher is present as an observer but does not participate in the proceedings or interrupt to ask questions for clarification during the meeting. However, after the meeting, the researcher could interact with the officials and other members to get more information.

In a covert study, the researcher becomes part of the community by concealing their role as a researcher. In such instances, the researcher does not interview the participants on matters relating to the research explicitly but may interact with them as a member of the community. Non-participant observation is suitable for either covert or overt observation. The nature or purpose of the research determines what type of observation is suitable for the research.

Informal Interviews

Researchers use informal interviews in participant observation to elicit local meanings. In informal interviews, the researcher uses questions that arise out of a conversation in a natural situation, such as when the person is attending an event and asks a local person for the significance and meaning of a particular practice. "A multitude of significant, nonthreatening questions can elicit the information the fieldworker seeks and create many golden moments in which to ask questions naturally as part of the general flow of conversation" (Fetterman 2010, 42). Such natural conversations are guided by the researcher's interest in a phenomenon. But "the researcher is not necessarily directing the topics for discussion, but is following, or following up on points raised by another person during the natural flow of conversation" (DeWalt and DeWalt 2011, 139). Tips on the art of interviewing for qualitative interview that were discussed above apply in conducting informal interviews.

Field Notes

In ethnographic studies, researchers record field notes based on their observations and informal interviews. Field notes contain jottings, descriptive notes, methodological notes, reflective notes, logs, analytic notes, and headnotes.

Jottings contain terms, phrases, and short sentences that the researcher came across while observing or taking part in an activity or event. The jottings are primarily made to help the researcher recollect the whole event or activity. DeWalt and DeWalt (2011) suggest that jottings could include words, phrases, sentences, names of people, sketches, maps, and logs. Any significant conversation that needs to be used verbatim must be noted accurately. It is also important to make note of the date and time of the event or activity, or conversation. The researcher must always carry a pen and small notebook to jot down notes while observing. Participants have mixed responses to note-taking. Initially, they may be apprehensive about it; over time, they will understand the role of the researcher and accept it.

Descriptive notes are the expanded notes based on the jottings. They are to be developed as soon as possible and at least by the end of the day. These notes must capture all the details of the activity or event, or conversation. "It should include description of the physical context, the people involved, as much of their behavior and nonverbal communication as possible, and in words that are as close as possible to the words used by the participants. . . . Specific words, special language, terms, and vocabulary should be recorded." (DeWalt and DeWalt 2011, 165-166). You should use words that are as close as possible to those used by the participants.

Field notes must capture the event or activity or conversation in detail and accurately, from the participants' perspective. The descriptive notes must have "sufficient detail to bring the scene to life" (DeWalt and DeWalt 2011, 167). Field notes must enable the researcher to recapture the event or activity or conversation as closely as possible.

Methodological notes contain the details of the methods chosen and how they were deployed. The researcher must record the effectiveness of the method in the field, challenges faced in using a particular method, and how they went about collecting data. If they adopted a new method, the reasons for the change of method and its usefulness in conducting field research need to be noted. Methodological notes are useful for the analysis of the field notes and can be used in the methodology section of the final report.

Reflective notes are also called journal or diary notes. Reflective notes help you clarify your position in analyzing the event or activity, or conversation. They also help you collect further data or explore new areas. Reflective notes record your feelings (joys, sorrows, frustrations), hunches, impressions, thoughts, and comments on what you have observed. You can also note your biases, anything that was not clear to you, anything that you wanted to follow up on, and anything new that you wanted to explore further with informal interviews or in-depth interviews, and so on. Reflective notes help you understand yourself regarding what you have observed and to track your progress.

Logs are the records of your daily activity: events to attend or attended, things to do or things done, people to meet or people met, documents (official records or informal documents) to be accessed or accessed, and weather of the day. Logs contain both what you planned to do in a day and any unplanned meetings, events, or activities in which you took part.

Analytic notes are the notes of inference and are called "meta-notes." Some researchers combine reflective notes and analytic notes. In qualitative research, data collection and analysis are performed simultaneously. You need not wait to complete the fieldwork to analyze the fieldnotes. You can start on the first day of your fieldwork and revisit them after the fieldwork to do a detailed analysis. "Summarization, inference, and new hypotheses form part of the body of analytic or meta-notes that are central to the enterprise, but sufficiently different from the more descriptive materials" (DeWalt and DeWalt 2011, 170), which are part of the descriptive notes. As you observe more and more in the field, you may find new interpretations, variations, and insights, and your inferences may change. Analytic notes keep a record of your train of thoughts or interpretation during the fieldwork. They record the progress of your interpretation.

Headnotes are the information that is stored in our minds that has not been recorded. Researchers have many things in their minds that are not possible to put in the field notes. It could be some sort of tacit knowledge: "the things we come to know without even knowing that we know them, the knowledge that is hard to put into words" (DeWalt and DeWalt 2011, 172). Tacit knowledge grows with the progress of the field research, and it helps the researcher to see the fieldnotes, sometimes, differently during analysis. If the researcher can translate the headnotes into words, then it becomes valuable to record them as part of the reflective notes; however, everything cannot be put down in words. The researcher will always have something more in their mind than the fieldnotes record, which could play a key role in telling the story.

In addition to using field notes, ethnographers collect documents, take photos, and record audios and videos of an event or activity in the field.

Documents

Documents, which were not produced to meet the purpose of the research can be another form of data. The documents must be related to the person, people, community, church, institution, or issue, which are the focus of the research. They could be personal letters or emails, testimonies, sermon notes, autobiographies, newsletters (personal, institution, church, organization), magazines, official communications, mission reports, and minutes of board meetings. They could also be, photographs, advertisements, flyers, audio/videos, blogs, tweets, YouTube videos, websites, archival materials, newspaper reports, television coverages, and social media posts. Bryman (2016) classifies this type of document as personal documents, official documents of the state, official documents of private sources, mass-media outputs, and virtual documents.

The focus of the research determines what kinds of documents would enrich your data. Let us assume you are researching racial violence against African Americans in a city. If your focus is on the victims of violence, you will approach the victims and interview them to capture the nature and effects of the violence. In addition to doing the qualitative interviews, you could collect photographs, videos, personal letters, emails, and any other documents the victims or the victim's families provide.

If the focus of your study is on the role of the church in response to the violence, then in addition to interviewing the victims, you would interview pastors or leaders. You would collect church reports or prayer letters, appeals for peace, minutes of church council meetings related to the violence, the church's representation to the government, and a copy of any memorandum submitted to government officials. Such documents help you explore how the church responded to the tragic incident.

If the focus is on the role of the government in dealing with an incident of racial violence, you will still interview the victims to bring out the intensity of the pain for them. In addition, you would collect documents from the state such as complaints filed with the police, action-taken reports of the police or other officials, their statements on the tragedy, statistical information on the damage caused to the people, and so on.

If your focus is on the media, then you would collect all the newspaper reports on the incident, clippings of television coverage, talk shows on the tragedy, and social media posts. Here, the focus would be on how the media covered this incident. Your analysis will bring out how the media was neutral or biased against African Americans in reporting, how the media was helpful to the victims, and how the media was helpful to restore peace between the communities.

If you are using a case study approach to studying the racial violence of a particular incident, you can make use of documents from many sources: victims, church, state, media, and social media. In the case study approach, you are looking at the issue from multiple angles.

Photographs

Photographs are another form of data to understand the world of participants. Researchers take photographs to capture the settings, activities, or events. Sometimes, they ask the participants to take photographs to serve the research purpose. Here the researcher or the participant takes photographs to meet the research purpose. Participants may also provide photographs related to their experiences, which are not produced for the purpose of research. Bryman (2016, 454) suggests that photographs are used in qualitative research in three ways: "aide-memoire," separate data, and prompts.

Ethnographers use photographs as part of their field notes. "Photographs are mnemonic devices" (Fetterman 2010, 78) that help the researcher recall the details for analysis. Photographs may be treated as a separate form of data because "the camera often captures details that the human eye has missed . . . Graphic representations of behaviors and locations can be illuminating and compelling" (Fetterman 2010, 78). Photographs provide information that supplements the fieldnotes or interviews.

Auto-photography lets participants capture images of their life through their own eyes instead of researchers taking photographs from their point of view. In this method participants decide how to capture their experiences, emotions, and perspectives in a deeper manner, which otherwise may not be possible for the researcher to access. It also helps participants to interpret their experience and articulate their perspectives contrary to the identity or perspectives imposed on them by others (Langmann and Pick 2018). This method is suitable to study marginalized communities and victims of some kind, from their perspectives. The advancement of digital technology enables participants to capture their life moments through a mobile phone camera or a digital camera.

Photo-elicitation involves using photographs to stimulate discussion and elicit deeper insights into participants' experiences and perspectives. "Photo-elicitation *elicits* . . . experiences and higher level values, assumptions, beliefs and cultures of participants" (emphasis original, Langmann and Pick 2018, 7). In photo elicitation, researchers show photographs to participants and ask them to reflect on the photos to talk about their feelings, meanings, and perspectives, of their own experiences. This method enables participants to subjectively interpret the photographs and reflect on them to express their meanings of their personal experience.

When using photographs, you must be aware of ethical and copyright issues. When you take photographs of participants, you need to obtain their consent to capture their images and to use them in your research reports. If participants own the photographs, then you will have to ask them for permission to use the photographs and to reproduce them.

Audio/Video

Audio/Video as data for qualitative research has been in use for a long time. Audio-visual data are generated by researchers and in some instances in partnership with participants. In qualitative research, audio and video data are complementary to other forms of data. However, the use of video as a method finds increased interest among researchers across disciplines (Harris 2016). Analysis of documentaries and movies is another field of research, which is different from video-based research.

Researchers from theology and religious studies could utilize video data and video as a method, for their research to explore many untrodden areas. For example, religion and food could be explored by capturing *langar*, food served in a *Gurudwara* (worship place of Sikhs), where anyone can walk in and participate in a community meal. In South India, churches celebrate *asanam*, in which congregation members cook and serve food to several thousands of people on the church's anniversary. This is a significant event for people in that region, which is unexplored by theological scholars thus far.

As discussed, qualitative interviews are always audio-recorded and transcribed for analysis. An audio recording of an informal conversation or an event may help the researcher reproduce a verbatim conversation when needed. However, the audio recording does not capture the body language, which can be essential to have. Moreover, the identification of speakers could be problematic. Yet, audio recordings can play a supplementary role in fieldnotes.

Video recording of events or activities help the researcher capture details. During analysis, the researcher can view the video repeatedly to get a full sense of the activity. By using multiple cameras, a researcher can capture both the bigger picture and minute details of an organized event in the community. But it may not be possible to capture daily activities or behaviors.

Video data could be researcher generated videos, participant generated videos, selfie videos, Vlogs (video blogs), screen recordings of online activities, videos/reels from social media, video footages from public domain, stack videos, and so on.

Having participants record videos of their lifeworld or any event or activity to which the researcher has no access is gaining interest among researchers. Such videos allow the researcher to access the life world or the events that would not be otherwise possible for them to investigate. Videos are useful "particularly in realms where the knowledge sought is beyond the range of language" (Banks 2007, 116). They can bring out the hidden or uncovered aspects of the phenomenon under study.

Online Data

With an increased interaction among people on the internet, the need arises to understand online cultures. Role-playing video games such as Second Life, World of Warcraft, and Lineage allow people to be active in virtual worlds. Each player creates an avatar and takes part in the community, which is not an imaginary or fictional world, but real. "Just as in the physical world, people within virtual worlds perform and cycle through different roles and identities. Virtual worlds make such shifts explicit, as well as introducing spaces for play and experimentation" (Boellstorff et al. 2012, 1). Social networking sites like Facebook, Instagram, YouTube, and Twitter are the other forms of socialization on the internet. A scholar can research online lived experience, online activities, online behaviors, perspectives, meaning, online communications with its structure, patterns, and content. They can also research online patterns and types of social relations, the interaction between online communities, and communication between online and offline communities (Kozinets 2010).

Many aspects of online culture may also be studied from a religious or theological perspective. Religious groups are increasingly using the internet to promote their beliefs and practices and followers of a religion use the internet to practice their faith. The Second Life, a virtual platform, has mosques, churches, Hindu temples, and Buddhist temples. Hindu virtual temples facilitate online *darshan* and rituals. Virtual churches such as Anglican Cathedral, i-church, and LIFE.CHURCH exist in the virtual world. At the virtual churches, people come together as a virtual community to have worship services, take part in communion, conduct baptisms, and organize mission trips to the real world (Estes 2009). Muslim Pal is an application for Muslims to interact virtually.

Because this internet world of religion is largely an unexplored territory for theological and religious scholars, it has great research potential. Researching online religion from a theological or religious perspective would add new dimensions to the understanding of virtual religious communities. Douglas Estes (2009), the author of *SimChurch*, observes that learning about virtual churches and people in virtual world will help us understand the churches and people in the real world. Therefore, researching religion in the virtual world also helps us understand religion in the real world.

Lorme Dawson and Douglas Cowan (2004) spell out six areas for studying religion online:

1. Who and how the internet is used for religion. How does the usage change over a period?
2. People's experience of online religion.
3. Comparative analysis of online and offline religious activities.
4. Studies on online religious practices.
5. Technology and religion and consequences of technology on religious life.
6. Suitability of technological and cultural aspects of the internet to the advancement of religion.

In addition to the above aspects, Kozinets, (2010) suggests studying online religious communities and virtual churches.

To explore online religion, you must choose the appropriate method of data collection based on the research purpose or research questions. The ethnographic approach uses participant observation as the primary mode of data collection, which is suitable to study online communities; it is called virtual ethnography or netnography. "Netnography is participant-observational research based in online fieldwork. It uses computer-mediated communications as a source of data to arrive at the ethnographic understanding and representation of a cultural or communal phenomenon" (Kozinets 2010, 60). Similar to an ethnographer who immerses in the culture, a virtual ethnographer also becomes immersed in the virtual community authentically by participating actively, not just by being an observer. Besides participant observation, online interviews, discussion forums, and email interviews/surveys could be used for online research.

Researching online requires scholars to manage many challenges. Brad McKenna, Michael D. Myers, and Michael Newman (2017) have made recommendations to address the challenges in using social media for qualitative research in the field of information sciences. I rely on them to make the following recommendations for studying religion online.

1. To tackle a huge amount of data, use a filter or data mining technique to reduce the volume of data.

2. A software program for analyzing qualitative data will be helpful for handling a large volume of data.
3. Screenshots can capture digital contents, like text and image.
4. Screen recording records sound and video of online activities.
5. In order to become immersed in the online culture, the researcher must be familiar with the online environment: skills of playing online games, the language of the community, and the visual cues.
6. To address the authenticity of the data, use different types of data: field notes, chat logs, discussion posts, data from external sources, and so on.
7. To address the authenticity of the data, where the users are anonymous or have masked their identity, design a study for which identity is not a key factor for answering the research question.
8. Obtaining informed consent from everyone may not be possible. But get permission from the gatekeepers to access private sites.
9. To take part actively in the virtual world, create an avatar. Some sites permit use of multiple avatars that would allow you multiple perspectives. Be mindful of the community's values and practices; some communities may encourage the use of real identity, but some may not appreciate real identity being disclosed by the members.
10. To bridge the digital divide, supplement traditional forms of data.

With social media technologies constantly emerging, new challenges will arise for researchers, but that should not deter theological or religious scholars from exploring online religion.

Qualitative Survey

People use the term "qualitative survey" broadly to refer to qualitative research in general (Kane 2008; Echchabi and Aziz 2014). I prefer to use the term to refer to self-completed open-ended questionnaires, which are a method of data collection for qualitative research. Some books discuss the use of email interviews in which the researcher sends out a set of open-ended questions for participants to answer in detail. Bryman (2016, 491) has a serious objection to asynchronous or email interviews and wonders, "whether it is appropriate to describe them as interviews at all and indeed whether they are experienced by research participants as interviews." Because they involve only writing with no interaction, no discussion between the researcher and the participants, they are more like a self-completed questionnaire than an interview. Therefore, I classify such a written form of "interview" as a qualitative survey.

Unlike a quantitative survey, which aims at measuring variables and generalization, the qualitative survey aims at understanding the "'depth and uniqueness' rather than breadth and representation" (Fink 2003, 68). A qualitative survey clearly instructs the participants to explain their experiences with thick descriptions.

At the outset, the questionnaire for the qualitative survey introduces the purpose of the research, states the credentials of the researcher and supervisor, and identifies the institution where the research is conducted. It also assures the participants that their participation is voluntary and that they have the right to decline to answer any questions. The second section deals with the demographic details of the participants and the third section presents the open-ended questions.

You could conduct a qualitative survey in person or through the post/email/online. If it is in person, you can explain the purpose of the research and answer any questions the participant has during the survey. Otherwise include the information as described above. Set a time to collect the answers. By sending out the questions through the post, you are asking the participants to use their own stationery to answer the questions. For an email survey, you can send the questions in a Word file as an attachment, which the participants could download and answer the questions and return as an attachment. Having the answers in a Word file makes it easy for the researcher to store them and analyze the text. Another option for an email survey is to send the questions in the email and ask the participant to answer by replying to your email. If needed, you could ask further questions or clarifications by email. Here, you can save the email as a PDF or copy the answers and paste them into a Word file for analysis. For an online (web-based) qualitative survey, you can create an online survey with open-ended questions either on a blog site or on any of the online survey sites. Then you email or text the link to the participants, asking them to click the link to answer the questions. You could also create an online qualitative survey with options for discussions between you and the participant.

I suggest you use the qualitative survey to gain data to supplement other forms of data. The qualitative survey allows you to include more participants than interviews do. It also helps you to include participants who are not available for an in-person interview due to distance or other factors that prevent them from discussing sensitive issues.

In this section on data collection, we have discussed data sources and types and data collection methods, such as qualitative interviews, participant observation, collecting documents, taking photographs, recording audio and videos, capturing online data, and qualitative survey. The next section deals with analyzing qualitative data.

Data Analysis in Qualitative Research

Data collection and data analysis are done simultaneously in qualitative research. The results of the analysis help the researcher collect new data and so on. Immediately after an interview, the researcher documents their reflective thoughts on the interview or on an event by making note of the salient features. When they are not clear on a particular factor, they collect more data or have an informal conversation to clarify it. When a new theme emerges from an interview or observation, they collect more data to understand the theme further in the subsequent interviews.

Although qualitative data deals with different forms of data as we have seen, the analysis basically deals with text: transcription of interviews, expanded field notes from participant observation, transcriptions of audio recordings of events or actions, and text documents from the field. To analyze other forms of data, such as photographs, videos, artifacts, screenshots, and other digital media, the researcher writes memos on them in text form. Memos are the researcher's reflective comments on the text or other forms of data.

As mentioned, the steps in qualitative analysis involve transcription of interviews and any other audio recordings, making sense of the data, coding the units of meaning, grouping the units together as categories, and grouping the categories under broad themes. In addition, each qualitative approach adopts certain steps to capture the elements that are peculiar to it. The ethnographic approach aims to tell the story to present the bigger picture of a culture; the phenomenological approach highlights the themes; the narrative approach presents the narrative structure.

Transcription

The conversion of audio recordings of interviews into text data is the first step in qualitative analysis. Transcribing is a tedious and time-consuming process, and it is estimated that an hour of audio recording takes four or five hours to transcribe. Researchers of large projects engage professional transcribers. If your research is for a doctoral or master's degree, engaging professional transcribers will cost you heavily and you will have to address ethical issues regarding confidentiality. Moreover, if you do it yourself, you will achieve better accuracy than someone else could; because you remember the interview and could recollect easily what is said or meant. Repeated listening to the audio while transcribing helps you make sense of the interview, which will be helpful in the analysis process.

You must transcribe the exact words of the participant, instead of a paraphrased summary of the interview. Seidman (2006, 114) warns us: "To substitute the researcher's paraphrasing or summaries of what the participants say for their actual words is to substitute the researcher's consciousness for that of the participant." Therefore, avoid paraphrasing or summarizing interviews for analysis.

You must transcribe the whole interview and cannot be selective in transcribing a portion of an interview. "Preselecting parts of the tapes to transcribe and omitting others tends to lead to premature judgments about what is important and what is not" (Seidman 2006, 115). Any portion of the interview that is not transcribed is considered lost data. While transcribing, it is essential to record not only what the participants said but also how they said it. You must record "all the nonverbal signals, such as coughs, laughs, sighs, pauses, outside noises, telephone rings, and interruptions, that are recorded on the tape" (Seidman 2006, 116). You must avoid the temptation to polish the language; it is good to preserve the messiness of the original conversation.

Be consistent in using symbols in the transcription, such as square brackets to indicate your comments or capitals to denote a loud voice and so on. Researchers who adopt conversation analysis follow the Jefferson Transcription System, which provides symbols to capture the complexity of conversation.

You need to translate the interviews that are conducted in local languages into English or the language in which you will write your research report. Institutions may require you to make the data available in English for supervisors and examiners to inspect if required. When using software for analysis, if the software does not process the local language, then you will have to translate the interviews into English. You must maintain accuracy in translating the interview data.

Many software packages are available for transcription; some are free. Transcription software allows you to play, pause, rewind, and forward to make the process easier. With a USB pedal, you can operate the player with your feet, so that your hands are free to type. Another option is using voice recognition software to transcribe the interviews. Paid versions of Zoom and other applications have transcription features. Online transcribing services are available, but confidentiality issues may arise. If you are planning to code manually, then Saldana (2013) suggests that you type on the left half of a page, leaving the right half for writing codes and memos.

Making Sense of the Data

Making sense of the data is the next step in qualitative analysis. Repeated reading of the transcription of interviews or fieldnotes or repeated review of the visual data or videos will help you make sense of the data. Reading the text a few times helps you capture the bigger picture of the interview or event. "By reading and rereading the corpus, you gain intimate familiarity with its contents and begin to notice significant details as well as make new insights about their meanings. Patterns, categories, and their interrelationships become more evident the more you know the subtleties of the database" (Saldana 2011, 95). You need to immerse yourself in the data to make sense of the details. Making sense of video data, for example, involves a repeated review of the videos to observe the enormous details they provide to the research. Having a bigger picture in mind helps you understand and interpret the smaller pieces in context. You will find this interesting because you are dealing with the real-life experiences of people, not with abstract ideas or concepts at this stage.

Coding

After making sense of the data, the next step is coding. A code is a label or name you assign to a unit of meaning or category. According to Corbin and Strauss (2015, 105) coding is a process of interacting with the data by raising questions, comparing data, and deriving and developing concepts by "digging beneath the surface to discover the hidden treasures contained within" the data. In other words, "Coding means naming segments of data with a label that simultaneously categorizes, summarizes, and accounts for each piece of data" (Charmaz 2006, 43). Coding is labeling a unit of meaning in the data.

A code is a name given to a unit of meaning. A unit of meaning could be an idea or action captured from a word or phrase or paragraph, or even the entire narrative. "A code is a researcher-generated construct that symbolizes and thus attributes interpreted meaning to each individual datum for later purposes of pattern detection, categorization, theory building, and other analytic processes" (Saldana 2013, 4). You can name a code based on your understanding of the segment of the data or you can use the same words or phrases used by the participants to name a code, which is called "in vivo" code.

What needs to be coded? You could code units of meaning, which refer to a segment of data that offers a description or an action or an idea or inferential meaning. It could be descriptions, processes, emotions, values, beliefs, practices, assessments, relational dynamics, causal connections, concepts associated with theories, and so on (M. B. Miles, Huberman, and Saldana 2014). As you progress with coding each interview or each data set, the same codes may appear frequently within or across the data sets, while some appear frequently only within a particular data set. Codes are helpful in retrieving portions of data from several data sets that share the same meaning.

Coding reduces the data to meaningful units for analytical purposes. "Coding is deep reflection about and, thus, deep analysis and interpretation of the data's meanings" (M. B. Miles, Huberman, and Saldana 2014, 72). Coding is subjective and reflective. Because "coding is not a precise science; it is primarily an interpretive act" (Saldana 2013, 4). You will approach the data from your position based on your theology/ religious philosophy, methodological approach, conceptual framework, and other orientations. These orientations operate as filters when you code the data.

Johnny Saldana (2013, 58) recommends two cycles of coding. The first cycle deals with, naming data segments while the second cycle deals with, "classifying, prioritizing, integrating, synthesizing, abstracting, conceptualizing, and theory building." Similarly, for the grounded theory approach, Charmaz (2006) suggests two phases of coding, the initial phase, and the focused phase. All qualitative approaches use two levels of coding.

During the initial phase, the researcher names the data segments. For initial coding, Charmaz (2006) advises researchers to be open-minded; she also warns that being open does not mean being empty. You may be aware of several possible codes in the literature. But if you go with the preexisting codes, you may miss out on the reality of the participants' life world, which goes against the logic of the qualitative method. One of the salient features of the qualitative method is that it aims to reflect the reality closer to the participant's world. Digging out the data with an open mind will help you discover treasures.

Nevertheless, some scholars suggest using preexisting codes or deductive coding (M. B. Miles, Huberman, and Saldana 2014); John Creswell (2013, 184) uses the term "lean coding" for deductive coding, in which the researcher starts with five or six preexisting codes. However, he suggests that in such cases, the researcher must be open to finding new codes emerging from the data. The downside of deductive coding is that the researcher may make the data fit preexisting codes.

Kathy Charmaz (2006, 49) has prescribed a set of principles for coding. 1. "Remain open": You must be open-minded in coding. 2. "Stay close to the data": Codes are to reflect the data and the reality of the participants' world. Participants' words could be used to name codes. 3. "Keep your codes simple and precise": Choose clear names for codes, not ambiguous ones. 4. "Construct short codes": Names of codes to be short, not a sentence; you can maintain the definitions of codes separately. 5. "Preserve actions": Participants' actions are to be preserved, instead of abstracting their actions. 6. "Compare data with data": Constantly compare codes with one another within an interview or fieldnotes and across the data sets. 7. "Move quickly through the data": Do not wait until completing data collection to begin the analysis. Start data analysis when you have completed the first interview.

Following these principles will immerse you in your data and help you use codes that reflect the data closely rather than making the data fit your codes. Bryman (2016, 583) advises that you need not worry about numerous codes emerging, but "the important thing is to be inventive and imaginative as possible." By repeating the process of initial coding, you will find repeated codes emerging, when sub-codes emerge, you begin to see patterns emerge.

At the second level, you will deal with the codes that were developed during the initial coding to find patterns or relationships among the codes. During the focused (second) phase, you "pinpoint and develop the most salient categories in large batches of data. Theoretical integration begins with focused coding and proceeds through all your subsequent analytic steps" (Charmaz 2006, 46). You must group the codes under a category or classify them under categories. Categories are like containers holding relevant data that share common properties (Bryant 2017). As you repeat the process, other categories will emerge.

During the second phase, you synthesize the open codes into patterns and themes so that they can be abstracted as concepts or theoretical blocks. You can use conceptual or abstract terms to label categories (Saldana 2013). By repeating this process, you further refine or recategorize the codes and this cycle goes on, you may rearrange and reclassify the codes and find new categories. As with creating sub-codes, you will need to create sub-categories. As you continue to code, you can start recording your thoughts as memos.

Similar to coding transcripts, other forms of data such as documents, photographs, audios, videos, and online data can also be coded. For coding these kinds of data, you must look for details instead of coding the entire document or photo or video. Fetterman (2010, 80) observes that repeated watching of videos helps the researcher find "new layers of meaning, including nonverbal signals among participants." However, he warns us it is possible to over-focus on something while missing the bigger picture or even a smaller one. You must identify units of meanings and categories from each document or photo or frame of a video. Follow the two cycles of coding as discussed above.

Memoing

Memoing and coding are parallel steps in qualitative analysis. Memos are reflective thoughts of the researcher on the participants and the phenomenon and are "one of the most useful and powerful sense-making tools" in qualitative analysis (M. B. Miles, Huberman, and Saldana 2014, 96). In memoing, you record everything that you are learning from the data and your thoughts on the analytical process. As you progress with coding, you document your reflection as memos.

What is recorded in memos? You can record your reflective thoughts by answering the following questions that are based on Saldana's (2013) recommendations.

1. How do you view the phenomenon under study?
2. What are your feelings and thoughts on the participants, their perspectives, and worldviews?
3. What are the definitions of codes?
4. What are the reasons for selecting a segment of data for a code?
5. How do the categories, patterns, and themes emerge?
6. What are the emerging concepts?
7. What are the claims that you could make from the emerging patterns, themes, and concepts?
8. How could the emerging codes and categories answer the research questions?

9. How are the emerging patterns, categories, themes, and concepts linked?
10. What explanations could you offer on the links among the patterns, categories, themes, and concepts?
11. How do the emerging claims and theories from the data relate to the existing theories or models from the literature?
12. What are the challenges or problems you faced during the study?
13. Are there any ethical issues that you are concerned about?
14. What are the recommendations for future research?
15. What are your reflective thoughts on the memos?
16. How could you incorporate all this into your research report or dissertation/thesis?

Your reflective thoughts on coding and the data, which tell the bigger story of your data, are important in constructing a theory. Memoing is a phase that lets you move from coding to writing your research report; memos are the link between data and the final report. Memoing is a vital process in qualitative analysis in which you reflect on making connections between research questions and codes; codes and concepts; the findings and participants' lifeworld; the findings and participants' perspectives; the findings and transferability; themes and theories; the findings and theoretical and practical implications; and the current state of research and future direction for research.

Developing Themes

Developing themes involves grouping or classifying categories under broad themes based on second cycle coding and memoing. Themes are "broad units of information that consist of several codes aggregated to form a common idea" (Creswell and Poth 2018, 262). You can derive themes from the data, literature, and research questions. I suggest you transform your sub-research questions into major themes. "It is crucial to tie your themes to your research question(s) and to the literature that relates to your research focus" (Bryman 2016, 588). The themes are the basis for constructing a theory and will help you advance knowledge. You must argue why your themes are significant, how they relate to one another, what the implications are, and how they are connected to literature (Bryman 2016). Methodologists (Creswell 2013; Saldana 2011) suggest that three to seven themes are manageable for writing the final report. However, the grounded theory approach prefers one central theme.

In this process, you decontextualize the classification of categories as themes; in other words, you conceptualize the categories as themes, so they are transferable, an aim of qualitative research. Transferability is decontextualizing the categories as concepts so that they are applicable elsewhere. "Concepts are abstractions that have more meaning to life outside the study" (Saldana 2011, 111). Saldana suggests that you use the "touch test" to differentiate a category from a concept. For example, a church is a building that can be touched, but worship cannot be touched, which makes it a concept. In your analysis, when you come across a tangible category, it must be transformed into an intangible to make it a conceptual theme. Let me illustrate the difference. "Praying" can be seen or listened to, which is tangible, but praying is actually a "religious practice," which is intangible. Praying is a category, but religious practice is a concept. When you develop concepts from the codes and categories, they become the building blocks for constructing a theory (Saldana 2011). Codes emerge from data, categories or themes emerge from codes, and theory emerges from themes.

A theory is an explanation of how categories are related and affect one another in the social world. Your research could offer several theories, or it could produce one, which accommodates all categories in its matrix. The grounded theory approach aims at explaining the whole process with a central theory or a model. Phenomenology aims at offering several themes that interact within a phenomenon. The qualitative case study offers multiple perspectives of a case. The qualitative approach chosen determines the kind of theory you would construct as the outcome of your research.

In addition, you must construct theories by interacting with the existing theories or models from the literature. You need to interpret your conceptual themes in comparison to the literature and vice versa to offer a model or theory to advance knowledge in the field of theology or religious studies. For more information, see the section on writing the discussion chapter in Chapter 8.

Using Computer Software for Analysis

Many researchers use computer-assisted qualitative data analysis software (CAQDAS), for analyzing qualitative data. Novice researchers tend to think that the software does the analysis. In quantitative research, the software can analyze data and produce results based on the statistical tests chosen by the researcher. But for qualitative research, the software does not do any analysis; the researcher does. However, the software is a convenient tool for storing and retrieving the data with ease.

The software for qualitative analysis aids researchers in many ways. It can handle different kinds of data, such as text, images, videos, audio, and documents on a large scale. The software can store the transcriptions of the interviews with pseudonyms to identify interviewees and store other demographic information about the participants and enable each interview to be accessed separately for analysis.

The search feature allows the researcher to look for a concept or term across the corpus of data and analyze how the factor is present or absent among the participants. This facility also helps researchers find patterns across the interview data and other data sets.

In the first cycle of coding, the program creates and stores codes with links to the data units. Researchers can access all data segments linked to a code across data sets. A code might have a link to the excerpts from an interview, an image that represents the code, a video clip that characterizes the code, a document that says something about the code, and so on.

In the second cycle of coding, the software facilitates the creation of a hierarchical structure for developing categories, patterns, and themes. You can assign open codes to a category and make it a parent code and group many categories under a theme. This will make it easier for you to access all categories and codes under a theme by opening a theme, or to access all codes by opening a category.

The software helps researchers create and store memos with a link to codes or data segments. It makes it easier to access all the codes, memos, and themes linked to a particular transcript or other forms of data. Researchers can easily access them for a quick review and reorganize the hierarchical structure. Qualitative analysis software can assist the researchers in making a creative visual presentation of the analysis.

It facilitates team research when multiple researchers analyze qualitative data. The software can keep a log of each one's activity and the changes made by whom and when. Above all, it speeds up the analysis process and saves a lot of time, which is the supreme contribution of any qualitative analysis software.

Some of the well-known software programs have features to analyze text, visuals, audio, video, and documents. All of them must be purchased, though there are discounts for students:

- ATLAS.ti (https://atlasti.com/)
- HyperRESEARCH (http://www.researchware.com/products/hyperresearch.html)
- MAXQDA (https://www.maxqda.com/)
- NVivo (https://www.qsrinternational.com/)
- QDA Miner (https://provalisresearch.com/products/qualitative-data-analysis-software/)
- Transana (https://www.transana.com/)

The following free programs are suitable for primarily analyzing text data, but some could code visual, audio, and video data as well. Free open-source programs for qualitative analysis are:

- RDQA: R package for Qualitative Data Analysis (http://rqda.r-forge.r-project.org/)
- QDA Miner Lite (https://provalisresearch.com/products/qualitative-data-analysis-software/freeware/)
- QualCoder (https://qualcoder.wordpress.com/)
- Taguette (https://www.taguette.org/)
- TAMS: Text Analysis Markup System (https://tamsys.sourceforge.io/)

You must acquire the needed skills to use them. If it seems challenging, you can use the tutorial videos on YouTube to learn how to use these programs.

Credibility and Trustworthiness

Qualitative research considers credibility and trustworthiness as key concepts in establishing authenticity. You may be familiar with validity and reliability that are associated with quantitative research. But qualitative research does not deal with them; instead, it deals with credibility and trustworthiness to produce authentic knowledge.

Trustworthiness in qualitative research is about that the findings are dependable or trustable by establishing credibility, transferability, dependability, and confirmability. Credibility is a quality the researcher establishes by showing that the findings are close to the real world of the participants and their perspectives. Transferability is about how the findings could be relevant beyond the participants to other context. Dependability shows the methodological rigor of the study that findings are trustable, while confirmability shows that the findings emerged from the data.

John Creswell (2014) suggests eight strategies for establishing credibility and trustworthiness: triangulation, member check, rich and thick description, clarifying bias, presenting negative or discrepant information, spending prolonged time in the field, peer debriefing, and external auditing.

Triangulation is a strategy that uses multiple data sets such as in-depth interviews, focus group interviews, and document analysis to increase the credibility and trustworthiness of findings. When common themes emerge across the data sets, they indicate the trustworthiness of the research.

Member check is a process in which you take your findings or themes back to a few participants to check whether they accurately reflect their experiences. When they do, they reflect the real world of the participants.

The rich or thick description helps the readers understand the context from which your findings have emerged. When you present a finding with excerpts from the transcripts or fieldnotes with thick descriptions, they authenticate the finding or theme.

Clarifying bias involves explicitly identifying and stating your theological or ideological position in addressing the phenomenon to help readers understand your position. By describing your background, culture, ideology, and theological/religious position, you can show how you have fashioned interpretation. This is called *epoche* in which you bracket your theological/ideological position to add credibility to your claims.

Presenting negative or discrepant information involves not neglecting to include an experience or finding or theme that does not fall within the emerging dominant theme or perspective. You should not be "satisfied by explanations that appear to explain nearly all the variance in their data. Instead, . . . every piece of data has to be used until it can be accounted for" (Silverman and Marvasti 2008, 265). In qualitative research, every experience is real and valid, including those that do not fit into your perspective or the dominant theme, because it is real to the participant. Presenting discrepant information makes your analysis authentic.

Spending prolonged time in the field for an ethnographic study helps researchers to understand the world of participants and their way of seeing the world to offer rich and thick descriptions in their reports. You can mention the period of time you lived with the community in the field, which will enable readers to understand the efforts that went behind data collection. Spending a prolonged time in the field is not applicable for other approaches in qualitative research.

Peer debriefing involves letting someone who is not part of the study review your findings and interpretations. This would help you assess whether your findings and interpretations make sense to another person. Students could have supervisors randomly check the codes and themes to verify if they are closer to the data.

External auditing involves letting another researcher or specialist review the entire process and the project for an objective assessment of the research. This is suitable for professors who could recruit a specialist to audit the analysis of their project. However, students may not find an external auditor for their master's or doctoral dissertation/thesis; however, they could invite fellow students to do the external auditing.

Qualitative researchers commonly use triangulation and member check to establish the credibility and trustworthiness of their research. I suggest you also use rich and thick descriptions, bracketing—clarifying your bias, and presenting discrepant information. If you are doing an ethnographic study, you must consider a prolonged stay in the field to add credibility to your study.

Chapter Summary

This chapter has presented the definition of qualitative research and its suitability for theological/religious studies. You have learned about the five approaches in qualitative research: phenomenological, grounded theory, ethnography, case study, and narrative. The chosen approaches determine the kinds of data required to answer your research questions and the methods for collecting them. You have understood qualitative research uses purposive sampling, and that the sample size is small because qualitative research requires in-depth analysis of narrative data. You have learned the procedures and steps to analyze qualitative data, which includes transcription, making sense of the data, coding, memoing, and developing themes. This chapter also introduced the steps for establishing credibility and trustworthiness for authenticity.

By reading this chapter, you have gained a comprehensive understanding of qualitative research and the techniques you can apply to your research.

Review Questions

1. What is qualitative research?
2. What is the phenomenological approach?

3. What is the grounded theory approach?
4. What is the ethnographic approach?
5. What is the qualitative case study approach?
6. What is the narrative approach?
7. What is the role of theories in qualitative research?
8. What are the different types of sampling used in qualitative research?
9. How to arrive at a sampling size for qualitative research?
10. What are the types of data collected for qualitative research?
11. What are the different methods of data collection for qualitative research?
12. What is a qualitative interview or an in-depth interview?
13. What is participant observation?
14. How to analyze data in qualitative research?
15. What are the steps to establishing credibility and trustworthiness?

Further Help

Creswell, John W., and Cheryl N. Poth. 2016. *Qualitative Inquiry and Research Design: Choosing Among Five Approaches*. 4th ed. London: Sage.

Seidman, Irving. 2013. *Interviewing as Qualitative Research: A Guide for Researchers in Education and the Social Sciences*. 4th ed. New York: Teachers College Press.

Saldana, Johnny. 2015. *The Coding Manual for Qualitative Researchers*. 3rd ed. London: Sage.

Chapter 5

QUANTITATIVE RESEARCH

Quantitative research is deductive and begins with a theory or hypothesis to investigate the relational dimensions among variables by collecting numerical data and analyzing them with statistical tools. As we have seen in Chapter 3, postpositivism is the philosophical base of quantitative research and reflects the natural sciences' approach to studying the social world.

Quantitative research identifies concepts, variables, or constructs based on a theory or hypothesis and measures them to examine the relationship or association among the variables. It collects numerical data using different methods from predetermined samples and analyzes them statistically to offer an explanation indicating the causal nature or the kind of a relationship that exists between variables and/or presents a descriptive explanation of the population.

Researchers choose quantitative research when the study aims at measuring fine distinctions among the variables under examination, establishing causal relationship among variables, discovering the nature of relationship among variables, generalizing the results of the sample to the population, offering statistical description of the population, and making the study replicable. For quantitative research, the researcher collects numerical data through survey instruments, structured questions, controlled observation, pretests and posttests, and texts and documents for content analysis. It analyzes the data using appropriate statistical tools to answer the research questions.

The main phases of quantitative research are the conceptual, data collection, data analysis, and reporting of results. Because quantitative research is deductive, based on a theory or a theoretical framework, you first develop a hypothesis that predicts the relationship between variables. Then you adopt a method to empirically test the hypothesis by measuring the variables. "Constructs are conceptualized at the theoretical (abstract) plane, while variables are operationalized and measured at the empirical (observational) plane" (Bhattacherjee 2012, 12). Before you step into the field to collect data, you must design the study with all clarity at the conceptual phase.

Although religion is complex, and many aspects of religion are not measurable, quantitative research is best suited to answer research questions that deal with measurable aspects of religion. Quantitative research can test any theory related to religion and hypotheses generated by qualitative studies on religion. Quantitative research can examine the effects and consequences of religious beliefs and practices as causal factors. Qualitative research deals with the meaning of religious beliefs and practices, while quantitative research addresses the scale and representativeness of the phenomenon. In other words, quantitative research can indicate how widespread and to what extent the phenomenon is found among the population. Quantitative research is appropriate for generalizing results and predicting outcomes. Therefore, which is the best method—qualitative or quantitative—to study a religious phenomenon is not the right question. Rather the right question is, which method is suitable for answering the research questions. The research purpose and research questions determine the choice of qualitative or quantitative method to study a religious phenomenon.

Sociology of religion, psychology of religion, and anthropology of religion use quantitative research to answer questions that can be answered only by numerical data. Practical theology and missiology adopt quantitative research to study religiosity, spirituality, religious practices, beliefs and practices, congregations, church/denominational growth, religious violence/conflict, and so on. Scholars of Biblical studies can use quantitative research to study biblical texts by using content analysis.

Types of Quantitative Research

The three major types of quantitative research are survey (non-experimental), experimental, and quasi-experimental. Researchers in the fields of theology and religious studies mostly use the survey method but nothing prevents them from being innovative and using experimental or quasi-experimental methods.

Survey Method

The survey method enables a researcher to study a large population. It is a technique for collecting numerical data from a sample (a small number) of the target population to examine the relationship between variables by using statistical tools to measure the variance and to offer a descriptive explanation of the sample. To establish reliability and validity, the same set of questions is asked in the same manner to every participant. Although, the entire population could be covered in a survey like a census, in scientific research, researchers select a sample out of the population. "Surveys are information collection methods used to describe, compare, or explain individual and societal knowledge, feelings, values, preferences, and behavior" (Fink 2009, 1). Surveys use questionnaires to collect data from people, either by letting them answer the questions on their own or with the researcher through structured interviews. Researchers also use mixed-mode surveys. Questionaries are distributed by mail, email, and websites, while structured interviews are done in person or over the telephone. The purpose of the survey and the objectives based on the purpose should be stated clearly in the questionnaire.

A cross-sectional survey describes the characteristics of the population from a predetermined sample based on a single survey. Longitudinal studies conduct more than one survey to measure the same variables with the same sample after a time gap, in which time is taken as a variable.

Experimental Method

The experimental method is a procedure in which the independent variable is manipulated to examine its effects on the dependent variable. The purpose of experimental research is to measure the outcome of the intervention by "providing a specific treatment [intervention] to one group and withholding it from another and then determining how both groups scored on an outcome" (Creswell 2014, 13). In an experimental study, the researcher randomly assigns the samples to one of two groups. One is called the intervention or experimental group, which receives the treatment or intervention, and the other is called the control group, which does not receive any interventions. Using a control group eliminates the possibility of any other factor causing the changes; it rules out the possibility of an extraneous variable influencing the dependent variable. In an experimental study, the researcher takes measurements twice, once before the intervention (pretest) and once after the intervention (posttest) and do it in a laboratory or in the field. When a study is conducted in a laboratory, extraneous variables are controlled to have a stronger internal validity; however, the ecological validity (relevance to the real world) may be weak for laboratory studies.

The suitability of the experimental method for theology and religious studies is debatable. Experimental designs are common in natural sciences, but are uncommon in social sciences, except for social psychology and organizational studies because "the vast majority of independent variables with which social researchers are concerned cannot be manipulated" (Bryman 2016, 44). The same is true in the fields of theology and religious studies. However, interdisciplinary studies, especially, can create opportunities to be innovative and use experimental method for theology and religious studies.

For example, in a study of the effects of intercessory prayer on cancer patients, Ian N. Olver, Emeritus Oncologist at the Royal Adelaide Hospital cancer centre, Australia, and Andrew Dutney, Professor in Theology at the Flinders University, Australia conducted an experimental study. In this study, a theology professor and an oncologist teamed up to do this experimental research. They randomly assigned the patients to two groups. During the experiment, patients from the intervention group received intercessory prayer from a group of Christians, whereas the control group did not. The researchers used quality of life (QOL) and spiritual well-being scales to take measurements before and after the intervention over six months. The study found that the experimental group significantly improved in their spiritual well-being, emotional well-being, and functional well-being (Olver and Dutney 2012). Spirituality and health are new fields of interest, with great potential for theological/religious scholars to enter.

Quasi-experimental Method

A quasi-experimental method is similar to an experimental method but done in a natural setting. Quasi-experimental methods "do not use random selection or allocation to groups but often recognize natural clusters in the population" (Gorard 2004, 177). In quasi-experimental studies, researchers cannot randomly assign participants to experimental and control groups and in some situations, it may not be possible to have a control group.

For example, Rachel Mash and Robert James Mash (2012) did a quasi-experimental study to assess the effectiveness of a church-based HIV prevention program for youth in Anglican Churches in Cape Town, South Africa. In this study random allocation was not possible, therefore, the churches were clustered. The churches, where this program was running were grouped together as the intervention group and other churches, where this program was not running were grouped as the control group. The researchers collected data from both groups with a preintervention questionnaire. After the intervention, data were collected with a postintervention questionnaire among the participants in the intervention group. For the control group, the preintervention questionnaire was served again to collect data. The study found "church-based peer education can raise the age of sexual debut for young people and increase the use of condoms among those who are sexually active" (5). Quasi-experimental studies are suitable for natural settings and can result in valuable outcome.

Conceptual Phase in Quantitative Research

Identifying theory and concepts, providing operational definitions, and choosing the scales for measurement are some of the key steps during the conceptual phase. Quantitative research is rigid in its design, unlike qualitative research, which is flexible. You must plan every aspect of the research process at the "conceptual phase." You need to do an extensive literature review to identify the theory you want to test or the concepts to create a hypothesis to test the relationship between variables. Decide on the type of research, whether it will be a survey or experimental or quasi-experimental research or content analysis or secondary analysis. Then you will choose the location of your study, identify the size of the population, and calculate the sample size before moving on to data collection and analysis.

Theory and Concepts

You need to identify a theory first and select the concepts associated with the theory to create a hypothesis for testing in your research. A theory is an explanation of how variables work together. "Theories provide meaning and significance to what we observe, and observations help validate or refine existing theory or construct new theory" (Bhattacherjee 2012, 3). You formulate your research question based on the theory.

All research is done in the context of past research; therefore, as discussed in Chapter 1, you must find theories or concepts relating to your research interest to define the research problem or research question in the literature. Literature review is vital in the conceptual phase of quantitative research.

Some researchers may forego a theory, but they identify the concepts to be studied and formulate their research questions based on the literature review. "Concepts are the building blocks of theory" (Bryman 2016, 151). A concept is a label that is used to explain a practice or action or an attitude or behavior. A concept is an intangible or abstract label that is attached to tangible things. As seen in Chapter 4, for example, attending worship in a church or going for namaz in a mosque or reading the Bible or Koran or Gita are tangible activities. However, they can all be grouped under an abstract label as religious practice or religiosity, which are concepts. Concepts are also called constructs. Each concept has various components or dimensions that need to be identified based on the chosen theory or literature review.

Variables

A variable is a measurable component of a concept or a construct that differs or changes from one entity to another. For example, gender is a variable with two attributes (male and female): to quantify these attributes, we assign them numbers: female is 1 and male is 2. Gender is a directly observable variable, but others require scales to be measured. Intelligence, for example, is a concept/construct; to measure it, we use the IQ score, which is a variable that differs from person to person. Religiosity is a concept in which prayer is a variable and the frequency of prayer in a month can be measured on a five-point scale from (1) Never (2) Rarely (3) Once in a while (4) Weekly (5) Daily. The frequency of prayer as a variable varies from person to person.

Variables can be "independent" or "dependent." The variable that acts on the other to make changes happen is the independent variable, and the variable that changes is called a dependent variable. The researcher manipulates the independent variable in an experimental study to investigate the effect. For example, a study on the effects of intercessory prayer on a group of inpatients admitted to the Coronary Care Unit found that intercessory prayer resulted in "a measurable improvement in the medical outcomes of critically ill patients" (W. S. Harris et al. 1999, 2278). In this study, the intercessory prayer was the independent variable, and the medical outcome of the patients was the dependent variable. This experimental study concluded that the independent variable of intercessory prayer affected the dependent variable of the medical outcome of the patients.

Hypothesis

A hypothesis is a prediction of how two variables are related and work together, which can be tested. In other words, a hypothesis predicts the anticipated outcome of the relationship between two variables in a testable form. Such a prediction is "not simply an 'educated guess.' Rather, researchers base them on results from past research and literature where investigators have found certain results and can now offer predictions as to what other investigators will find when they repeat the study with new people or at new sites" (Creswell 2012, 111). A hypothesis is formulated based on research questions or a research problem, which are derived from the literature. A good hypothesis defines the focus of your research clearly and guides you in choosing the methods and measures.

Testing a hypothesis involves creating a research hypothesis, which predicts the existence of a relationship between two variables, and a null hypothesis, which predicts the absence of a relationship between the two variables. The research hypothesis is also called the alternative hypothesis because it is opposite to the null hypothesis.

Researchers create a null hypothesis to test a hypothesis. In hypothesis testing, although researchers test the research hypothesis, they, in fact, falsify the null hypothesis. By falsifying the null hypothesis, researchers establish that the research hypothesis is accepted. These days, all researchers do not state the null hypothesis explicitly, but this is how probability of knowledge is established.

Researchers formulate directional or non-directional hypothesis for testing. A directional hypothesis predicts the outcome of the testing as positive or negative changes for the two groups. This is also called the one-tailed hypothesis because it flows in one direction. It indicates the direction of the impact of the independent variable as greater or lesser, and higher or lower in comparison of the two groups. A hypothesis can be non-directional, because it predicts a difference but does not state in which way it will change, because the researcher could not find any study to predict the direction. This is also called the two-tailed hypothesis. Box 2 presents examples of different hypotheses.

Box 2: Examples of Research Hypotheses and Null Hypotheses

Example 1: Null Hypothesis and Research Hypothesis

Null Hypothesis:
There is no significant difference between information technology professionals and other professionals attending virtual churches.

Research/Alternative Hypothesis:
Information technology (IT) professionals are more likely to attend virtual churches than are other professionals.

Here, the researcher predicts the relationship between IT professionals and their attendance in virtual churches compared to other professionals. Two groups are compared to test the relationship between the types of professionals and their participation in virtual churches.

Example 2: Directional Hypothesis

Null Hypothesis (Directional):
There is no significant relationship between the use of contemporary music in worship and the growth rate of emergent and traditional churches.

Research/Alternative Hypothesis (Directional):
Using contemporary music in worship will bring about a higher growth rate in emergent churches than in traditional churches.

Here, the researcher predicts that the effect of contemporary music in worship results in a higher growth rate in emergent churches. The independent variable of contemporary music brings positive changes to the dependent variable of church growth in emergent churches as compared to the traditional churches.

Example 3: Directional Hypothesis

Null Hypothesis (Directional):
There is no significant relationship between regular churchgoers and subjective well-being (SWB) scores and non-churchgoers.

Research/Alternative Hypothesis (Directional):
Regular churchgoers are likely to have higher SWB score than non-churchgoers.

The research hypothesis predicts a positive effect of church attendance on the SWB score among churchgoers than non-churchgoers.

Box 2 continued

Example 4: Non-Directional Hypothesis

Null Hypothesis (Non-Directional):
The SWB score does not differ between regular churchgoers and non-churchgoers

Research/Alternative Hypothesis (Non-Directional):
The SWB score differs between regular churchgoers and non-churchgoers

In this example, the research hypothesis predicts a relationship between SWB score and regular churchgoers and non-churchgoers but does not indicate which direction the change will happen.

Measurement

Measurement reveals the extent to which two concepts are related and how it varies among the sample. To measure a concept, the researcher needs indicators that are tangible items that are directly or indirectly observable.

Measuring items is common in our daily life. In quantitative research, the researcher measures concepts to describe the characteristics of the relationship between two variables. Extreme variations can easily be recognized; for example, differences between students who are highly successful academically and those who are not, and between students who are highly religious and those who are not. However, measurement allows us to find finer variations in the differences and helps us have *"precise estimates of the degree of relationship between concepts"* (emphasis in the original, Bryman 2016, 152). Measurement helps us see to what extent two concepts are related. For example, how intercessory prayer and medical outcome of patients are related and how it varies among the sample.

To measure a concept, you need to identify the dimensions and indicators. The operational definition identifies the dimensions or components or aspects of a concept/construct, along with the indicators for each dimension to be measured. Each indicator will have one or more items for measuring the concept.

Indicators are tangible items that are directly or indirectly observable. "Indicators operate at the empirical level, in contrast to constructs [concepts], which are conceptualized at the theoretical level"

(Bhattacherjee 2012, 44). Direct indicators are gender, income, age, race, caste, and so on. Indirect indicators are those that are not directly observable such as belief in God, meaning of prayer, sense of guilt, and so on. See Box 3 for examples of concepts, dimensions, and indicators.

Box 3: Example of Concepts, Dimensions, and Indicators

Religiosity is a concept, which can have religious beliefs, religious practices, and lifestyle as dimensions and each dimension can have several indicators that can be measured. The dimension of religious belief could have belief in God, belief in sin, belief in salvation, belief in life after death, as indicators. The dimension of religious practices could include personal prayer, church attendance, Bible reading, and so on as indicators. Lifestyle dimension could include ethical practices, attitude toward one's profession, social concerns, and so on as indicators.

Concept	Dimensions	Indicators
Religiosity	Religious Beliefs	Belief in God Belief in sin Belief in salvation Belief in life after death
	Religious Practices	Personal prayer Church attendance Bible reading Praying with others
	Lifestyle	Ethical practices Being sincere in work Concern for others

You can identify the dimensions of a concept from the literature and from your observations. De Jong, Faulkner, and Warland (1976), in a comparative study of religiosity between American and German students, used six dimensions: belief, experience, religious practice, religious knowledge, individual moral consequences, and social consequences. Lisa D. Pearce, George M. Hayward, and Jessica A. Pearlman (2017) used five dimensions of religiosity in their study on religiosity of adolescents. Each dimension of religiosity can include several indicators and each indicator can have one or more items. You must formulate questions to measure each indicator. Using multiple dimensions and indicators will help you obtain better measurements of a variable. Quantitative research uses four scales of measurement: nominal, ordinal, interval, and ratio to measure variables.

Nominal Scale

The nominal scale is a naming scale that labels the variables that are categorical or mutually exclusive like gender, religious affiliation, race, and caste. "Nominal scales merely offer *names* or *labels* for different attribute values" (emphasis in the original, Bhattacherjee 2012, 46). They give unique identifier to a category. Nominal scale is suitable for identifying mutually exclusive categories. The numbers do not carry any numerical value but are only countable. For example, we can assign a number to Female as 1 and Male as 2 on the scale; the values of 1 and 2 are just labels and do not carry any importance.

Ordinal Scale

An ordinal scale is used to rank the order of variables, but the distance between the order is unknown. At the ordinal level, "the actual or relative values of attributes or difference in attribute values cannot be assessed" (Bhattacherjee 2012, 46) but only indicates the order of quality or quantity. This scale helps the researcher tag the samples in an order. Ordinal scale helps researchers categorize and rank the data that deal with frequency, satisfaction, and so on. In ordinal scale, the order is the important element and is suitable for measuring educational level, income level, scales of rating to indicate "poor" to "excellent," scales of frequency/occurrences indicating "not at all" to "very often," scales of agreement like, Likert scale ranging from "strongly disagree" to "strongly agree," and ranking scales. The central tendency (the central position within the distribution) can be measured by calculating mode or median, not mean in ordinal scale. Box 4 gives examples of ordinal scale.

Box 4: Examples of Ordinal Scale

Example 1:

A scale to measure the range of income could be:
Low: 1
Medium: 2
High: 3
Here, each range is assigned with a number by maintaining the level of importance, from lower to higher. This measurement does not identify the exact income, for example, but only the order of variance in range. It indicates that the medium income range is higher than the lower-income range and the higher-income range is higher than the medium income range.

Example 2:

How are you satisfied with your church?
1. Very unsatisfied
2. Unsatisfied
3. Neither
4. Satisfied
5. Very satisfied
In this order, rank 2 is better than rank 1 and rank 5 is better than rank 4.

Interval Scale

An interval scale indicates the equal distance between two attributes and the order. "Interval scale allows us to examine 'how much more' is one attribute when compared to another, which is not possible with nominal or ordinal scales" (Bhattacherjee 2012, 46). Descriptive statistics and correlation analysis use interval data. A researcher uses an interval scale when the distance between attributes is important for analysis. Interval scale helps researchers calculate mode, median, and mean; central tendency, and standard deviation. See Box 5 for examples of interval scale.

Box 5: Example of Interval Scale

A scale of measuring income with the following options:
Less than $5,000
$5,001 to 10,000
$10,001 to 15,000

In this scale the distance between each attribute is $5000.

Ratio Scale

A ratio scale is similar to interval scale but has a zero value. The zero value is known as "true zero" with a meaning. This scale has all the features of nominal, ordinal, and interval scales, as well as "a zero point on the scale that indicates the absence of the attribute being measured" (Balnaves and Caputi 2001, 47). The ratio scale is used in social sciences to measure age, employee strength, revenues, and so on. Researchers can use descriptive and inferential statistical tests on the data. It allows researchers to calculate central tendency by mode, median, and mean; standard deviation, and coefficient variation. See Box 6 for examples of ratio scale.

Box 6: Example of a Ratio Scale

To measure the age of the participants a ratio scale can have the following options:
0 – 5 years
6 – 10 years
11 – 15 years
16 – 20 years

The above scales have been discussed in order of importance to research: nominal scale and ordinal scale are used for descriptive statistical analysis, whereas interval and ratio scales can allow sophisticated statistical analyses.

Validity

Quantitative research aims for validity and reliability; both are key quality factors that demonstrate the rigor of the study. Researchers must demonstrate how the measures are valid and reliable to establish the accuracy, consistency, and authenticity of the results in quantitative research.

Validity is about the accuracy and integrity of the results. Validity ensures the appropriateness of the instrument in measuring a variable accurately. In other words, whether the instrument measures what it intended to measure, and validity is "concerned with the integrity of the conclusions" in the research (Bryman 2016, 41). There are many kinds of validity, but the three main kinds are construct or concept validity, internal validity, and external validity.

Construct Validity

Construct validity is about how accurate the operational definitions are in identifying the dimensions and defining the indicators of the concept or construct to be measured. You need to ask yourself whether the variables really represent the concept, and the operational definitions are accurate in measuring the variables. One way of establishing construct validity is to test the questionnaire with two or three groups that are likely to score differently. For measuring religiosity among students, you might administer the instrument to one group of believers who attend a Bible study on campus and another group of students who are part of the atheist club on campus. If the students who attend the Bible study score high and the students from the atheist club score low on the religiosity scale, then the instrument has construct validity. If, however, the atheist club students score high on the religiosity score, it indicates that your operational definition is not representing the concept of religiosity.

Internal Validity

Internal validity is about the causal relationship between variables. In an experimental study, if the conclusion says X causes Y, then the researcher needs to ensure that something else or an extraneous variable is not the cause of the changes in the dependent variable. To establish internal validity, researchers use experimental and control groups. In a study assessing the effectiveness of online theological education, you would randomly assign the samples to two groups, for example, and have one group of students take a fully online course and the second group take only traditional classes. The first group is called experimental group and the second is called the control group. By randomly assigning the students to two groups, you ensure that all internet savvy students do not end up in the online classes. This way you eliminate the extraneous variable, internet savvy, as the cause for higher scores in the experimental group. If the experimental group scored higher, then you can conclude that online classes are more effective than traditional class and establish internal validity.

External Validity

External validity is the extent to which results can be generalized to the population or other contexts. A representative sample of the population guarantees generalizability. Therefore, the definition of population, the sample frame, the sample size, and random sample selection are key elements in establishing external validity. (See sampling in quantitative research in this chapter for more.)

Ecological Validity

Ecological (contextual) validity is about how closely the findings of a study are to the real world and is used because findings may be technically valid but may not reflect the social reality. Bryman (2016, 42) warns us, "if research findings are not ecologically valid, they are in a sense *artifacts* [emphasis in the original] of the social scientist's arsenal of data collection and analytic tools." The knowledge that is produced through research must reflect the social world. Donna Mertens (2015) suggests that researchers must clearly explain the context of the study for others to assess the suitability of the findings to their contexts.

Reliability

Reliability is a criterion used for assessing the consistency in measuring a variable/concept. Reliability indicates the repeatability of the results. If the same questionnaire is administered to the same people at different times, it should yield the same results; if it does not, then the questionnaire is not reliable. Reliability has three aspects: internal reliability, test-retest reliability, and inter-rater reliability.

Internal Reliability

Multiple indicators are used to measure a concept and they must be consistent. "Internal consistency reliability is a measure of consistency between different items of the same construct" (Bhattacherjee 2012, 57). Each item in the scale must be positively related to the variable, which ensures high scores on most of the items, if not all, or vice versa. When all items of an indicator are not related to each other, the instrument is not reliable internally. The split-half method can check internal reliability. It randomly splits the indicators into half or bases them on odd and even numbers and administers the measurement. Then the correlation between one half of the test with the other half can be calculated; if they are consistent, then it is internally reliable. These days, researchers use Cronbach's alpha test to check internal reliability with the help of software.

Test-retest Reliability

Researchers use test-retest to establish the external consistency of the instrument. It is about the stability of the measure in different situations. If for example, you measure your weight on the same scale at different times, the scale shows a different weight each time, we know the scale is not reliable, assuming you have not actually put on weight between the tests. To test consistency, researchers give the same test to the same people at two different times. If the respondents score at the same level at both times, then the instrument is reliable. The longer the time gap between tests, the better because the respondents are less likely to remember their earlier answers.

Inter-rater Reliability

Inter-rater reliability is suitable for studies that use content analysis or structured observation, in which an observer or rater makes a subjective call on categorizing an item or behavior. This is also known as inter-observer reliability. In this process, two observers or raters observe or categorize items. When both of their observations match, then the reliability is higher. When the two observers' findings lack consistency, operationalizing categories (defining the categories for observation) helps the observers to categorize an item or behavior consistently.

Sampling in Quantitative Research

Sampling is a technique for selecting a small number or subset of the target population. Quantitative research uses two major sampling logics: probability and non-probability sampling.

In sampling for quantitative research, you first identify the research site and the universe of your study, which could be a geographical location (city/town/village) or institutions or churches, and so on. Further, you must specify the characteristics of people who have the information, experience, or access to the needed information for your study to define the population. When you have identified the population, you need to come up with a sampling frame, which is a list of people who constitute the target population from which you will draw the sample. A sampling frame is the master list of the target population.

For example, in a study of the religiosity of university students in Pretoria, South Africa, we defined the population by specifically choosing university students, not school students. Then, we must choose whether we are going to study students from all universities in Pretoria or only one; let us say all the universities in Pretoria. The next question is, are we studying all students or only undergraduates or only graduate students? We choose only graduate students. Therefore, the unit of analysis is the graduate students. The population for this study is the graduate students from all universities in Pretoria. The attributes of the population are: graduate students and those registered with any university in Pretoria.

You must obtain a list of graduate students from all universities in Pretoria and make a list of them for the sampling frame. The sampling frame is the list of graduate students from all universities in Pretoria.

Probability Sampling

Probability sampling is selecting of a sample from a population using random selection so as to represent the population. With probability sampling everyone in the population has an equal chance of being selected as a sample. When you want to generalize the results of a study you must use probability (representative) sampling. In probability sampling, four methods are used: simple random sampling, systematic sampling, stratification sampling, and cluster sampling.

Simple Random Sampling

Simple random sampling is a technique commonly used in probability sampling. To have random selection of the participants from the sampling frame, you could write each number from the sampling frame on pieces of paper, place them in a container and pick out the required number of slips to make up the samples. You can also generate random numbers in Microsoft Excel or other computer programs or online. Traditionally, researchers use the random table for random selection. When you have the random numbers generated, then identify the corresponding numbers in the sampling frame with the random numbers to contact the persons for the survey. Simple random sampling is suitable when the configuration of the population is uniform. Generalizability of the results to the population is higher with random selection.

Systematic Sampling

Systematic Sampling is suitable when a numbered list is not available but only a list of names. In systematic sampling, you divide the sample size by the total number in the list to get a fraction. For example, the total number in the sample frame is 100 and your sample size is 20; you divide 20/100, in this case, select one in every five. For a randomized start, start with any number from 1 to 5; so, if you start with the number 4, then your sample sequence will be 4, 9, 14, 19, 24, 29, 34, 39, 44, and so on. But if the list is arranged based on some attributes like, males and females alternatively, then all the odd numbers would be male and even numbers would be female, which would affect the principle of random selection. In such a case, reorder the list.

Stratification Sampling

Stratification sampling is appropriate when the population varies in several aspects. "A stratified sample involves breaking the population into mutually exclusive subgroups or strata" (Clark-Carter 2010, 154). Researchers identify subgroups within the population to have a proportionate representation of samples from each subgroup. Religious identity could be a factor, for example, in identifying subgroups in a population. In a mixture of the religious population, if Sikhs are only 5 percent, in such a case, the researcher takes only 5 percent of the sample size from the subgroup of Sikhs. This technique is called proportionate stratified sampling. But if the nature of the research has a special interest in such a small group or the researcher does not want a proportionate representation of the subgroup population for some reason, then an equal percentage of the sample size is distributed among the various religious groups. This is called disproportionate stratified or non-proportional stratified sampling. However, researchers adopt simple random selection within the subgroups.

Cluster Sampling

Cluster sampling is a technique to divide the population into groups, especially when the population is widespread geographically. In a study of theological students in India, instead of finding out all theological students in India, the researcher could identify the institutions affiliated to the Senate of Serampore College and institutions accredited by the Asia Theological Association (ATA). By using simple random sampling, the researcher can select a required number of institutions under each stream. Then the researcher could survey all students or use simple random selection for selecting students from each institution selected randomly; this is called multistage cluster sampling. If the researcher studies theological students from only one stream, Asia Theological Association, then the institutions under ATA can be randomly selected, in which case, the researcher can include all students from the selected institutions. This is known as single-stage cluster sampling.

Non-Probability Sampling

Non-probability sampling is a technique used by researchers to select sample using their subjective judgment. The sample is chosen non-randomly; hence, not everyone in the population has an equal chance of being selected. Non-probability sampling is cost effective, less time consuming, and the response rate may be higher. Non-probability sampling is not representative of the population and is not suitable for generalizing the results of a study.

Non-probability sampling is used when a sampling frame or population size is not available, or generalizability is not the aim of a study. For example, in a study of religious conversion in Thailand, you cannot get a list of all the people who changed their religions. Therefore, the researcher would use non-probability sampling and select samples non-randomly. Because of the non-random selection, generalizability to the population is not possible. However, no one can disregard the value of the study because this would be the only way to measure certain variables like religious change. In non-probability sampling, four methods are used: purposive or judgmental sampling, convenience sampling, quota sampling, and snowball sampling.

Purposive or Judgmental Sampling

For purposive or judgmental sampling, quantitative researchers use personal judgment in selecting the sample based on the purpose of the research. If, for example, the total number of the population is not known, then purposive sampling is suitable for selecting whoever is available. In other instances, it is easier to include an institution, which is willing to be a part of the study, rather than including an institution by random selection, and finding out it is not willing to be a part of the study. Purposive sampling is suitable when only a few people qualify to be part of a study. The limitations of purposive sampling in quantitative research are the issues of reliability and generalizability.

Convenience Sampling

Researchers deploy a convenience sampling technique to recruit available participants. This is suitable for pilot testing of a questionnaire. Some studies with convenience sampling could also provide valuable insights that otherwise could not be studied. Such a study could open avenues for further research.

Quota Sampling

Quota sampling is similar to stratification sampling but uses non-random selection. The researcher divides the population into subgroups and allots a quota proportionately to the size of each group, which is known as proportional quota sampling. If proportionate quotas are not allotted to the subgroups, this is called non-proportional quota sampling. Therefore, neither type of quota sampling is representative of the population. "The non-proportional technique is even less representative of the population but may be useful in that it allows capturing the opinions of small and underrepresented groups through oversampling" (Bhattacherjee 2012, 69). Quota sampling is more common in market research than in academic research.

Snowball Sampling

Snowball sampling is more suitable for qualitative research under purposive sampling (see Chapter 4). In snowball sampling, the present participant introduces future participants. This is suitable for studying a rare population that could not have a sampling frame, such as secret followers of a faith, victims of some form of discrimination, and so on.

Sample Size

A sample size is a small number or subset of the population, which is calculated by using a sample size formula or is chosen by the researcher. For probability sampling, researchers calculate the sample size by using a statistical formula that uses the population size, the margin of error, and the confidence level. For non-probability sampling, the researcher determines the sample size by taking various factors into consideration.

Sampling error is one of the factors to be taken into consideration in determining the sample size. Sampling error is the mismatch between the sample mean and the population parameter, which is the mean of the population, which cannot be calculated because it is not possible to sample the entire population. Sampling error is about the gap between the sample and the population. "Even with a well-crafted probability sample, a degree of sampling error is likely to creep in" (Bryman 2016, 176). Therefore, researchers allow room for error in determining the sample size.

Several formulas are available for calculating the sample size by taking into account, the margin of error and confidence level. The website The Research Advisors (2006) has a sample size table to determine sample size matching the size of the population by choosing a margin of error and confidence level. Use the following link to access the table: https://www.research-advisors.com/tools/SampleSize.htm

Alan Bryman (2016) suggests that, when random sampling is used, a larger sample size decreases the sampling error. He further recommends taking the cost and non-response factors into consideration while deciding the sample size. He advises students to be truthful in stating the sampling procedures instead of making a false claim about probability sampling. With limited time and resources "truly random approach to sample selection may not be open to you. The crucial point is to be clear about and to justify what you have done. . . . People will be much more inclined to accept an awareness of the limits of your sample design than claims about a sample that are patently false" (Bryman 2016, 183). He further recommends that students highlight the positive features of their sample while acknowledging the limitations.

For non-probability sampling, researchers arrive at a sampling size based on the type of sampling technique, size of the population, availability of resources and time, and the response rate. The researcher may choose a percentage of the population or allot a quota for different segments of the population. Otherwise, researchers proceed without a predetermined sample size and the final count of the responses stands as the sample size. Larger sample sizes are better for non-probability sampling.

Data Collection in Quantitative Research

The data collection methods in quantitative research vary according to the nature or purpose of the study. Quantitative research uses questionnaires to measure variables through surveys and structured interviews; structured observation in place of a survey; pretests, and posttests for experimental and quasi-experimental methods; texts and documents for content analysis; and existing data for secondary analysis.

Questionnaires for Survey and Structured Interview

The survey method and structured interview primarily use questionnaires to collect data. A questionnaire is also called a "survey instrument" or a "research instrument." Designing the survey instrument well is vital and the success of the project depends on this. It must cover all research questions. You must establish the validity and reliability of the instrument by conducting a pilot study for a new instrument. If you are using an existing instrument, you must discuss the validity and reliability of the instrument as presented by the author/s who produced it.

Variables can be measured in survey instruments. "The questions in your questionnaire are your variables. Your operational definitions— your choices on how to measure your constructs—should be reflected in the variables in your questionnaire" (Balnaves and Caputi 2001, 77). The researcher must incorporate the appropriate scales (nominal, ordinal, interval, and ratio) to measure the variables. It is advisable to find a preexisting questionnaire to use in a survey if they have good validity and reliability scores.

Before writing the questions, researchers need to be clear on several aspects of conducting a survey, such as "what concepts need measured, what type of information the question is asking for, what survey mode will be used, whether changes can be made to questions, and whether respondents will be willing and motivated to answer" (Dillman, Smyth, and Christian 2014, 107). Surveys can collect information related to demographics, beliefs, attitudes, opinions, behaviors, and events. For demographic information, participants will have the answers ready, but for other types of information, they will have to think through the questions to answer them. The context of the questions and the wording play a key role in helping participants to answer correctly.

Questions

David de Vaus (2002) gave a set of principles to use in designing questions: 1. Reliability will ensure the same participant answers a question every time in the same manner. 2. Validity is about whether the question measures what it meant to measure. 3. Discrimination offers fine variations to measure a variable with "sufficient response alternatives to detect meaningful variation and to avoid using extreme or absolute statements" (97). 4. Response rate depends on the nature of questions. "Intrusive, sensitive, irrelevant or repetitive questions as well as those that are poorly worded, difficult to understand, difficult to answer or have insufficient response categories can frustrate respondents and produce non-response" (97). 5. Same meaning for all will address the differences in the meaning of a word. The meaning of a word could differ from person to person, especially with cultural variations. If every participant understood the meaning of a word differently, they would be answering different questions. 6. Relevance means that each question must have a purpose in being part of the questionnaire.

In designing a questionnaire, wording questions is central to the success of a survey. De Vaus (2002, 97–99) provides a checklist of seventeen questions about wording the questions. Here I have explained ten of them with examples for the fields of theology and religious studies:

1. Is the language simple?

You need to avoid all theological terms and jargon and use common words that are familiar to the public. For example, how often do you use glossolalia in your prayer? Glossolalia is a theological term for speaking in tongues. Using such a term in a question will not work. Instead, a question like, how often do you speak in tongues while praying? will be easier for participants to respond to.

2. Can the question be shortened?

If the question is long, then it could lead to confusion.

3. Is the question double-barreled?

How often do you pray and read the Bible? This type of question carries two questions within; participants will be confused about whether to answer about the frequency of prayer or Bible reading. Make sure you have a single question in each question.

4. Is the question leading?

In leading questions, the wording hints at a particular answer. An example of a leading question is, would you agree that Pentecostalism has damaged the growth of traditional churches? This question prompts the respondent to affirm what is implied. This can be reworded as, what is the effect of Pentecostalism on the growth of traditional churches? to make it a neutral question.

5. Is the question negative?

Avoid the use of negatives and especially double negatives in your question. A question like, don't you disagree with the court's verdict on abortion? will confuse the participants. This can be reworded as, do you agree with the court's verdict on abortion?

6. Is the respondent likely to have the necessary knowledge?

When a question does not apply to all participants, first use a filter question to determine whether the participant is eligible to answer the next question. For example, do you speak in tongues while praying? with "Yes" or "No" options. If "Yes," they can answer the subsequent question, how often do you speak in tongues? If "No," then instruction would be given to skip the subsequent question and move to the next question.

7. Will the words have same meaning to everyone?

The meaning of words differs with people and contexts. A question like, 'Does your church have elders in the church committee?' could mean differently to participants from different denominations. For congregational denominations, elders are the key leaders, but in episcopal churches, elders could mean older people being part of the church committee.

8. Is the question ambiguous?

A question like, how often do you pray at home? may appear straightforward, but it is not clear whether the question is about one's personal prayer, frequency of family prayer, or frequency of prayer led by the participant at home. Be specific and clear in your question to avoid ambiguity.

9. Is the question too precise?

Asking for very precise answers might lead to erroneous answers. For example, how many times have you prayed alone during the last one month? may not yield an accurate answer, because participants may not remember the exact number of times they prayed during the last one month. It is good to provide a range for them to choose such as monthly once, once in two weeks, weekly, and daily.

10. Is the frame of reference for the question sufficiently clear?

A frame of reference is missing in a question like, how often do you go to church? It is not clear whether the frequency is in a week or month or year. It should be reworded as, how often do you go to church in a month?; here, "in a month" is the frame of reference for this question.

A survey questionnaire can have open-ended or closed-ended questions. Open-ended questions do not offer the participant any choices for answering but expect the participants to come up with their answers, which are called "descriptive answers." Closed-ended questions provide choices from which participants choose the answers. Both have advantages and disadvantages.

During analysis in quantitative research, descriptive answers will be challenging to reduce them into statistically analyzable categories. However, open-ended questions for fixed categories, like numerical values or a list of items, will not be a problem for analysis. Responses to closed-ended questions are easier for coding and analysis.

Participants may hesitate to answer a sensitive question about age or income; in such cases, a closed-ended question with multiple ranges makes participants more comfortable. For example, for a question on what is your age, the options could be 1) 21 to 30; 2) 31 to 40; 3) 41-50; 4) 51 and above.

The types of closed-ended questions may vary according to the response options. For fixed categories, you can provide mutually exclusive multiple options for participants to select the group they belong to, for example, Male and Female, and there is no order in them.

Questions with an ordinal scale, offer the choices in a rank from lower to higher. For a question on income, what is your income range per annum? The choices are listed in a rank:

> 1. Less than $5,000
> 2. $5,001 to 10,000
> 3. $10,001 to 15,000
> 4. $15,001 and above

The above options are mutually exclusive as well. For a question on age, if the options are given as 1) 10 to 20; 2) 20 to 30; 3) 30 to 40; 4) 40 to 50; 5) 50 and above, they will confuse the participants who are at 20/30/40/50. They will wonder whether to choose the lower band or the higher one. For categorical answers, the response options must be mutually exclusive.

Likert scale responses give the participants the option to choose from a five or seven-point scale. The Likert scale is named after the inventor Rensis Likert. "It provides a measure of intensity, extremity, and direction" (D. A. de Vaus 2002, 107). This scale is used to measure attitudes and opinions on a continuum and the scale must be balanced with the neutral option in the middle. Some researchers do not use the neutral option to force a choice. Researchers write Likert scale questions as single or multiple items. A single statement is used to obtain a choice of the agreement (see Box 7), or a set of multiple statements are used to obtain choices of agreement (see Box 8). When a set of statements are given, they all need to be mutually connected.

Ranking questions have a list of items that require the participants to rank them by giving a numerical score such as 1, 2, 3, and so on. As well, the participants can be asked to rank only the top two or three items.

Multiple-choice questions with the option of choosing more than one option are also used but it is better to avoid such questions. Instead, each item can be listed with yes/no options, which forces the participant to make a choice that is easier for analysis.

Avoid vague quantifiers like, do you attend church regularly? People can understand regularity in many ways. Attending church every day is regular for some; once in a week is regular for others, and once in a year is regular for some others.

Knowledge questions or questions seeking opinion or attitude based on awareness must have a 'don't know' option, because every participant may not know everything. Having a don't know option for a question can be problematic because there is a possibility of some participants choosing that option instead of thinking through the question to really respond.

Response Rate

The response rate, which researchers want to be high, depends on many factors related to the questions and response categories, such as "question content, question construction, method of administration, and questionnaire length. Intrusive, sensitive, irrelevant or repetitive

Box 7: Examples of Single Statement

"I believe in the doctrine of transubstantiation in which the bread and wine turn into the flesh and blood of Jesus Christ" can have the following options on a five-point scale:
1. Strongly disagree
2. Disagree
3. Neither disagree nor agree
4. Agree
5. Strongly agree

On a seven-point scale the options for answers would be:
1. Strongly disagree
2. Disagree
3. Somewhat disagree
4. Neither disagree nor agree
5. Somewhat agree
6. Agree
7. Strongly agree

Box 8: Examples of Multiple Statements

Indicate to what extent you disagree or agree to the following statements by checking the appropriate cell.

(1. Strongly disagree, 2. Disagree, 3. Neither agree nor disagree, 4. Agree, 5. Strongly agree):

	1	2	3	4	5
1. I believe in Jesus					
2. My thoughts revolve around Jesus					
3. I know my prayers are always answered					
4. I feel I am always loved by Jesus					

All the above statements about Christian spirituality are mutually connected.

questions as well as those that are poorly worded, difficult to understand, difficult to answer or have insufficient response categories can frustrate respondents and produce non-response" (De Vaus 2002, 97). The length of the questionnaire is another factor that affects the response rate; it should not be too short or too lengthy. The ideal length is based on the purpose of the survey; as a researcher, ask yourself, "Will it be a pleasant experience for the participants taking the survey?" While designing a questionnaire, take these factors into consideration to increase the response rate.

A well-designed questionnaire with a good layout increases the response rate. A cramped questionnaire with a small type size or without proper space may put off respondents. In a good design, response options are listed either horizontally or vertically, not in a haphazard manner. Grouping the questions into different sections enhances readability.

Sections of a Survey

The first section of a questionnaire must briefly state your credentials, the institution in which the study is being conducted, the purpose of the survey, the voluntary nature of participation in the survey, the participants' right to refuse to answer, time likely required for taking the survey, and assurance of anonymity.

Introduce each of the other sections. Provide clear instructions for questions on the number of options to choose, on how to answer a particular type of question such as ranking a list, and on skipping questions when the option 'No' is selected to a filter question, and so on.

Start with easy questions that are directly related to the purpose of the survey. "Choosing the right question to start the survey off is absolutely crucial, as the first question strongly influences whether sample members choose to participate" (Dillman, Smyth, and Christian 2014, 230). Place the sensitive and demographic questions toward the end of the questionnaire.

Experts' Review

It is good to get reviews of your draft questionnaire from subject specialists, experts on questionnaire design and statisticians to avoid failure of the survey (Dillman, Smyth, and Christian 2014). Subject specialists can review the content of the questionnaire in terms of the concepts being measured, facts, and knowledge relating to the field of study. Experts in questionnaire design could review the question order, measuring scales, instructions, response options with bias, and so on. Statisticians could review the questionnaire from the analytical point of view of whether a particular type of question or response could yield worthy or meaningless results. They can see the possibility of using a variety of statistical tools to analyze a set of questions and how changing the wordings of questions or response options could make way for sophisticated statistical analysis.

Pilot Test

When you are ready with a questionnaire, the next step is to do a pilot study by choosing a smaller group from the samples. "The goal is to determine whether the proposed questionnaire and procedures are adequate for the larger study" (Dillman, Smyth, and Christian 2014, 251). A pilot study will help you know how participants understand each question and the entire questionnaire and respond by answering the questions. A pilot study is essential when you have developed a questionnaire for your study.

A questionnaire is an instrument in a survey to collect data. As we have seen earlier, quantitative research is rigid in its design; if the instrument fails to collect the intended data, then the entire research is a failure. You cannot modify a questionnaire in the middle of a survey when you find something wrong with the questionnaire. Therefore, it is very important to design the questionnaire based on the research question or hypothesis to measure the concepts.

Instead of developing an original questionnaire, a researcher could use an existing questionnaire, especially for research that tests a theory, because the author/s of the theory would have already established the validity and reliability of the questionnaire. Some research may require a modification of the questionnaire; for some, a combination of several questionnaires will serve the purpose. If the researcher modifies or combines questionnaires, they must establish its validity and reliability. They need to obtain permission from the authors to use an existing questionnaire.

Administering Surveys

You can administer a survey in two ways: as a self-administered questionnaire and as a structured interview. You can provide the questionnaire in person, by post, email, or a link to web survey or a mobile app and let participants fill in the self-administered questionnaire. A structured interview can be conducted face-to-face or online or over the telephone, in which you fill the answers given by the participants.

Supervised Self-Administered Survey

In a supervised self-administered survey, researchers distribute the questionnaire to the participants, as individuals or a group, and they complete the survey in the presence of the researcher or administer. If a participant has questions, the researcher/administer is available to provide clarity.

Postal Survey

A mail or postal survey is a common method in some countries. Researchers send the questionnaire to the participants by mail with a stamped return mail envelope. The participants take the survey and return the filled-in questionnaire by mail. In terms of cost, this method is cheaper. But the participants cannot ask the researcher for clarity, therefore, it is very important to make every question self-explanatory. The response rate is debatable for this type of survey; it depends on factors like literacy rate, medium of language, cultural factors, and so on. In North America, people are used to mailed surveys and the response rate is usually high, but now on the decline. Some researchers offer a monetary incentive, but in some countries, researchers cannot send money along with a questionnaire. Thus, the postal survey requires an effective follow-up plan to boost the response rate.

Email Survey

Email surveys are more frequently used than postal surveys, depending on access to email. Researchers send the questionnaire by email either as text within the email or as an attachment. For in-text email, the participants answer the questions within the email itself. Another form of email survey attaches the questionnaire as a Word file; the participants answer the questions and send the file back as an attachment. This is cost effective, but participants may find it difficult to fill in the answers as new text changes the layout. A fillable PDF file may solve this issue. The free version of Adobe Acrobat Reader DC has a form fill option, which is often used for email surveys. An email survey would not be suitable for those who have no access to email. Medium of language could be an issue, but many email providers will send messages in local languages.

Web Survey

Web surveys are becoming more popular. Researchers design the questionnaires using templates from survey sites to create surveys and to analyze or extract data for sophisticated statistical analysis. Researchers send the link/URL of the survey by email or text message or as a QR code, asking the participants to take the survey by clicking the link or scanning the QR code. A web survey has several advantages, especially because the survey can be designed with visual elements and a variety of response options. Many participants access websites through smartphones; therefore, it is essential that the website is mobile-friendly. There are free and paid versions of online survey tools; Google Forms [https://www.google.com/forms/about/] is a free online survey provider with many features and is responsive to mobile devices. In some countries, internet availability could be an issue. Language barriers may be addressed with advanced web technology that will translate the survey into a local language. However, it would be good to have a translated questionnaire verified by a native speaker rather than relying on the translation done by web technology.

Mobile Survey

A mobile survey is an option. Researchers can develop a mobile application for the survey and distribute the application or make it available to be downloaded by the participants from an app store and opened. However, having to download and install the application might deter people from taking the survey.

Face-to-face Structured Interview

In a face-to-face structured interview, the interviewer asks the participant the questions as they are in the questionnaire to get their responses and the interviewer fills up the answers in the questionnaire. The main advantage of this method is that the interviewer can clarify participants' questions.

Telephone Interview

Researchers conduct telephone interviews in which the interviewer asks the questions and fills in the participant's answers. The interviewer can use a paper copy or an electronic copy of the questionnaire to fill in the answers. A telephone survey is advantageous because no travel costs are incurred, and it makes rescheduling possible according to the availability of the participants.

Mixed Mode Approach

In the mixed mode approach, the researcher uses more than one method to administer the survey. Using a different approach for different types of participants could enhance the response rate. Researchers sometimes give participants multiple options to choose from to take the survey. The advantages of the mixed-mode approach are cost-effectiveness, the short time span for conducting the survey, increased coverage, and improved response rate, reduced non-response error, and reduced measurement error (Dillman, Smyth, and Christian 2014). When the mixed-mode approach is used, the questionnaire needs to be designed in such a way that it is suitable to all modes of the survey.

Data for Structured Observation

Structured observation, a method for studying the social behaviors of people, is highly organized and based on an observation schedule, which defines the rules for observation. Despite the increased interest in studying "religion as practised," structured observation is not a popular choice among scholars in the field of religious studies (Stausberg 2011, 384). However, this method is suitable for studying religious practices, rituals, festivals, and visit to worship places, where external behavior is a key factor.

In structured observation, the researcher directly observes the behavior of the participants. Structured observation is different from participant observation in qualitative research, where the researcher aims to capture the bigger picture with small details. Contrarily, structured observation observes specific aspects of the observed. "Structured observation selects some acts, actors, objects or places, separating them out from the totality of the field, but even these units of observation cannot be studied in their totality" (Stausberg 2011, 387). The focus is on the specific aspects of what is observed, rather than on capturing every detail about everything.

Structured observation "requires a precise definition and protocol of the observed behavior" to make "the observation measurable" (Stausberg 2011, 384). The observation protocol is known as the observation schedule. Researchers frame the rules of observation based on the focus of the research to identify mutually exclusive categories of behaviors and record them systematically with numerical codes. The observation schedule "specifies the categories of behaviour that are to be observed and how behaviour should be assigned to those categories" (Bryman 2016, 269). The observer must categorize the behaviors uniformly to measure the observed behaviors. The schedule makes a list of behaviors and assigns a number to each category for observers to record the number when such behavior takes place.

The structured observation could record "incidents," "short periods," "long periods," and "time sampling" (Bryman 2016, 273).

Observers record the behaviors of the sample when an incident happens. For example, if you were observing devotees visiting a Hindu temple, the focus of research could be on what happens when the priest rings the handbell, (not a bigger bell in a temple, which the devotees ring). You would observe the devotees' behavior whenever the priest rings the handbell; the ringing of the bell is the incident in this case. You make a list of behaviors based on a literature review or on your initial observations. The list could include the following behaviors:

1. Bowing down
2. Closing eyes
3. Stretching both hands toward the *deepam* (sacred light) that is brought by the priest
4. Opening eyes
5. Stretching both palms upside down over the *deepam* (sacred light)
6. Taking sacred ash from the bowl
7. Applying the sacred ash on the forehead

Because this is not corporate worship, the priest rings the bell for every individual or group. Through structured observation, you can scrutinize the variance in behavior among different people: men and women, boys and girls, and so on. Each behavior or action is recorded with a numerical code. Researchers statistically analyze the recorded numerical data from the structured observation.

Structured observation can be short or long. Observing a child in a church for a few minutes during the sermon and recording the child's behavior every five seconds for five minutes is a short period of observation. A long period of observation involves observing selected participants during the entire sermon and recording their behaviors. Time sampling is the recording of the participants' behavior for a fixed interval of time, such as after every thirty seconds.

Structured observation can be used as a data collection method in an experimental study by artificially creating a situation to observe the behaviors of participants. It is also called field stimulation. Structured observation follows probability or non-probability sampling.

Pretest and Posttest in Experimental and Quasi-experimental Studies

Both experimental and quasi-experimental methods use pretest and posttest designs to collect data for analysis. The tests are based on the scales chosen for the experiment. If the study is about spiritual well-being (SWB), then the researcher uses the SWB scale or any other related scales to measure the SWB of the participants.

Single-group Posttest

In a single-group posttest experiment, the researcher introduces an intervention to a single group and measures the outcome with a posttest. Without a pretest, the results cannot be compared and hence any causal claim is dubious.

Single-group Pretest and Posttest

A single-group pretest and posttest study measures a single group twice, before and after intervention. If the score after the intervention is higher, then the researcher infers that the intervention caused the increase. Even if the scores are different before and after the treatment, without a control group, there is no possibility of ruling out other causes.

Pretest-posttest Control

In a pretest-posttest control group study, researchers assign the participants randomly to two groups and measure both groups before and after the experiment. The researcher serves a pretest questionnaire to both groups before the experiment. After the experiment, the control group takes the pretest questionnaire again, while the experimental group takes the posttest questionnaire. The researcher measures the participants of both groups and compares the results before and after the experiment. If the score of the experiment group has increased, then the causal relationship between the treatment and its effects is established. If the scores do not change, then the researcher concludes the causal effect is nil.

As mentioned, experimental designs are not common in the fields of theology and religious studies. However, a cross-discipline team of researchers from theology and other sciences could produce innovative experiments.

Data for Content Analysis

Quantitative content analysis is a research method that quantifies and measures message units in texts. Message units are concepts, themes, portrayals, coverage, tones, and so on. Researchers analyze the text and quantify them with "predetermined categories and in a systematic and replicable manner" (Bryman 2016, 283). The text for content analysis could be verbal, written or printed or digital forms, images, audios, and videos.

Quantitative content analysis differs from a thematic analysis in qualitative research that generates themes from narrative data. The quantitative content analysis quantifies the units of analysis based on predetermined categories. Quantitative content analysis is not about assessing the totality of the text or its meanings. Doing content analysis is not doing a literature review or critical analysis of literature or rhetorical analysis of writings but is about quantifying message units.

Media studies have been the main field to use content analysis, but now researchers in other fields use it widely. In most cases, researchers use the existing data for content analysis, instead of generating new data, because the researcher is interested in examining messages that are part of communication; the mode of communication could be in various forms.

For content analysis, text and documents come in many forms such as printed texts, speeches, lyrics, case narratives, photos, films, radio or television programs, blogs, comments to blogs, social media posts, social media comments, and websites (Bryman 2016). In addition, the list could include YouTube videos, tweets, newsletters, news items in print media, television, and online media, cartoons, artwork, advertisements, and so on. For theology and religious studies, the content analysis could analyze sermons, songs and hymns, liturgy, periodicals, manuscripts, speeches recorded in the scriptures, and many other items.

Clear research questions and hypotheses based on the literature review will help you identify the content of the analysis and the need for it. "All decisions on variables, their measurement, and coding rules must be made before the observations begin. In the case of human coding, the codebook and coding form must be constructed in advance. In the case of computer coding, the dictionary or other coding protocol must be established a priori" (Kimberly 2002, 11). The researcher needs to operationalize the concepts and variables with a clear definition for measuring. The next step is developing a coding scheme based on the operational definitions. The coding scheme contains a codebook with clear definitions of variables and their measures and a coding form to record the coding. Researchers can do the coding manually or digitally.

Then the researcher decides on a sample using the random selection of period or themes, mediums, and so on; all the sampling principles discussed earlier are used in selecting data for content analysis. But here, the unit of analysis is not the individuals, but message units. Message units refer to the "communication *content*" (emphasis in the original,

Kimberly 2002, 14). Researchers analyze the numeric data by using statistical tools like those used in other forms of quantitative research.

For example, Stephen Gray, Alexandra Inglish, Tejinder Singh Sodhi, and Tien-Tsung Lee (2017) did a study on the commercials aired during religious television programs in the USA. For this study, they identified terror management theory from the literature and associated fear of death with Christian fundamentalists as their theoretical framework. Based on this conceptual framework, the researchers formulated the research questions and hypotheses. They had the following research questions and hypotheses:

RQ1: What are the dominant product categories being advertised during religious programming?

H1: Advertised products will appeal to Christian fundamentalists' religious beliefs and sense of fear.

RQ2: What are the dominant appeals in the advertisements aired during religious programming?

H2: Appeals related to fear are frequently used in advertisements aired during religious programming.

RQ3: What is the level of religiosity demonstrated in the advertisements aired during religious programming?

RQ4: Do the advertisements tend to be casual/relaxed or serious/tense? (109)

Based on their research questions, they developed a coding sheet that has both a coding form and codes. The variables in this study are appeals, several themes that are listed in the coding sheet, and the tone of the commercial. They chose three Christian television programs: The 700 Club, CBN Newswatch, and Christian World News. Based on the literature review, they developed a coding sheet with the following items:

1. date coded
2. air date
3. program title
4. product being advertised
5. length of commercial
6. how strongly the ad appeals to a viewer's religiosity
(1 = strongly, 2 = somewhat or moderately, and 3 = little or not at all)
7. whether the ad mentions any of the following items
(health, religion/God/salvation, death, financial/material loss,

secular culture, safety, fear, pain, isolation, rejection, and being bad)

8. the overall impression and tone of the ad

(1 = casual/relaxed, 2 = middle, and 3 = serious/tense) (110)

For content analysis, the coding sheet is the instrument like a questionnaire for a survey for collecting data. All the commercials that were aired during the religious programs were the population for this study, but the coders worked out a set of criteria to select three programs. The coders carried out the study by watching selected episodes either live or online, based on a prearranged plan. Three coders watched 205 commercials and coded. One of the message units in this study was "fear." They analyzed the numerical data by using statistical tools and found that appeals relating to fear (81%) dominated the commercials. Content analysis in quantitative research enables researchers to examine message units in a text. Scholars of theology and religious studies could adopt quantitative content analysis for studying various forms of texts as mentioned above.

Data for Secondary Analysis

The secondary analysis deals with the data that were collected by others. Alan Bryman (2016, 310) appeals to all, especially undergraduate and postgraduate students, to consider using secondary analysis for their research projects because of the following advantages: "cost and time," "high quality data," "opportunity for longitudinal analysis," "subgroup analysis," "opportunity for cross-cultural analysis" and "reanalysis [to] offer new interpretations." The researcher looks for the existing data based on the research question. They may consider public data, government data, census, and data from other researchers for secondary analysis. With the internet, they can find valuable data online.

Some of the websites that hold data related to religion in the Western world are:

The Association of Religion Data Archives
http://www.thearda.com/

US Religion Census
http://www.usreligioncensus.org/index.php

Pew Research Center
http://www.pewresearch.org/

United States Census Bureau
https://www.census.gov/en.html

UK Data Service
https://www.ukdataservice.ac.uk/

European Data Portal
https://www.europeandataportal.eu/en

Robert D. Woodberry (2012) did an interesting study using secondary data; he statistically analyzed the censuses of several countries and matched them with the data on the presence of Protestant missionaries. The results established that the presence of Protestant missionaries was instrumental in promoting "religious liberty, mass education, mass printing, newspapers, voluntary organizations, [and] most major colonial reforms," that shaped democracy (244). This article won the best article award of the American Political Science Association in 2013. With secondary data, one can come up with innovative ideas for research and the results could result in far-reaching consequences.

Data Analysis in Quantitative Research

Quantitative research uses descriptive and/or inferential statistical tools to analyze the numeric data. Descriptive statistics describes the basic characteristics of the sample and provide a summary of the data in a meaningful manner. Inferential statistics helps researchers to infer from the data and generalize to the population. Inferential statistics analyzes the relationship between variables when testing a hypothesis.

For statistical analysis, researchers mostly use software programs like IBM SPSS or SAS or R, or Microsoft Excel. Student projects can be done in Microsoft Excel or Google Sheets. Many books and YouTube tutorials are available for each statistical software program for analyzing quantitative data.

As a first step in statistical analysis, the data need to be prepared. Data preparation steps involve coding, data entry, and dealing with the missing data. After preparing the data, you choose from several statistical tools for analyzing the data to answer your research question. This section will introduce the basic statistical tests for quantitative analysis. For more information on statistics, consult books on statistics.

Coding

Coding is assigning a numerical value to items in the questionnaire. For example, gender has two categories female and male, and these categories are to be translated into a numeric form by assigning 1 to female and 2 to male. For a multiple-choice question, each response option is to be coded with a numeral. Similarly, for a five-point Likert scale, numeral 1 is assigned to strongly disagree, 2 for disagree, 3 for neutral, 4 for agree, and 5 for strongly agree. For a question that requires participants to choose more than one item, each item is to be coded with 1 for yes and 2 for no. Open-ended questions like age or income may require that a range be created and coded: for example, with age, 1 for less than 20, 2 for 21 to 30, 3 for 31 to 40, 4 for 41 to 50, and 5 for 51 and above. When multiple researchers are involved in large surveys, they need to use a codebook to ensure uniformity in coding by each coder.

Data Entry

All quantitative software programs have the provision to enter data directly into their database for analysis. But it is advisable to enter the data into Microsoft Excel or other spreadsheets that will make it easier to reorganize, share, and deal with a portion of data than entering data directly into the software program (Bhattacherjee 2012). Spreadsheets can also be saved as comma-separated values (CSV) files which could be imported into any statistical software for analysis. Researchers do not need sophisticated software for small projects; Microsoft Excel is sufficient (Salkind 2017). In Microsoft Excel or spreadsheets, each column represents a variable or question, and each row represents a participant.

Missing Data

Participants may inadvertently or deliberately miss answering a question, which results in missing values. Some statistical software programs can read the blank entries as a missing value, or some software requires that you assign a number like 999 to indicate a missing value. You need to be aware of the method to accommodate the missing value in the software.

Univariate Analysis

Univariate analysis, the simplest form of data analysis, analyzes one variable. The univariant analysis offers a descriptive explanation of the sample by presenting the frequency distribution, central tendency, and measures of variation or dispersion. Univariate analysis helps researchers to summarize the data in a meaningful manner by revealing patterns.

Frequency Distribution

Frequency distribution presents the percentage of each category with the number of participants. "A frequency distribution is a method of tallying and representing how often certain scores occur" (Salkind 2017, 98). Let us assume in response to a question on the frequency of prayer, table 4 is the frequency table for a sample of 131:

Table 4: Frequency Distribution of Prayer

Category	Frequency	Percent
Daily	60	45.8
Weekly	31	23.6
Once a month	17	13
Never	20	15.3
Missing data	3	2.3
Total	131	100

Central Tendency

Central tendency is a single value that indicates the central position in a data set. Central tendency deals with different averages such as mean, median, and mode. Average is "the 'middle' space or as a fulcrum on a seesaw. It's the point where all the values in a set of values are balanced" (Salkind 2017, 52). Central tendency helps you understand the distribution of values across the sample from the middle value.

Mean

Mean is the simple average that is used commonly; it is also known as the arithmetic mean. To calculate the mean, you add all the values and divide them by the number of values. For example, a test score of seven students is 12, 25, 20, 18, 17, 15, and 19. The sum of the values is 126; the mean, 126 divided by 7, is 18.

Median

The median is the middle value in a distribution. We identify the median by arranging the values in numerical order and then choose the middle value. For example, the test scores are arranged in increasing order: 12, 15, 17, 18, 19, 20, 25. The median for these values is 18. With even number of values, the two middle values are added and divided by 2. Let us add one more value to the test score: 12, 15, 17, 18, 19, 20, 22, 25. In this, the middle values are 18 and 19; so, the median is 18+19= 37/2= 18.5.

Mode

Mode is the most frequently occurring value in a distribution. For example, in these test scores, 12, 15, 17, 17, 18, 19, 20, 25, the mode is 17 because it occurred twice.

Measures of Variation

Measures of variation or dispersion is about how the values are spread around the central tendency. Dispersion is measured by range or standard deviation.

Range

The range is derived by deducting the lowest value from the highest value in a distribution. For a set of test scores, 15, 17, 17, 18, 19, 20, 25, 32 the range is 32-15 = 17.

Standard Deviation

Standard deviation (SD) shows the variation of dispersion from the mean. Standard deviation is "the average amount of variation around the mean" (Bryman 2016, 338) or the "average distance of each score from the mean" (Salkind 2017, 82). Standard deviation is more accurate in measuring the dispersion than range; especially when a distribution has an outlier. For example, for these test scores, 15, 17, 17, 18, 19, 20, 25, 32, we derived 17 as the range. But if the test score has 48 as one of the values, 15, 17, 17, 18, 19, 20, 25, 32, 48, then the range is 48-15= 33. The outlier 48 made the range inaccurate. But standard deviation corrects this. Standard deviation can be derived by using a formula; all software programs have the feature to find the standard deviation for a set of values.

Bivariate Analysis

Bivariate analysis analyzes the existence of any relationship between two variables by using correlation. For example, the relationship between the variable age and religiosity or women and spiritual well-being could be examined by using correlation test.

Correlation

Correlation is one of the ways of examining the relationship between two variables, but this does not establish a causal relationship between variables. One of the common correlation coefficients is called Pearson's product-moment correlation, which carries the name of the inventor Karl Pearson; it is also referred to as 'Pearson's r' or simply 'r'. We measure the strength of relationship between two continuous variables between -1 and $+1$. A correlation of $+1$ indicates the perfect relationship between the variables; a score of 0 indicates the absence of any relationship between the variables, whereas -1 indicates the perfect negative relationship between the variables. Thus, correlation indicates the kind of association between the variables.

Statistical Significance

Statistical significance is the claim researchers make that the results are true. Researchers cannot be totally certain of their results because other factors or chance could have caused the results; so, it is claimed the results are 95% true. But in statistics this is stated differently; instead of saying 95% true, researchers say that the results have a 5% chance of not being true. Researchers choose the level of 5% chance of not being true to accommodate other factors or sampling error. A researcher cannot be certain that the results based on a sample will be the same for the population.

Statistical significance is about the confidence level and the level of risk the researcher will take to claim the result is generalizable to the population with probability sampling. Statistical significance is not about the practical significance of the results.

Significance level is the value the researcher chooses while designing a study to indicate the risk the researcher is willing to take to accept that the results could go wrong. The significance level is known as alpha (α). Alpha could be 1% (.01) or 5% (.05) or 10% (.1). Commonly, researchers choose alpha as 0.05 (5%) significance level.

P-value

Statistical significance is determined by p-value or probability value. In statistics, probability is a key factor. Probability indicates the chance of being incorrect in rejecting or failing to reject the null hypothesis and the researcher can never be 100% certain in claiming the association between variables. If the probability value or p-value is less than α 0.05, then it is considered statistically significant because the chance of being wrong is less than 5%.

Statistical significance plays a vital role in testing a hypothesis. The researcher creates a null hypothesis for the research/alternative hypothesis. Contrary to the research hypothesis, the null hypothesis claims that there is no relationship between the variables or groups. If the p-value of the statistical test is less than 0.05, the predetermined significance level (α), it is considered statistically significant; therefore, the null hypothesis is rejected and the research hypothesis is accepted. If the p-value is greater than α 0.05, then the null hypothesis is not rejected and the research hypothesis is rejected. Smaller p-value means the evidence is stronger for rejecting the null hypothesis.

Type I and Type II Errors

Type I and Type II errors are possible while dealing with the significance level in rejecting or accepting the null hypothesis. A Type I error is a false positive and is also known as alpha (α), in which the null hypothesis is rejected when it is actually true, because the p-value is less than α 0.05 which is statistically significant. To reduce the chances of Type I error occurring, you lower the α value (significant level). But making the α level lower will lead you to a Type II error. A Type II error is a false negative and is known as beta (β), in which you accept the null hypothesis when it is actually false. To reduce the chances of Type II error, you can increase the sample size or be lenient with the α level. These errors are interrelated; decreasing the chances for Type I error increases the chances for Type II error and vice versa.

Chi-square Test

The chi-square test is used to analyze statistical significance. It examines the relationship, the probability of independence between two categorical variables or mutually exclusive categories; it is not suitable for analyzing parametric or continuous data. It does not deal with percentages or ratios, only numerical values. Commonly, it is used in cross-tabulation, in which how a particular category answered a question is known as a test of independence. For example, the chi-square test can examine the probability of independence between gender and frequency of prayer. The chi-square test is also used to analyze the observed values and expected values, which is called the goodness of fit test. The expected value can be calculated by dividing the total of the observed value by the number of categories.

Degrees of freedom

Degrees of freedom (df) is calculated by $n-1$; here, n refers to the sample size or a number of values. Degrees of freedom is the number of values that are free to vary in data. For example, for a mean of 5 based on three values, the values could be 5, 7, (or any other numbers you can choose for the first two values), but the third value must be 3 in this case, it cannot vary, because the mean is 5. So, the degrees of freedom is 3–1 = 2. By using the degrees of freedom and significance level (usually 0.05), you can obtain the critical value from the chi-square table; the statistical software will do this for you. If the obtained value is equal to or greater than the critical value, then the null hypothesis is rejected, and the research hypothesis is accepted.

T-test

A t-test is also called the Student T-Test; William S. Gosset developed the t-test and used the pseudo name "Student" to publish his article due to the restriction by his employer. T-test examines the difference of statistical significance between the averages (means) of different variables while taking the variation into consideration. A paired t-test tests the difference between two means of the same sample. An independent t-test is used to test the means of two different groups. A one sample t-test tests the means of the sample to the standard means of the population. In addition, researchers may choose either a two-tailed or one-tailed test. The two-tailed test compares both positive and negative differences between the groups. One-tailed test tests the direction of the difference, for example, whether women scored higher in IQ scores than men. With the computed t value (t-test statistic), chosen significance level of 0.05, and the determined degrees of freedom, you calculate the p-value by looking up at the t-table; the statistical software will do this for you. If the p-value is not greater than the chosen significance level of .05, you reject the null hypothesis.

Analysis of variance (ANOVA)

Analysis of variance (ANOVA) is like a t-test that deals with two groups. ANOVA deals with more than two groups. The statistic value of ANOVA is referred to as the F value; F refers to the name of the inventor of this statistic, Ronald A. Fisher. ANOVA tests the differences in means among multiple groups. ANOVA examines how the "variance due to differences in performance is separated into variance that's due to differences between individuals within groups and variance due to differences between groups. Then, the two types of variance are compared with one another" (Salkind 2017, 286–88). The F statistic or F value is calculated by taking the variance between samples, the variance within samples, and the sample sizes. Then the researcher looks at the F distribution table for critical value; for each α level there is a separate F table. By choosing the appropriate F table, with the degrees of freedom of the numerator and degrees of freedom of the denominator, you can find the critical F value. If the F value is greater than the F critical value, then the null hypothesis is rejected. All these can be done with a few clicks in statistical software. One-way ANOVA tests one independent variable among multiple groups. Factorial ANOVA tests the variance of two or more independent variables in multiple groups; it analyses the main effects of each factor and the interaction between the factors as well.

Regression analysis

Regression analysis helps predict the value of the dependent variable based on the value of the independent variable. Prediction is possible by using a "set of previously collected data (such as data on variables X and Y), calculat[ing] the degree to which these variables are correlated with one another, and then use that correlation and the knowledge of X to predict Y" (Salkind 2017, 328–29). Regression analysis is used to examine the strength of the relationship between the variables, predict the effect or impact, and forecast a trend. See Chapter 8 for reporting of the results of analysis.

Chapter Summary

This chapter presented the definitions of quantitative research and the three types: survey research, experimental research, and quasi-experimental research. You have learned the importance of the conceptual phase of quantitative research, which involves identifying theories, concepts, variables, hypotheses, and measurement scales. In quantitative research, numerical data are collected through survey, structured observation, pretests, posttests, identifying message units for content analysis, and existing date for secondary analysis. You have understood the importance of designing a questionnaire and establishing the validity and reliability of the instrument before conducting a survey. You also know the principles and procedures of sampling and data collection for quantitative research. This chapter introduced you to univariate analysis and bivariate analysis to analyze data in quantitative research.

You can now confidently and skillfully design and conduct a quantitative study.

Review Questions

1. What is quantitative research?
2. What are the different types of quantitative research?
3. What are the different scales of measurement?
4. How to establish validity and reliability?
5. What is probability sampling?
6. What is non-probability sampling?
7. How to arrive at a sample size in quantitative research?
8. How to design a survey questionnaire?
9. What is structured observation?
10. What is quantitative content analysis?
11. What is univariate analysis?
12. What is bivariate analysis?
13. What is Pearson's correlation coefficient test?
14. What is statistical significance?

Further Help

Bhattacherjee, Anol. 2012. *Social Science Research: Principles, Methods, and Practices.* Textbooks Collection. 2nd ed. http://scholarcommons.usf.edu/oa_textbooks/3

Dillman, Don A., Jolene D. Smyth, and Leah Melani Christian. 2014. *Internet, Phone, Mail, and Mixed-Mode Surveys: The Tailored Design Method.* 4th ed. Hoboken, NJ: John Wiley & Sons.

Salkind, Neil J. 2016. *Statistics for People Who (Think They) Hate Statistics: Using Microsoft Excel 2016.* 4th ed. London: Sage.

Chapter 6

MIXED METHODS RESEARCH

Mixed methods research is an emerging strategy, in which the researcher combines both qualitative and quantitative strategies to minimize the limitations of each strategy and to augment the strengths of both strategies. Recently it has gained a lot of interest across disciplines. The researcher must be well versed in both qualitative and quantitative research to design and conduct mixed methods research (Creswell 2015). Since this approach combines both qualitative and quantitative research strategies, it requires research skills to handle narrative and numerical data and needs more time because it amounts to conducting two research projects in a single study.

Definition of Mixed Methods Research

Authors who promote mixed methods research provide further understanding of this strategy. R. Burke Johnson, Anthony J. Onwuegbuzie and Lisa A. Turner (2007, 129) say: "Mixed methods research is an intellectual and practical synthesis based on qualitative and quantitative research." It will "provide the most informative, complete, balanced, and useful research results." These authors emphasize synthesizing both research strategies together to arrive at all-inclusive results. In mixed methods research, according to Abbas Tashakkori and John Creswell (2007, 4), the researcher "collects and analyzes data, integrates the findings, and draws inferences using both qualitative and quantitative approaches or methods in a single study." Tashakkori and Creswell stress the integration of the findings from both approaches. Mixed methods research for John Creswell and David Creswell (2018, 41–42) is "an approach to inquiry involving collecting both quantitative and qualitative data, integrating the two forms of data, and using distinct designs that may involve philosophical assumptions and theoretical frameworks. The core assumption of this form of inquiry is that the integration of qualitative and quantitative data yields additional insight beyond the information provided by either the quantitative or qualitative data alone." This definition considers mixed methods research a separate strategy in social research while stressing the integration of the data for deeper insights.

Based on the above definitions, we conclude that mixed methods research combines qualitative and quantitative strategies to systematically collect narrative and numerical data and to rigorously analyze different data sets in a single study, the researcher integrates the findings to answer the research questions holistically.

As discussed, both qualitative and quantitative research are suitable for theology and religious studies because they can address different kinds of research questions related to religion and theology. In some cases, a study in theology/religious studies could ask questions that require both qualitative and quantitative data to answer them. M. Nel and W. J. Schoeman (2015, 91) argue for the need to study the "complexity of congregational life" by taking both inductive and deductive approaches by using mixed methods research. Niko Kohls, Anna Hack, and Harald Walach (2008) argue for the need to use a mixed methods approach to study exceptional and spiritual experiences. Many areas relating to theology and religious studies can potentially be researched by using mixed methods research. Mixed methods strategy could open avenues for scholars of theology and religious studies to raise questions creatively and find answers relevant to the context.

Characteristics of Mixed Methods Research

John Creswell and Vicki Clark (2018) have identified core characteristics of mixed methods research and I have adapted them for ease of understanding.

1. Research questions/hypotheses guide data collection

A researcher may use mixed methods research sensing the need for a second strategy because the first one may not answer a particular dimension of the problem and the research questions require answers from both quantitative and qualitative data. For example, a quantitative study on racial discrimination may indicate how widespread it is in a particular location. But this data cannot reveal the victims' feelings, the effects on different aspects of their life, and the lived experience of being discriminated against. To capture these aspects, the researcher could use qualitative research in addition to quantitative research.

2. Scrupulous collection and analysis of both qualitative and quantitative data
Mixed methods research systematically collects and rigorously analyzes both qualitative and quantitative data. It maintains scientific rigor in both phases of research.

3. Integration of data and findings
Mixed methods research integrates data and findings to obtain deeper or additional insights. Integration is a key component of mixed methods research.

4. Logic and procedures of each strategy upheld
Mixed methods researchers, in a single study, design and conduct qualitative and quantitative research according to each strategy's logic and procedures in a single study. They collect and analyze data according to the respective methodology, research design, and procedures without compromising scientific rigor.

5. Grounded in the paradigms of social research and theories
Researchers do not design mixed methods research in a philosophical vacuum. The methods may, for example, bring postpositivism and constructivism together in a study. However, scholars differ on the paradigms of research for mixed methods research. The pragmatic paradigm is the bedrock of the mixed methods research (J. W. Creswell and Clark 2018); though, interest is growing in the use of transformative paradigm (Mertens 2015). The choice of theoretical lens is a key component in mixed methods research because the research engages deductive and inductive reasoning.

Purposes of Mixed Methods Research

Using mixed methods research depends on the purpose and nature of the study and research questions. 'Which is the best method?' is not the right question in selecting qualitative or quantitative or mixed methods research. The right question is 'Which is a suitable strategy?' to find the answers to the research questions. John Creswell and Vicki Clark (2018) provide the rationale for mixed methods research. I have adapted some of them here.

1. To address the limitations of one approach

Qualitative data provide insights into the process but is based on a small sample size and does not offer data on how two variables are related or how widespread a factor is among the population. Quantitative research explains the association between two variables and offers descriptive information about the population but lacks insights into the process or meanings of the phenomenon for individuals. Mixed methods research is suitable to address the limitations of one approach and complement each other to gain a holistic understanding.

2. To explain the meanings of quantitative results

Quantitative research establishes the association between variables and descriptive information on the population of the study based on statistical analysis. But providing an understanding of the meaning of the association of variables for individuals requires using qualitative research with its narrative data. Here, statistical results are complemented by the meanings the participants attribute to the phenomenon.

3. To develop an instrument

In instances where variables and theories are not available in the literature for a problem, qualitative research needs to be used to explore the phenomenon. An exploratory study of a small number of participants highlights the variables, the kind of questions to be asked, and the hypotheses to be tested. Based on the findings of qualitative research, mixed methods researchers design an instrument to conduct quantitative research among a larger sample.

4. To enhance the understanding of intervention in an experimental study

In an experimental study, researchers test the intervention, and the results indicate its effectiveness. However, the participant's experience of the intervention, its effectiveness for them, what it means to them, and their feelings cannot be captured in an experimental study. This requires a qualitative study.

5. To compare qualitative findings and quantitative results

Mixed methods researchers collect and analyze qualitative and quantitative data simultaneously and compare the results for in-depth understanding.

Research Designs in Mixed Methods Research

John Creswell and Plano Clark (2018), in the third edition of their book, *Designing and Conducting Mixed Methods Research*, suggest research designs for mixed methods fall broadly into three systems. They modified their earlier typologies to arrive at three major designs: convergent, the explanatory sequential, and the exploratory sequential.

Convergent Design

In convergent design, the researcher uses qualitative and quantitative strategies simultaneously to understand how the results come together and are similar. Convergent design values both qualitative and quantitative data equally. Researchers collect data separately, analyze them separately, present them separately or in parallel, and finally integrate them for a holistic understanding. They use the two data sets for triangulation in convergent design. The integration takes place in the discussion chapter where the themes from the qualitative analysis and results from the quantitative analysis are compared side by side to identify any convergence between the two data sets.

Convergent findings show the holistic understanding of the problem because they augment the strengths of both qualitative and quantitative research while reducing the weaknesses of each strategy. But when results are divergent, the researcher must justify the outcome with an explanation (Creswell 2015) by finding a solution in the data or by collecting new data. Another option is to simply state the divergent results as the limitation of the study (Creswell and Creswell 2018).

Explanatory Sequential Design

Explanatory sequential design is a two-phase study. In this design, the quantitative research is completed in the first phase, followed by the qualitative research in the second phase. Quantitative research takes priority and qualitative research is secondary in this design. The qualitative findings are used to expand on quantitative results to provide a better and more detailed understanding of them. Quantitative results portray the bigger picture of the research problem, while qualitative findings "refine, extend, or explain the general quantitative picture" (Creswell 2015, 545). Although quantitative research takes priority in this design, qualitative findings add significance to the study (Bryman 2016).

The researcher designs the qualitative research based on the results of the quantitative research. The researcher determines the aspects of the quantitative results that require follow up with qualitative research and the participants of the study, whether they are to come from the sample of the quantitative research or from others in the population (Heiselt and Sheperis 2010). Researchers prefer similarity in the sample so that the qualitative findings will add more details to the results of the quantitative research. This design is preferred by researchers who come from a postpositivist background and are not well versed in qualitative research (Creswell and Creswell 2018). It is a complex design for beginners.

Exploratory Sequential Design

Exploratory sequential design is also a two-phase study. In the first phase, qualitative research is used to explore a research problem; the quantitative research is then used to explain the relationship between variables related to the problem. Qualitative research identifies themes and variables for developing an instrument to be tested in quantitative research. The exploratory sequential design uses a different set of samples drawn from the same population for the qualitative and quantitative phases.

This design is ideal when variables or instruments, or suitable measures are not available to study a population or to identify a suitable intervention (Creswell and Clark 2018). This design is suitable to test a hypothesis or theory, or model developed through qualitative research, generalize the qualitative findings to a larger population, and offer a clear understanding through quantitative research. Qualitative research assumes priority in this design.

The advantage of this design lies with the instrument being culturally relevant to the population because it emerged from the participant's experience of the phenomenon based on qualitative research. The second phase tests the theory or model developed by the qualitative research in the first phase, with a larger sample representing the population. Unlike the explanatory sequential design, the exploratory sequential design uses a different set of samples drawn from the same population for the qualitative and quantitative phases. Mixed methods researchers first collect qualitative data and analyze them. Comparison of data in this design is irrelevant, but data integration takes place in the phase of designing the instrument for the survey (Creswell and Creswell 2018). Based on the qualitative findings, researchers design the survey instrument for the quantitative research. Quantitative results indicate the generalizability of the qualitative findings.

Quality Concerns for Mixed Methods Research

Mixed methods research must meet quality measures (O'Cathain 2010; Bryman 2016; J. W. Creswell and Clark 2018) and preferably, follow the quality criteria of quantitative and qualitative research. The following factors can address the quality concerns of mixed methods research.

1. Rigor in planning and designing

Researchers must ensure that they have followed the steps and procedures rigorously in planning and designing each strand (quantitative and qualitative) of research. At the planning stage, researchers must spell out how conflicting research paradigms are to be discussed and dealt with in their study.

2. Rationale for mixed methods research

Researchers are required to provide a clear rationale for the choice of mixed methods research. It should not be simply based on the researcher's preference or on a false notion that mixing two methods is better than a single method.

3. Guided by research questions and purposes

Research questions and purposes should guide the choice of mixed methods research. The link between research questions and the type of research must be spelled out clearly to help readers understand that the research questions have guided the choice of mixed methods. Research questions and purposes must be appropriate for each strand.

4. Rationale for research design

An explanation of the intended outcome of the study and its link to the chosen design (convergent or explanatory sequential or exploratory sequential design) is required. Researchers must offer reasons for the choice of a particular design and show how the design meets the intended outcome of the study. The intended outcome is the end product of integrating data sets.

5. Rigor in data collection and analysis

Data collection and analysis are to be carried out rigorously as per the steps and procedures for qualitative and quantitative research.

6. Integration of data

The core element of mixed methods research is the integration of data. In convergent design, data are integrated to complement the results; in explanatory sequential design, qualitative findings explain the quantitative results; and in exploratory sequential design, qualitative findings contribute to the design of a quantitative instrument to test and generalize qualitative findings. The researcher must explicitly state how the data are integrated.

7. Validity, reliability, credibility, and trustworthiness

Each strand must address quality concerns on its own terms. Quantitative research must establish the validity and reliability of the instrument and results. Qualitative research must demonstrate the credibility and trustworthiness of data collection and interpretation.

Chapter Summary

This chapter helped you understand the emerging strategy of using mixed methods research for theology and religious studies. Mixed methods study combines qualitative and quantitative research strategies to collect and analyze narrative and numerical data to find holistic answers. You have learned the characteristics of mixed methods research and its purposes, such as triangulation, complementarity, and development. The chapter discussed different research designs of mixed methods research. In convergent design, the researcher uses qualitative and quantitative research simultaneously, whereas the explanatory sequential design uses quantitative research in the first phase and qualitative research in the second phase. On the other hand, the exploratory sequential design uses qualitative research in the first phase and quantitative research in the second phase.

You have understood quality concerns in mixed methods research. You have also gained a good understanding of mixed methods research and its potential benefits in addressing complex research questions in theology and religious research.

Review Questions

1. What is the definition of mixed methods research?
2. What are the characteristics of mixed methods research?
3. How to determine the suitability of mixed methods research?
4. What is convergent design?
5. What is explanatory sequential design?

6. What is exploratory sequential design?
7. How to address quality concerns of mixed methods research?

Further Help

Creswell, John W., and Vicki L. Plano Clark. 2018. *Designing and Conducting Mixed Methods Research*. 3rd ed. London: Sage.

Teddlie, Charles, and Abbas Tashakkori. 2009. *Foundations of Mixed Methods Research: Integrating Quantitative and Qualitative Approaches in the Social and Behavioral Sciences*. London: Sage.

WRITING A RESEARCH PROPOSAL

Research is a journey. Unfortunately, some begin their research journey without knowing their destination. But you are ready for a research journey only when your research proposal is ready, meaning writing a research proposal is the first and the most important step in your research. If you can produce a good research proposal, then your research journey will be smooth.

Importance of Research Proposal

A research proposal is like a travel plan for a journey. The destination is the purpose of the research, which you identify by defining the research problem and framing research questions on your topic. Until you find a research problem and the primary question, you will not know where you are heading. Once you decide the destination, you must decide the route, which is a methodological approach and then you must select the mode of travel, which is the method. You will also have to come up with reasons for taking on this journey and its importance. A good research proposal lets you start your journey with the confidence that you will reach the destination, and it makes the journey successful and satisfying.

In addition to giving you clarity, your research proposal must convince the department committee/authorities about the value of your research and your potential to execute the research project with the available resources and within the time frame. The purpose of the research proposal is to inform the authorities about your research, anticipated findings, and the efforts required to complete the project; and convince them about the significance of your research, that deserves committee's approval (Weiss 2019).

Therefore, you describe the proposed research in detail, the need for and the importance of the research and explain how the research will be conducted. A research proposal is a document that provides a clear picture of every aspect of a research project. A research proposal can also be described as the blueprint of your research project (Denscombe 2012). The research proposal provides clarity on the background or rationale for the study, presents the research questions, states the purpose of the research, and defines the research problem, the methodological approach, and the methods that will be used to collect and analyze data. The proposal also discusses ethical issues and presents the significance, scope and limitations, and the practical implications of the research.

Elements of a Research Proposal

Because a research proposal is not a simple description of the project, rather a justification for the study (Punch 2016), it must answer the following questions to convince the committee.

- What is the area of research?
- What is the focus of the investigation?
- What is already known about the topic in the literature?
- What is not known yet about the topic?
- What kinds of data are needed to find an answer for the unknown?
- How will the data be collected and analyzed?
- How will the ethical concerns be addressed?
- What will be the contribution of the research to the advancement of knowledge?
- What will be the practical implications of the results?
- Will it be significant enough for a doctoral/master's level research?
- How long will it take to complete the research?

The answers to the above questions can be seen as various elements in a research proposal. You must logically connect the following elements to argue for the need for your research:

1. Title
2. Abstract
3. Background

4. Statement of the Problem
5. Statement of the Purpose
6. Research Questions/Hypotheses
7. Literature Review
8. Methodology
   - Philosophical/Theological Assumptions and Social Research Paradigm
   - Research Design and Approach
   - Primary Source
   - Sampling
   - Role of the researcher/Instrument
   - Data Collection Procedures
   - Data Analysis Procedures
   - Credibility/Reliability
   - Trustworthiness/Validity
   - Justification of the Methodology
9. Significance
10. Limitations and Delimitations
11. Definition of Terms
12. Organization of Research Report and Dissemination
13. Timeline
14. Ethical Concerns
15. Working Bibliography
16. Appendices

Title

The title is the first part of the proposal one reads. The main title must present the concepts or the variables to indicate the focus of the investigation (see Chapter 1). It should be formulated with keywords to help your work be found by others. A subtitle may be used to indicate either a specific aspect of the study or the significance or methodology or method or location.

The title should not be too generic or too broad. For example, "A Study of Persecution" is too broad and lacks clarity. This title presents only one concept but needs to have one or more concepts associated with the idea of persecution to clarify the focus. One example is "Socio-economic Impact of Persecution against Tribal Christians in Kandhamal District in India." This title deals with two concepts: persecution and socio-economic impact, which clearly states the focus of the research; it also indicates the location of the research site. Nor should a title be too narrow. For example, "Church dropouts among 13-year-old teens in AG Churches in Kothanur, Bangalore." Here, the age factor of 13 is too narrow and the geographical location is a small area in the city of Bangalore. With such a narrow focus and a small geographical location, finding sufficient data to have credible results would be challenging.

The research title must say as much as possible about the research but in a few words. John Creswell and David Creswell (2018) suggest not having more than twelve words for a research title; however, up to fifteen words are acceptable.

A good title includes a main title and subtitle with any or some of the following features. Box 9 presents examples of titles.

Main Title:
- Uses a descriptive phrase instead of a sentence
- Accurately presents the focus of the study
- Introduces key concepts or variables of the research
- Indicates the relationship among the variables
- Contains keywords
- Is comprehensive yet precise to indicate key aspects of the research
- Uses words to stimulate the interest of readers

Subtitle:
- Present the specific aspect of the study
- State the theory
- Indicate the approach/methodology
- Specify the participants
- Identify the research site
- Inform the significance
- Suggest the implications

Avoid the following in a research title:
- Punctuation marks
- Abbreviations
- Italics or boldface or capitalization for emphasis
- Redundant phrases like "a critical study" or "an examination of" or "a study of"

Abstract

The abstract summarizes the essence of your research proposal. An abstract is not an introduction (Punch 2016) or a background to the study but an overview of the research proposal. The abstract also gives

---

Box 9: Examples of Titles

The first two examples below show how titles could be worded to indicate the focus and other aspects of a study and the third example shows how not to coin a title.

Example 1

Christian Women's Pornography Usage: The Role of Perceived Addiction, Social Anxiety, Shame, and Grace (Bohannon, 2021)

The main title presents the main topic of Christian women and pornography. The subtitle indicates the specific aspects such as perceived addiction, social anxiety, shame, and grace that the study covers.

Example 2

The Experiences of Students with Disabilities: A Phenomenological Study of Postsecondary Students in Ghana (Agyekum 2021)

The main title introduces the topic of the experiences of disabled students. The subtitle presents three elements of the study:
- Approach: phenomenology
- Sample: postsecondary students
- Research site/location: Ghana

Example 3

An Examination of Religiosity, Spirituality, and Psychological Wellbeing Among Pagan Women: A Mixed Method Approach (Reed 2016)

The main title presents the specific aspects of the study (religiosity, spirituality, and psychological wellbeing) and the sample: pagan women. The subtitle indicates the methodological approach as mixed methods.

The phrase "an examination of" in the main title is redundant and could have been avoided. The term "pagan" carries a negative connotation; it is always good to avoid such derogatory terms in a research title and writing. Moreover, the title simply says pagan women, so the reader knows little about them because it says nothing more about the participants or the research site of the study.

---

readers their first impression of your research. For many, the first impression is the last. Therefore, you must cover all essential elements of the proposal in the abstract. The abstract should briefly present the purpose, research question/hypothesis, objectives, methodology and methods, and the significance of the study.

A well-written abstract catches the interest of a reader, so they read further. A good abstract answers the following questions:

- What are the reasons for doing this research?
- What will be studied?
- How will it be studied?
- What are the likely findings/results expected?
- What is the significance of the study?

Although the abstract appears at the beginning of your research proposal, you should write it only after writing the entire research proposal because only then will you be able to have clarity on all aspects of the proposal. An abstract provides evidence about clarity in the research design and the plan for executing the research project, in a few words. Institutions vary in limiting the word count in an abstract to between 150 and 250 words.

Background

The background introduces the research and also helps readers know how well versed you are in the literature related to your topic and the value of your research for the field of study. The background could include the research setting for the topic, the reason you are interested in the topic, and the context for your research. The first is vital to include and the latter two are optional.

In the background you must present the research setting for the topic in the existing literature. The research setting, which is based on scholarly literature, indicates how the topic has been researched in the past, what the current interests are, and in what direction the research is moving. However, the background is not about reviewing the literature but to indicate how your research "fits into what is already known, and to locate it in relation to present knowledge and practice" (Punch 2016, 315). You can provide an overview of the literature related to the topic in this section.

Second, you may describe how you became interested in the topic and present your personal experience (C. Dawson 2009) or concerns that led you to select this topic.

The background section may also describe the relevance of the topic to the context of the research. It could deal with the social, cultural, political, economic, and religious contexts. Let us assume that a study is about spiritual resources for health care professionals amid COVID-19.

For this study, you could present the statistics about the number of health care professionals infected with COVID-19, the number that recovered, and the number of deaths among them in your region. This statistical information presents the social context of the study. Similarly, you can present the appropriate context for the issue or phenomenon that you plan to study to indicate the relevance of the study to your context.

Statement of the Problem

In this section, you present the research problem. As discussed, this is a conceptual problem, which is a gap in the literature. You could identify several gaps like a knowledge gap, disciplinary gap, theoretical gap, relationship gap, methodological gap, analytical gap, sampling gap, contextual gap, and theory-praxis gap. Because research is a matter of solving a puzzle, finding an academic puzzle or controversy in the literature about your topic is a key step in moving forward.

This section must present the various kinds of gaps that you have identified from the literature. You must offer evidence by citing specific studies to support your claim of the existence of gaps in the literature.

Statement of the problem for professional doctoral research presents a real-world problem in ministry practice. Therefore, you describe the problem or issue in ministry for which your research will find a solution. Describe the contextual factors with details to offer clarity on what your research is about. Also, you must state the theory/theology/explanation that you plan to apply in your research to solve this problem by citing literature.

Statement of the Purpose

In statement of the purpose or purpose statement section, you state the intent/aim of the study, which must be achieved by the end of the research. The purpose statement will eventually become the thesis statement in your dissertation/thesis. After stating the purpose in one sentence, briefly describe the aim of the study, the participants, and the research site (Creswell and Creswell 2018). See Box 10 for examples of purpose statements.

While your research topic may be based on a practical problem in the church or society, the purpose of your research is not about solving it, but the intent of the research project and what the research will achieve in the end. To clarify further, academic research does not solve a problem in the church or society but contributes knowledge to solve a practical problem.

Box 10: Examples of Purpose Statements

Purpose Statement of a Qualitative Study:

The purpose of this qualitative research is to understand the lived experience of persecuted Christians from selected villages in the state of Uttar Pradesh, India, where religious violence against Christians was unleashed. Persecuted Christians are those who have faced some form of violence or abuse that includes physical, psychological, verbal, and social for being a Christian. This qualitative study will interview persecuted Christians about their suffering to understand how they make meaning of it.

The above statement reveals that the research is a qualitative study, and the aim is to understand the lived experience of persecuted Christians. It indicates that the method of data collection is interview and the participants are the persecuted Christians from the villages where religious violence took place against Christians.

Purpose Statement of a Quantitative Study:

The purpose of the study is to test the church growth principle of homogeneity among the selected Church of South India (CSI) churches in Chennai, India, by using a survey method. The homogeneity principle claims that caste networks play a key role in the growth of churches in India. This study will examine the link between caste networks and composition of the congregation among the selected CSI churches in Chennai city.

The above statement states that the study will aim to test the principle of homogeneity for church growth; the keyword here is "test," which indicates that this is quantitative research. The variables are identified as caste network and composition of the congregation and this study will examine the relationship between these variables. The research site is the CSI churches in Chennai city.

Purpose Statement of a Mixed Methods Study:

This mixed methods study will test the homogeneity principle of church growth and explore the perceptions of members of the Church of South India (CSI) churches in Chennai city on caste networks within the churches. This study will adopt convergent design, in which both quantitative and qualitative data will be collected and analyzed separately but simultaneously. Finally, the results will be integrated to gain an overall understanding of the link between caste network and composition of the congregation among the CSI churches in Chennai city.

The above statement identifies that this is a convergent mixed methods study. It aims to test the theory of the homogeneity principle of church growth in composition of the congreation and also aims at understanding how the members perceive the existence of caste networks within their churches.

However, the purpose of professional doctoral degrees like, Doctor of Ministry, Doctor of Missiology, and so on is not about generating new knowledge, but about applying the existing knowledge to find a solution to a practical problem the researcher faces in their ministry context. Therefore, professional doctorate students can state the purpose of the research, as to resolve a problem in the context of ministry by applying a theory/explanation/theology from literature.

Purpose statements differ for qualitative, quantitative, and mixed methods studies. The purpose statement for a qualitative study employs terms like "understand," "explore," "construct," and "develop." The statement could indicate the specific approach adopted for the qualitative study such as phenomenological, grounded theory, ethnographic, and so on.

The purpose statement of a quantitative study identifies the type of research such as survey, experiment, quasi-experiment, longitudinal, and so on. Quantitative purpose statements use terms like "theory," "test," "independent variables," "dependent variables," "measure," and "instrument."

Purpose statement of mixed methods research specifies the overall aim of both the quantitative and qualitative studies and the rationale for using the mixed methods approach. It also denotes the type of mixed methods design, whether it is convergent or explanatory sequential or exploratory sequential.

Research Questions and Hypotheses

The research questions or hypotheses are described in a separate section (see Chapter 1 for a discussion on formulating research questions and the role of hypothesis). Research questions emerge from the literature; however, "they move things from the realms of the abstract to the realms of the concrete" to be researched empirically (Denscombe 2012, 73). Research questions clarify the focus of the investigation, the type of data required, and the method of collecting and analyzing the data to make a credible claim. Therefore, you must make your research questions clear and precise. The types of research questions vary for qualitative (Box 11), quantitative (Box 12), and mixed methods studies (Box 13).

Qualitative Research Questions

Qualitative questions cover the broad aspect of the phenomenon under study to understand various perspectives of participants. Qualitative research has one primary or central research question that indicates

Box 11: Examples of Qualitative Research Question

Example 1

For a phenomenological study of the lived experience of postsecondary students with disabilities in Ghana, Shadrack Agyekum (2021) raised the following questions.

Central Question:
How do postsecondary students with disabilities at Golden Technical Institute in the eastern belt of Ghana describe their lived experiences? (25)

Sub-questions:
What are the academic experiences of postsecondary students with disabilities at Golden Technical Institute in Ghana? (26)

What are the social experiences of postsecondary students with disabilities at Golden Technical Institute in Ghana? (27)

What institutional factors impact the persistence of postsecondary students with disabilities at Golden Technical Institute in Ghana? (27)

What personal factors impact the persistence of postsecondary students with disabilities at Golden Technical Institute in Ghana? (28)

Example 2

Russell Joseph Allen (2021, 22) studied evangelical students in public schools processing the content areas and had the following research questions.

Central Question:
How do evangelical students in public high schools interpret content areas through their worldview?

Sub-questions:
What philosophical assumptions about content information are informed by the lived experiences of evangelical students in public high schools?

How do the lived experiences of evangelical students impact the way they relate the Bible to topics presented in public high school classrooms?

How do evangelical students' lived experiences influence the way they comprehend the multiple worldview perspectives involved in a content presentation at a public high school?

the focus of the study, and several sub-questions that address different components or aspects of the primary question (Creswell and Creswell 2018). They are open-ended questions suitable to understanding, exploring, describing, and discovering a phenomenon. They are not guided by any theory.

Quantitative Research Questions

For quantitative research, you either present research questions or hypotheses (Creswell and Creswell 2018). Quantitative research uses three to seven questions that are related to each other and are logically progressive. Researchers derive them from a theory and the questions reflect the hypotheses of the study.

Box 12: Examples of Quantitative Research Questions

Example 1

Andrea M. Tom (2021, 17) for a quantitative descriptive study of the impact of Bible reading on evangelical pastors had the following research questions:

RQ1: Excluding reading for vocational purposes (such as sermon or teaching preparation), how much time do Christian leaders spend in regular Bible reading for personal growth and development?

RQ2: What perceived impact, if any, do Christian leaders identify that Bible reading has on their personal lives?

RQ3: What perceived impact, if any, do Christian leaders identify that Bible reading has on their family lives?

RQ4: What perceived impact, if any, do Christian leaders identify that Bible reading has on their leadership approach and behaviors?

RQ5: What is the perception Christian leaders have on the link between Bible reading and their understanding of God?

RQ6: What perceived impact, if any, do Christian leaders identify that biblical and historical, Bible-centered role models have on their leadership approach and behaviors?

Example 2

In a quantitative study on the relationship between servant leadership and age on organizational commitment in faith-based organizations, Frank Deno (2017, 8) had the following research questions and hypotheses.

Research Questions:
R1: What is the relationship between leadership style and organizational commitment in faith-based organizations?

R2: What is the relationship between age and organizational commitment in faith-based organizations?

Null Hypothesis for R1:
$H_0$1: There is no statistically significant relationship between servant leadership and organizational commitment in faith-based organizations.

Research/Alternative Hypothesis for R1:
H_A1: There is a statistically significant relationship between servant leadership and organizational commitment in faith-based organizations.

Null Hypothesis for R2:
$H_0$2: There is no statistically significant relationship between age and organizational commitment in faith-based organizations.

Research/Alternative Hypothesis for R2:
H_A2: There is a statistically significant relationship between age and organizational commitment in faith-based organizations.

The above questions measure the independent variables of servant leadership and age on the dependent variable of organizational commitment in faith-based organizations.

Example 3

Ashlie M. Leste (2013, 15) for a quantitative study that examined religious similarity and quality of relationship among couples had only the research hypotheses:

H1: Religious similarity will be positively associated with couples' relationship quality.

H2: Joint religious activities will mediate the relationship between religious similarity and relationship quality.

H3: Social support will mediate the relationship between religious similarity and relationship quality.

This dissertation neither presented research questions nor null hypotheses but only research hypotheses.

Mixed Methods Research Questions

Mixed methods research must deal with qualitative questions and quantitative questions separately. Not many studies state their mixed methods questions separately; however, John Creswell and Vicki Clark (2018) suggest doing so. Separate questions offer clarity on integrating the results from both quantitative and qualitative studies.

Box 13: Examples of Research Questions for Mixed Methods Research

---

Example 1

Michelle L. Weibel (2011, 8) in a convergent study on teachers' attitudes and concerns about educational field trip had the following research questions:

Quantitative Research Questions:
> *1. Do teachers' environmental attitudes change following the Forever Earth field trip?*
> *2. What teacher demographic characteristics are related to a change in environmental attitudes?*

Hypotheses for Quantitative Research Questions:
> *1. Teachers' environmental attitudes will change following the intervention of the Forever Earth field trip.*
> *2. Teacher demographics will not have an impact on changes in teacher attitudes.*

Qualitative Research Questions:
> *1. What concerns do teachers have toward an outdoor environmental education field trip?*
> *2. How does the experience of an outdoor environmental education field trip impact teachers?*

Example 2

Kyle Murbach (2019), in a mixed methods study on self-efficacy in information security (SEIS) of deaf, had one central question and three hypotheses for the quantitative phase and one question for the qualitative phase.

Primary Mixed Methods Question:
> *To what extent and in what ways have semi-structured qualitative interviews explained quantitative survey results to provide a better overall understanding of variances in SEIS and overall security practice behavior in the deaf population?* (10)

Box 13 continued

The above mixed methods question deals with integrating both quantitative and qualitative results.

Hypotheses for Quantitative Research:
$H1_0$. *There is no statistically significant difference between deaf and hearing end-users' SEIS. (10)*

$H2_0$. *There is no statistically significant difference between deaf and hearing end-users on security practice behavior. (11)*

$H3_0$. *A positive SEIS does not predict the facilitation of improved security practice behavior for deaf and hearing end-users. (11)*

Qualitative Research Question:
Q1. What is the essence of the deaf end-user's lived experiences when engaging in security practices and their confidence levels in doing so? (11)

This study followed the explanatory sequential design and had one central question for mixed methods research. The researcher had three hypotheses and did not have any research question for the quantitative research and had one research question for the qualitative phase.

Research Objectives

The research objectives section states what will be achieved at the end of the research. The objectives deal with several aspects or components that you intend to cover in your investigation. You must show at the end of your research that you have achieved the research objectives. Since objectives reflect the research questions, you may convert the research questions into declarative statements to formulate objectives. The objectives are not the anticipated outcome of your research in the real world.

Qualitative research proposals do not mention research objectives, but they use only research questions. Quantitative proposals that are seeking grants require research objectives. However, academic research proposals do not require a section on the research objectives (Creswell and Creswell 2018). The researcher should follow their supervisor's advice or institution's guidelines to meet the committee's expectations regarding a section on research objectives.

Literature Review

In a research proposal, the researcher presents a preliminary review of the literature; the comprehensive review of literature will appear as a separate chapter of the dissertation/thesis. In the proposal, you demonstrate that you have identified relevant literature, and can critically engage them to locate your study in a larger context. The literature review shows how familiar you are with the authors' concepts, approaches, models, and theories related to your topic. A literature review in a research proposal establishes the need for the study and establishes that the proposed study will meet the need. A literature review must demonstrate how the proposed study will contribute "something different in relation to the topic, method, theory, data, application, or analysis" (Denscombe 2019, 57). This section deals with the definition of key concepts related to the topic and discusses how the concepts evolved over a period or are being dealt with by various researchers differently. You should be able to analyze the literature and synthesize literature by grouping the material. In your analysis, you can discuss the methodology, results, and the current debate among the scholars. The literature review section must establish that the proposed research is significant and timely.

In theological/religious research, this section must include a scriptural/biblical basis, theological/religious perspectives of the problem, and empirical studies from theology/religious studies and social sciences relating to the topic. See Chapter 2 for a discussion of reviewing the literature.

Methodology

The methodology section is the most important in a research proposal because it apprises the readers of how the proposed research will be executed. This section helps the committee in assessing whether the proposed research will fill the gaps identified by the literature review and assess your competence to execute the research project successfully. Therefore, you need to show readers that your research design and methods are appropriate and sound to achieve the purpose. "Design is *what* will be done. Method is *how* it will be done" (emphasis in the original, Ogden and Goldberg 2002, 101). You must explain the philosophical/theological assumptions and the paradigms of social research before introducing the research design. Explain each element of the research project: the primary sources, sampling logic and size, data collection methods, methods of data analysis, and validity and reliability or trustworthiness, and show how you will follow each step in your research. Then you must justify the choice of research design and discuss the suitability of the chosen methodology compared to other designs and approaches.

This section must address the following concerns:
- What are the philosophical/theological assumptions of this study?
- What paradigm of social research is adopted?
- What will be the research strategy and design?
- What kinds of data will be needed?
- Who will be the participants?
- What is the role of the researcher or the instrument?
- What will be the methods of data collection?
- How will the data be analyzed?
- Are the chosen methods suitable for answering the research questions?
- Will this plan be practically executable?

You must address these concerns with all the required details, with specifics. Specific details will help you execute the research project successfully. You must cite the methodology texts to present the plan of execution of your research project.

Philosophical/Theological Assumptions

You can present the philosophical or theological/religious assumptions you have adopted to study the topic, in a separate section. In theology, there are several approaches like liberation, feminist, and so on, and methods you can chose from. You must also offer the rationale for choosing social research for theology/religious research. You present this first and then present the paradigm of social research for the field-based research.

Research Strategy and Approach

In the research strategy and approach section, present your choice of strategy and whether your study will use a qualitative or quantitative or mixed methods strategy. Based on the chosen research strategy, you will state whether numerical or narrative or document or other forms of data or a combination of these data will answer the research questions.

You must explain the chosen approach or type of research. For qualitative research, it could be one or a combination of the following approaches: phenomenological or grounded theory or ethnography or case study, or narrative. For quantitative research, it could be a survey or a longitudinal study or quasi-experimental, or experimental. For a mixed methods study, it could be convergent or exploratory sequential or explanatory sequential design.

Primary Source/Population

For qualitative research, define the characteristics of people who share the phenomenon under investigation, allowing them to be the participants of the study. They must be people who can contribute data from their experience to answer the research questions. If the focus is on the lived experience of individuals, then location is irrelevant; for an ethnography or a case study approach, you can describe the research site, location, institution, and community.

For quantitative research, define the characteristics of the population of the study. You can describe the research site, location, institution, and community from which the sample will be drawn.

Sampling

For a qualitative study, you will use purposive sampling based on your research purpose and describe it under the sampling section. In addition, if you are using other sampling methods like saturation or snowball sampling or multi-variant sampling, you must explain them. You may cite the authors of methodology texts to justify the small sample size used in a qualitative study. Describe who qualifies to be a participant in your study. You can state the criteria for inclusion and exclusion.

For quantitative research, you must explain the sampling logic—whether you will use probability or non-probability sampling. For probability sampling, you must describe the population framework and explain the random selection process in identifying the participants for your study. For non-probability sampling, you must describe the chosen sampling methods, whether it is quota sampling or cluster sampling or convenient sampling, or another method. Explain the procedures for arriving at the sampling size. Present the criteria for the selection of participants for your study in the sampling section.

Role of the Researcher/Instrument

Based on the chosen method, this section is titled "Role of the Researcher" for a qualitative study, "Instrument" for a quantitative study, and with both terms for a mixed methods study.

For qualitative research, it is vital to describe the role of the researcher under this section. The researcher's socio-cultural background, values, and religious beliefs or theological position contribute to the overall approach taken to the research. These subjective elements are not negated in qualitative research but are considered subjective resources that contribute to the interpretive process. The integrity of the researcher is the key ingredient in establishing the credibility and trustworthiness of a qualitative study. Therefore, the researcher must consciously recognize any subjective elements to avoid bias. You can make a statement in this section about your theological/ideological position regarding the phenomenon under investigation. This is known as bracketing or *epoche* in qualitative research.

For quantitative research, you must discuss the instrument design under this section. Instrument design is a critical phase in quantitative research, because the instrument is the key factor in establishing validity and reliability. You must state whether you are adopting an existing instrument or developing a new one; the former is recommended for students. When you use an existing instrument, describe the origin and history of the use of the instrument, its features, and its validity and reliability (Punch 2016). If you are modifying an existing instrument, describe the kind of changes you are making. If you are designing a new instrument, describe the procedures for developing the instrument and establishing the validity and reliability of the instrument. Unlike qualitative research, quantitative research is rigid; if the instrument design fails, then the whole project will be stalled.

In a mixed methods research proposal, you must include both sections, "The Role of the Researcher" and the "Instrument" separately as part of qualitative/quantitative research methods.

Data Collection Procedures

Methods of data collection vary for the research strategies. You must explain the appropriate methods to be used for gathering data for each form of data in the data collection section. You need to explain how you will have access to data. If you need to get permission from an authority or a gatekeeper to do the research, submit the permission letter as an appendix to the research proposal. You need to describe the location, time, and procedures of data collection under this section (Decuir-Gunby and Schutz 2017).

For qualitative research, interviews, focus group interviews, participant observation, document collection, and qualitative survey are the common methods of data collection. You must explain the steps of each method and state how you will follow them in the field. You need to explain how you plan to obtain informed consent from the participants and attach a copy of the consent form in the appendix.

For interviews and focus group interviews, you must state whether you will use semi-structured or unstructured interviews. State whether you will use an interview protocol. For participant observation, state what you will observe, how you plan to observe, and how long you will stay in the field to collect data. Explain the procedures you plan to use such as taking field notes, informal conversations, and audio/video recordings. If you plan to use document collection, you must identify the kinds of documents, whether they are formal or informal, images or videos, or digital data. For a qualitative survey, you must state how you will develop a questionnaire. (See Chapter 4 for more about qualitative data collection.)

For quantitative research, you will describe how the survey/experiment will be conducted. If a survey is involved, then state whether it will be a self-administered or assisted or a telephonic survey or email survey, or web survey. You need to describe the plans to contact the participants and also check whether they have access to technology for taking the survey. (See Chapter 5 for more about quantitative data collection.)

Data Analysis Procedures

The section on data analysis procedures describes the techniques of data analysis you are using, which need to be appropriate to the chosen research strategy. Readers would expect specific details about the techniques and the steps for analyzing data.

For qualitative research, you must spell out the steps involved in coding, categorizing, and developing themes from the qualitative data. Because data analysis for qualitative research involves interpreting the narrative form of data, you must show the steps you will adopt to establish the credibility of the analysis. You may indicate the software that you plan to use for qualitative data analysis. (See Chapter 4 for more details about qualitative data analysis.)

For a quantitative study, you must name the statistical procedure and whether you will use descriptive statistics or inferential statistics, or both. The choice is based on the nature of the research problem. For a mixed methods study, you will describe the procedures for each phase of the study and show how you plan to integrate the results.

Reliability/Credibility

Reliability is about consistency in measuring variables in a quantitative study. Credibility is whether the findings are authentic and believable in a qualitative study. You must present the procedures that will be adopted to establish the reliability of a quantitative study and the credibility of a qualitative study.

Validity/Trustworthiness

Validity is about the accuracy in measuring variables in a quantitative study. Trustworthiness for qualitative research involves how far the findings confirm the reality based on the data. You must explain the procedures that are appropriate for the chosen design.

Justification of the Chosen Methods

The justification section offers the rationale for the choice of research strategy and methods, so readers can assess whether the chosen design and methods are suitable for achieving the purpose of the study and produce quality results. You will discuss the strengths and weaknesses of the chosen methods as compared to the other methods.

Significance

Significance in a research proposal is a statement of the theoretical and practical importance of the research. In the significance section, you explain the value that your research will add to the field of study by filling in the gaps in the literature. Describe in detail how your research will advance or modify the current knowledge or break new grounds in theology/religious studies. You may indicate the implications of the findings that could transform the world. You will specifically state how your research will help practitioners or religious leaders to address the problem in the field. If you are expecting your study to offer new insights to policymakers, then state the insights specifically.

Limitations and Delimitations

In the limitations and delimitations section, you will define the scope of your investigation. Limitations are the constraints related to the chosen research design over which the researcher has no control. For example, we cannot eliminate subjectivity in qualitative research, because the study is about lived experience. In a quantitative study, if a population framework is not available, probability sampling is not possible, which is a limitation.

Delimitations are the limits set by the researcher on the scope of the study. Although a research project is a detailed piece of work, it cannot be a complete survey of the field. The topic may be broad, but you will have to limit the scope by excluding some of the potentially relevant aspects/factors of your topic.

Definition of Terms

This section on terms will present the operational definitions of key terms or concepts. These definitions are not simply meanings of terms but are conceptual definitions. Quantitative studies rely on the definitions from the literature. If you are using a term in a limited or different sense, then explain how the terms are used in the literature and how you will use them in this study. For qualitative research, you may offer tentative definitions, which can be modified as you progress in your research. You must arrange the terms alphabetically.

Organization of Research Report and Dissemination

This section is about the organization of the research report and the plans for dissemination of the research findings. In the research proposal, students may present the chapter divisions and title this section as "Chapterization" or "Chapter Divisions." You can present a list of chapters in your dissertation and briefly describe what each chapter will cover. For social research in theology/religious studies, I recommend the following seven-chapter structure:

Chapter 1: Introduction
Chapter 2: Theological Framework or Religious Perspective
Chapter 3: Literature Review
Chapter 4: Methods
Chapter 5: Findings/Results
Chapter 6: Discussion
Chapter 7: Conclusions and Recommendations

Apart from these chapters, a dissertation/thesis has the front matter and appendices (see Chapter 8 for details of writing a dissertation/thesis).

For journal articles, the journal prescribes a style format and structure. The parts of an article include title page, abstract, keywords, introduction, methods, findings/results, discussion, and references.

Scholars can indicate in the research proposal how the results of the research will be disseminated, whether it will be presented at a conference or published in a journal or as a monograph and so on.

Timeline

In the proposal, you will provide a timetable for executing the research project with the specific period for each stage of the research. Because research is a long journey, it may not be possible to stick to the timeline, especially a tight one, so allow some buffer time for each stage. This could also be placed as an appendix in the research proposal.

Ethical Concerns

Social research involves people as the participants of the research, so your research proposal will be reviewed by your institution's ethics committee. In the ethical concerns section, you will state the steps you will take to ensure no harm is caused to the participants and that the safety of the data is maintained. Some institutions also require their students to submit an ethical approval form along with the research proposal. Research proposals are approved only after being cleared by the ethics committee before the start of the project. (See Chapter 1 for more details about ethical concerns.)

Working Bibliography

A working bibliography is not a complete list of the sources consulted for the project but is a tentative list to show the readers that the researcher has identified several credible sources in addition to those cited in the research proposal. This list will grow as you progress in your research. In this section you must list all the literature you have cited in the research proposal and include studies you plan to consult for your research project. You must follow the departmental style for formatting the working bibliography.

Appendices

You may include a consent form, permission letters to conduct the research, ethical application, and other supporting documents in the appendices.

Chapter Summary

Research proposal is a blueprint of your research project. From this chapter you have understood the importance of a research proposal and the various elements that constitute it, which include the background to the study, statement of the problem, statement of purpose, research questions and hypotheses, research objectives, literature review, methodology, and timeline. You have learned what each element in a research proposal deals with and how to write it. In addition, you have learned about developing research questions that vary for qualitative, quantitative, and mixed methods research.

Furthermore, you have understood the importance of addressing ethical concerns in your research proposal and a working bibliography. Now you are better equipped to write a compelling and effective proposal for your research project.

Review Questions

1. What is the role of a research proposal in a research project?
2. How to write a title?
3. What is an abstract?
4. What should be included in the background section?
5. How to present the statement of the problem?
6. How to write the statement of the purpose?
7. How to present research questions and hypotheses?
8. How to state the research objectives?
9. What to include in the literature review?
10. How to present the methodology?
11. What to include under philosophical/theological assumptions?
12. What is research design and approach?
13. What is the significance of research?
14. What are limitations and delimitations?
15. How to present the definitions of terms?
16. How to address ethical concerns?
17. How to structure a dissertation/thesis?
18. What to include in working bibliography?
19. What can be placed in the appendix?

Further Help

Denscombe, Martyn. 2019. *Research Proposals: A Practical Guide.* 2nd ed. Berkshire: Open University Press.

Punch, Keith F. 2016. *Developing Effective Research Proposals.* London: Sage.

Decuir-Gunby, Jessica T., and Paul A. Schutz. 2017. *Developing a Mixed Methods Proposal: A Practical Guide for Beginning Researchers.* Thousand Oaks: Sage.

Chapter 8

WRITING A RESEARCH REPORT

A research report is a channel for disseminating the research findings, which it does by expounding on why readers should believe certain claims. For students, a research report could be a dissertation or a thesis. The American system of education considers a doctoral research report as a dissertation and a master's research report a thesis, whereas the European system considers doctoral research report a thesis and a master's as a dissertation. For scholars, a research report could be a journal article, monograph, chapter in an edited volume, or conference presentation. This chapter discusses writing doctoral/master's dissertation/thesis, professional doctorate dissertation, and journal article.

A research report must be objective in reasoning out the claims based on evidence for readers to accept them and to "test and judge it before making your claims part of their knowledge and understanding" (Turabian 2013, 6). It follows the methods and structure accepted in a discipline.

A quality research report demonstrates the researcher's expertise in the field of study, enhances the credibility of the research, and triggers readers' interest in the topic. Examiners assess your research only on the basis of the dissertation/thesis you produce, otherwise, they do not have any other means of knowing how you have conducted the research. Unless you produce a quality dissertation/thesis, examiners and readers will not appreciate the hard work that went into executing your research, the meticulous pains you took to collect and analyze the data, and the significance of the contribution. See Chapter 9 to learn more about examiners' expectations and quality assessment criteria of a dissertation/ thesis.

Research Argument

Research writing is persuasive writing. A research argument is not simply a report about your project but a presentation of your case to convince the readers that your conclusions are valid (Bryman 2016). In research writing, you introduce your claim with no ambiguity in the introduction and maintain a logical flow to support the claim. The main claim of your argument is the thesis statement or the answer to the research question. The core elements of your argument include the claim, reasons for accepting the claim, and the supportive evidence for the reasons (Turabian 2013). Your argument must also address any opposing points of view and differing perspectives.

In a research argument, a claim is made about a fact, which could be contested. Therefore, the researcher must make a case, providing reasons and evidence to support the claim. Reasons are abstract ideas that are the basis for a claim or the explanations that support a claim (Turabian 2013). However, reasons cannot stand on their own, but need the support of evidence, which comes from research. You may draw evidence from literature or data from the field. Therefore, research writing involves making a claim and arguing about it by reasoning with evidence. Box 14 provides examples of research argument.

Academic Tone

Tone is the writers' use of language to express themselves to evoke a particular feeling or perspective in the readers. Informal language is appropriate for an email to a family member, but academic tone requires you to use formal language that adopts a neutral tone. Formal language avoids emotional words ("wow," "awesome," "depressing"), superlative terms ("best," "simplest"), colloquialism ("gonna," "buck," "cheers"), and contractions ("don't," "can't"), which are common to informal writing.

Academic tone does not mean using heavy jargon, which is understood only by a few experts in the field of study. You need to define unfamiliar conceptual terms to help readers understand the

---

Example 1

Writing a literature review on the role of spirituality and religiosity in the subjective well-being of individuals, the authors (Villani et al. 2019, 3) have used literature as the evidence.

Claim:

> *The literature about the relationship between religiosity, spirituality, and SWB [subjective well-being] has not yet achieved consistent results.*

Here, the claim is that existing studies do not offer consistent results on the relationship between religiosity, spirituality, and SWB, a claim that could be challenged. To provide a basis for the claim the authors offered reasons.

Reasons:

> *There are three main general flaws in this research field.*

The explanation or the basis of the claim is that there are flaws in the research conducted so far. This could be challenged with a question, what is the evidence for this explanation? Therefore, the reason needs external support—evidence, which the authors offered to support the reason and the claim.

Evidence:

> *First, the theoretical framework used to define and measure SWB as associated with religiosity and spirituality has often been too broad and focused only on the cognitive or the affective dimension of SWB, thus leading to an incomplete investigation (Lim and Putnam, 2010).*

> *Second, religiosity and spirituality constructs appear in the literature as distinct even if interconnected (Zinnbauer et al., 1999; Hill and Pargament, 2008), and the studies have typically considered only one of the two and its association with SWB (Fabricatore et al., 2000; Lun and Bond, 2013; Kim-Prieto and Miller, 2018).*

> *Third, we noticed that the grouping of religious experience reported on a subjective level was not univocal (Galen and Kloet, 2011; Kitchens and Phillips, 2018).*

The authors provided the evidence from the literature for three flaws by grouping the studies they analyzed into three categories. They cited them as evidence to support their reason and in turn to support their claim that literature does not provide consistent results with regard to religiosity, spirituality, and SWB.

> **Box 14 continued**
>
> **Example 2**
>
> In a qualitative study on faith and belief as expressions of spirituality, Eva Natsis (2017) made a claim and provided supporting evidence from the interview data.
>
> Claim:
> > *One of the prevailing themes in the findings of this study was a preoccupation with one's mortality.* (9)
>
> Natsis claimed that participants were preoccupied with the idea of mortality and explained why.
>
> Reason:
> > *The thought of mortality became a preoccupation with dying. Underlying this preoccupation for Joumana was a religious perspective in a God of judgment, and that if one did not perform righteous acts on the earth, their eternity would be doomed. The afterlife was very much categorized by a belief in judgment day.* (9)
>
> Natasis gave a reason that the idea of mortality is linked to dying and life after death. Unless this is supported by evidence, this reason can be contested. Therefore, she offered evidence from the data.
>
> Evidence:
> > *… it's like when you get judged by God and then you go to either hell or heaven. We've got these kind of beliefs and the more like you read Qur'an and the more you do your religious beliefs and stuff, the more you'll go – like the more good deeds you'll do, and you'll end up going to heaven and stuff. Joumana*
> >
> > *… so as Christians we believe we will end up in heaven when we finish. My friend, he's Buddhist and he believes in life after death, reincarnation. Simon* (10)
>
> Natsis offered evidence by presenting excerpts from the interview data by citing two of the participants of her research to support the reason, which supports the claim.

meaning (American Psychological Association 2020). You should be familiar with the conceptual terms and use of language in your field of study. The choice of words is a key factor in communicating your research results. Therefore, use appropriate words and terms that are in use in your discipline, while avoiding heavy jargons.

Academic tone avoids sermonizing in research writing. Theology students tend to be preachy in research writing; but, "the language of the pulpit is not the language of the thesis" (Vyhmeister and Robertson 2014, 170). You must avoid prescriptive, judgmental, and dogmatic language in research writing.

Academic Style

In writing, "style" refers to the way in which writers express their ideas. Academic style is formal and yet intended to be clear, which requires you to write concisely and precisely and communicate clearly without losing meaning. Good academic style avoids "wordiness, redundancy, evasiveness, overuse of the passive voice, circumlocution, and clumsy prose" (American Psychological Association 2020, 129). Succinct clear writing makes your research report readable.

Writing precisely requires discernment in word choice. The word must communicate the intended meaning. If it carries multiple meanings, then you must indicate the intended meaning. However, you should not use synonyms when referring to the same object to avoid confusion for readers.

Academic style consistently follows the triad of research writing: introduction, body, and conclusions. You must follow the triad for the entire dissertation and at every level, and in every chapter, every section, and every paragraph.

The introduction for a thesis is the first chapter, chapters 2 to 6 may serve as the body of a dissertation, and the conclusion chapter is the conclusion of a dissertation.

The same pattern follows for a chapter and a section. Introductory paragraphs orient the reader and provide context, the body of a chapter or section comprises the main arguments, and the concluding paragraphs are the conclusion of a chapter or a section.

For a paragraph, the topic sentence is the introduction, the sentences in the middle of a paragraph constitute the body, and the last sentence is the conclusion.

Providing logical consistency is another facet of academic style. It involves maintaining continuity in ideas, developing ideas into themes, and stating the relationships among the concepts. Liberal use of transition words and phrases, such as "then," "consequently," "furthermore," "however," "on the contrary," "subsequently," "as mentioned earlier," "first of all," and "to conclude" maintain the continuity and flow of your writing because they indicate the relationship between ideas and arguments. Transitions help you in writing a cohesive essay.

You must use unbiased or inclusive language to avoid offending or demeaning or excluding any section of society. Box 15 gives examples of unbiased language.

Box 15: Examples for Unbiased Language

Biased: God created *man*.
Unbiased: God created *human beings*.

Biased: Everyone must submit *his* thesis on . . .
Avoid: Everyone must submit *his/her* thesis on . . .
Unbiased: *All students* must submit *their* thesis on . . .

Biased: The *chairman* gave permission to conduct this study.
Unbiased: The *chairperson* gave permission to conduct this study.

Biased: The sample included eighty Christians and ten *non-Christians*.
Unbiased: The sample included eighty Christians and ten *people from different religions*.

Biased: One *blind man* was part of the study.
Unbiased: One *visually challenged male* was part of the study.

Biased: I interviewed five *rich men* for this study.
Unbiased: I interviewed five *males with an annual income of above $ 500,000* for this study.

Currently, the use of personal pronouns is acceptable in research writing but avoid overusing them. Some scholars use the passive voice to avoid personal pronouns, but research writing prefers the active voice. You can avoid using personal pronouns by using the names of parts of the paper. Instead of saying, "I describe the methodology in this chapter," you could say, "This chapter describes the methodology." Another example: instead of saying, "My concluding remarks are . . .", you can write, "The concluding remarks are . . .". Some authors use the first-person plural "we," instead of "I"; but you must not use "we" when you are the only author because it may confuse readers.

Avoid plagiarism at any cost. Plagiarism is presenting others' words or ideas or work as your own by not acknowledging the source. This includes presenting another author's words without quotation marks or paraphrasing ideas without citing the source. Plagiarism is an integrity issue and may result in you not being awarded your degree or having it revoked.

Writing a Dissertation/Thesis

Unlike theoretical research, in which the researcher organizes the chapters thematically to present the arguments for a dissertation/thesis, social sciences follow a structure of five chapters for a dissertation/thesis:

Chapter 1: Introduction

Chapter 2: Literature Review

Chapter 3: Methodology

Chapter 4: Findings/Results

Chapter 5: Discussion

However, this structure is not rigid. Some institutions combine chapters 4 and 5 as one chapter with separate sections for findings/results and discussion. Some institutions add a separate chapter on conclusions, instead of presenting them as part of chapter 5.

The logic behind this structure is that the researcher introduces the research in the introduction chapter, chapter 2 deals with the existing body of knowledge from the literature, chapter 3 describes the methodology and methods, chapter 4 presents the findings or results from data, and chapter 5 presents the new knowledge or the solution to the research problem by interpreting the findings or results in comparison to the literature review chapter.

This structure helps readers understand the different components of the research with no ambiguity. The reader can get an overview of the research from chapter 1, understand the current status of the research in the literature from chapter 2, know how the research was conducted from chapter 3, identify what emerged from the data in chapter 4, and understand the new knowledge or the solution, which is based on the interaction between the findings/results and the literature review from chapter 5.

In addition, theological/religious research needs to accommodate the theological/religious frameworks or perspectives to locate the study in the discipline. An interdisciplinary study in theology using social research requires students to engage in field-based studies across disciplines from the literature. Moreover, since the trend in theology/religious studies is to apply the new knowledge to transform real-world conditions and draw practical implications from the study, the implications could be part of the conclusions. Therefore, I recommend a seven-chapter structure for the dissertation/thesis in the fields of theology and religious studies using social research methods. They are:

Chapter 1: Introduction
Chapter 2: Theological Framework/Religious Perspective
Chapter 3: Literature Review
Chapter 4: Methodology
Chapter 5: Findings/Results
Chapter 6: Discussion
Chapter 7: Conclusions and Recommendations

The overall structure of a dissertation/thesis includes the following components:

Title Page
Dedication
Acknowledgments
Abstract
Table of Contents
List of Figures
List of Tables
Chapter 1: Introduction
Chapter 2: Theological Framework/Religious Perspective
Chapter 3: Literature Review
Chapter 4: Methodology
Chapter 5: Findings/Results
Chapter 6: Discussion
Chapter 7: Conclusions and Recommendations
References
Appendices

Title Page

The title page carries the title of the paper, your name, degree, name of the institution and department, and year of submission. Some institutions may require the student registration number, supervisor's name, and logo of the institution. You must follow the guidelines recommended by your institution.

Dedication

If your institution allows you to have a page for dedication, you may use it to dedicate your dissertation/thesis to someone or a group that you value greatly in your personal life.

Acknowledgments

The acknowledgments section provides you with an opportunity to acknowledge those who offered professional and personal help during your research journey. This could include your supervisor, doctoral committee members, other professors and staff who have extended their support, participants in your study, donors and grant-making agencies who have extended financial support, and your family and friends who stood with you during your research studies. In theology dissertations, students acknowledge God's favor and help to complete the research successfully. Be specific in stating the reason for thanking someone. Be concise in writing acknowledgments, keeping them within a page.

Abstract

The abstract is a summary of the dissertation/thesis. The abstract presents the research problem and research questions briefly, states the purpose or thesis statement, explains the methods concisely, and describes the key findings, significance, and implications briefly. Many read only the abstract and not beyond. Therefore, it is vital to write the abstract concisely, to let readers determine whether the dissertation has any value for them. I recommend that you write the abstract after writing all chapters so that you can write concisely, with clarity.

Table of Contents

The table of contents (TOC) presents the list of chapters and major sections with the corresponding page numbers. You may include up to three levels of headings, but two levels are a must. You must number different levels appropriately in the TOC, and they must match the levels in the body of the dissertation.

The TOC does not include dedication, abstract, and acknowledgments as they precede it. You must follow the instructions given by your institution in preparing the TOC.

List of Figures

If you have more than three figures in the dissertation/thesis, you can have a separate page to list them; otherwise, you may combine it with a list of tables as a "List of Figures and Tables."

List of Tables

More than three tables require a separate list; if you have three or fewer, combine the list with the list of figures and title it "List of Figures and Tables."

Chapter 1: Introduction

Chapter 1 introduces the research, which covers many elements of the research proposal. The introduction chapter in a dissertation/thesis must be written in the past tense because you are reporting what you have completed. This will involve revising the research proposal from future tense to past tense. Chapter 1 has the following sections from the research proposal:

- Background
- Statement of the Problem
- Statement of the Purpose
- Research Questions or Hypothesis
- Significance
- Limitations and Delimitations
- Definition of Terms
- Chapter Divisions

See Chapter 7 for more about writing these sections as part of the research proposal. The literature review and methodology sections from the research proposal will be expanded as separate chapters for your dissertation/thesis.

Chapter 2: Theological Framework or Religious Perspective

The purpose of the chapter on theological framework or religious perspective is to locate the study in the field of theology/religious studies and offer a rationale for a field-based study. For a theology dissertation/thesis, chapter 2 provides a theological framework for the study, presents the review of literature in theology, and locates the study in the field of theology. In presenting the theological perspective of the issue, you can critically analyze various theologies dealing with the topic under study. You can present the biblical, theological, historical-theological, ministerial, and missiological perspectives on the topic. Thus, this chapter creates an opportunity for you to integrate the sub-disciplines of theology in researching the phenomenon. For a dissertation/thesis in religious studies, this chapter offers a religious-philosophical framework of the study, presents the religious perspectives on the topic, and locates the study in the discipline of religious studies. The studies cited in this chapter will be useful for interpreting the findings/results in chapter 6 to establish the contribution of your study to the field of theology/religious studies.

In addition, this chapter establishes the methodology gap in theological literature that requires a field-based study. Generally, theological research is speculative, reflective, and analytical of theological concepts. But when theology engages in social research, a critical analysis of the research topic creates a framework to offer a new perspective based on the data collected from a field study. Therefore, it requires you to justify the need for a field-based study to raise new questions, use new methods and data, and to offer new perspectives, answers, and solutions. This chapter sets the stage for a field-based study using social research methods in theology/religious studies.

Chapter 3: Literature Review

The literature review chapter locates your study in the literature and shows how your study will contribute to the existing knowledge. This chapter deals with key concepts, models, and theories to present the current state of knowledge and must include current and landmark studies from across disciplines. This chapter must demonstrate your ability to critically analyze and to synthesize the related studies and your command over the literature.

You must make your claim or state your main position at the start of the review. You must link all studies to your argument. Your argument must progress logically, so check for any inconsistency. The introductory paragraph provides a road map of your argument in the chapter and presents the organization of the chapter. The conclusion of your review justifies the need for your study based on the gaps in the literature.

Writing a literature review involves synthesizing the literature based on critical analysis. You can structure the chapter based on themes or research questions, or disciplines. In a thematic review, you discuss each theme that emerged from various empirical studies. Otherwise, you can group the studies based on research questions or disciplines. Either way, the review must be a cohesive essay, not annotations. You may also present a summary of the studies and their results in a table or chart to enable readers to get a quick overview.

Be selective in citing studies. When you refer to a landmark study, tell the readers why it is significant. When you come across a literature review published in a journal, analyze the review in the light of your research and show how your review is different from that or is advancing the argument. You may be tempted to include all the studies that you have consulted, which is the practice in theology. But a dissertation/thesis based on social research does not require extensive citations, it requires you to cite only relevant studies. Relevant studies are the ones that support or oppose your point of view. You may come across many studies that deal with your topic, but the utility value of the study in your argument determines whether to include it or not. Thus, you can avoid including unrelated references in your review. (See Chapter 2 for more on a literature review.)

Chapter 4: Methodology

The title of this chapter can be "Methods" or "Methodology," and it must cover everything about the theological/philosophical assumptions, paradigms of social research, research design, procedures for data collection and analysis. This chapter offers a rationale for the chosen research design and methodology. You must explain the choices you made at every stage of the research and justify them and explain how you went about executing each step in your research. Discuss the advantages and disadvantages of the methods retrospectively after completing the project. You must write this chapter in the past tense because you are reporting on how you have carried out the research project.

For a qualitative methodology, the chapter restates the primary research question and the sub-questions. Explain the chosen paradigm of social research and justify it with reasons for choosing qualitative research strategy rather than other strategies. Describe the chosen approach. After presenting the approach, describe the sampling procedures and sample size with the parameters for selecting the participants. For a case study approach, explain the reasons for selecting the case and provide more details about the case in this chapter. Describe in detail the procedures for data collection and explain how you went about collecting data. Similarly, describe the procedures for data analysis and explain how you have analyzed the data. Mention the name of the software you have used for data analysis. Discuss the steps taken to establish credibility and trustworthiness of your research and finally, present ethical concerns.

For quantitative research, restate the research questions and the hypothesis. Explain the chosen paradigm of social research and justify it with reasons for choosing quantitative research strategy rather than other strategies. If you are using an existing instrument for the survey, then describe the study that produced the instrument. If you have developed a new instrument, explain the details of instrument design, and show how the instrument covers all objectives of your research. Discuss the validity and reliability of the instrument. If you have conducted a pilot study, then describe and discuss the results. Spell out the sampling procedures, details of population, sample size, and criteria for selecting the participants. Describe the research site where you have conducted the research. Explain the data collection methods and how you have collected data as well as the procedures for data analysis and the statistical tests/tools and the software that was used in analyzing data. Discuss the reliability and validity of your research and present the ethical concerns last.

For a mixed methods dissertation, explain mixed methods design and justify the choice of it. This chapter must explain each design separately and tell the readers how you have integrated the results.

Chapter 5: Findings/Results

Chapter 5 is titled "Findings" for qualitative research and "Results" for quantitative research. For a mixed methods dissertation, it can be "Findings and Results" or "Results and Findings," based on the approach. This chapter presents what emerged from the data without making any reference to the literature and is written in the past tense.

Chapter 5 in Qualitative Dissertation/Thesis

In a qualitative dissertation/thesis, the findings chapter presents the themes, patterns, and relationships among the themes/subthemes that emerged from the data analysis. First present the aim and research questions, then the demographic details of the participants with tables and charts; you may present the tables as an appendix and refer to them here. If your study dealt with a small number of samples, you may present a brief profile of each participant by highlighting the salient features of the interview. You can structure this chapter by using the themes of research sub-questions as the main sections in which to present the themes and subthemes from the data. Show the reader that you have analyzed the data systematically and thoroughly according to the methods chosen. Each theme and category are to be supported by excerpts from the data. Thick descriptions and the number of narratives from data indicate a systematic analysis. If you have used multiple sources such as in-depth interviews, focus group interviews, document analysis, and so on, to collect data, do not present the findings separately but rather thematically. This chapter occupies a large space in your dissertation/ thesis.

When you quote the participants, use pseudonyms instead of real names or codes. You cannot use the real names of the participants to protect their anonymity and codes will depersonalize the stories. As part of the introduction of the chapter, you can state that you have used pseudonyms and changed or omitted identifiable information to protect the anonymity of the participants. However, for a narrative approach and research using transformative paradigm dealing with human rights violations or victims of some kind, researchers would use the real names of the participants, because the identity of the participants play a vital role in knowledge production and finding solutions.

I recommend using the TIQC formula for presenting a finding. In TIQC formula, the "T" stands for *Theme*, "I" for *Introduction*, "Q" for *Quote*, and "C" for *Comment*. This formula will show readers that you have done a systematic and deeper analysis of qualitative data.

T: Theme

Present a theme (finding) in your own words and explain what the theme is.

I: Introduction

Introduce the quote from data. When you quote a participant for the first time, mention the pseudonym, gender, age, education or any other relevant information about the participant or image or document; for subsequent references, use the pseudonym. Also provide some contextual factors that would help readers understand the quotation.

Q: Quote

Present a quote from data. The quote can be large quotations or smaller quotations or paraphrased summary of an experience or images or excerpts from documents, or other forms of data; it is good to have a mixture of them. You can provide more than one quote to support a theme. The credibility of qualitative findings depends on how well you use narratives to support the findings. Therefore, be generous in providing thick descriptions of narrative data. Short quotations are placed within a paragraph, while longer quotations are presented as block quotes. You must follow the reference style to format quotes and cite participants.

C: Comment

State your comment on the quote/s to help readers understand how the quote/s support the theme and how the finding emerged from data.

The philosophy behind qualitative research, values every participant's experience as real and significant. Some scholars recommend counting the number of participants who share a particular theme to show how dominant the theme is. However, you must avoid downplaying a theme that is not common among the participants. Less frequency of a theme does not make an experience unreal to the participants. A single participant's experience may differ from the rest of the participants, which requires your special attention to show the uniqueness or provide a context to understand, rather than ignoring it totally. You must present all relevant findings to answer the research questions, not only the dominant themes that have emerged from data analysis.

Toward the end of this chapter, you may briefly restate the trustworthiness of your research. Summarize the major findings and indicate that you will discuss these themes in the next chapter. Place the interview protocol and the data matrix, if you have one, as part of the appendix and refer to them in this chapter. A data matrix for qualitative research presents the summary of the findings in a table, which is different from numerical summary of data in quantitative research.

Chapter 5 in Quantitative Dissertation/Thesis

For quantitative research, you will present the results from the statistical analysis of the data in this chapter. At the beginning of the chapter present the research questions and hypothesis. Describe the sample and present the demographics of the sample in tables and charts or place them in the appendix and refer to them in this chapter. The summary of the demographics helps readers understand who the participants are and the contextual factors of the results. For example, in a survey on religiosity of university students "religious affiliation" is a demographic factor; if a large number of samples is from students who are affiliated to religious groups in the campuses, the result will show that university students are religious. But the demographic information on "religious affiliation" would show that the sample is skewed toward students with religious affiliation. Describe the instrument briefly.

Use section headings to present the results of descriptive statistics and inferential statistical tests if you have used them. Present the results of each statistical test with tables and charts related to research questions or hypotheses. Interpret the tables and charts in words to help readers understand the numbers and figures. Interpretation, here, means explaining the table or the statistical test results; it is not about discussing the results with the literature, which you will do in the next chapter.

Towards the end, discuss the validity and reliability of the instrument, summarize the results, and indicate what lies ahead in the following chapter.

Chapter 5 in Mixed Methods Dissertation/Thesis

For a mixed methods dissertation, present the findings and results according to the approach chosen. For the explanatory sequential design, you will present the quantitative results first and then qualitative findings. For exploratory sequential design, you will present the findings from qualitative research first and quantitative results second. For the convergent approach, you can juxtapose the results and findings for each research question or hypothesis. For all approaches, the results and findings are not integrated in this chapter but only in the next one. Discuss the validity and reliability of the quantitative study and the trustworthiness of the qualitative study. Finally, summarize the key findings and results and introduce the next chapter.

Chapter 6: Discussion

The discussion chapter presents the main contribution of your study to the knowledge base in the fields of theology, religious studies, and social sciences. Chapter 6 presents the findings/results in dialogue with chapter 2 (theological framework/religious perspective) and chapter 3 (literature review). You will interpret the findings or results in congruence with the literature. In this chapter, situate the findings or results in the larger body of literature, comparing and contrasting the findings or results with the existing theologies/religious perspectives, biblical perspectives, theories, and models. Show how this study contributes by way of adding new perspectives or challenging existing paradigms/perspectives in theology/ religious studies and theories/models in other disciplines. In this chapter, you make meaning of your findings/results, present the relevance, and state the significance of your research for theology and religious studies.

You cannot add new literature here; if you want to use a new study to interpret your findings/results, then incorporate it first in the literature review chapter. In chapter 6 it is better to use the same sections that are in chapter 5 to ensure consistency in interpreting the findings/results.

Chapter 6 in Qualitative Dissertation/Thesis

For a qualitative dissertation, begin the discussion chapter by restating the purpose and research questions of the study. The themes of research sub-questions could be the broad sections of this chapter. You need not discuss every finding but must discuss the major findings that are relevant to the research questions.

The findings are to be decontextualized. In the previous chapter, you have presented the findings concerning the data in the past tense. But the same findings or themes are presented in the present tense for decontextualization. For example, chapter 5 presents a finding like this: Terminally ill cancer patients perceived that the Biblical promises were quite alive to their condition. This finding is decontextualized in chapter 6 as: Terminally ill cancer patients perceive that the Biblical promises are quite alive to their condition. This is to show the transferability of the findings to other contexts.

When you discuss a theme, you must refer to the specific aspects or the claim of a study from the literature and biblical/theological/religious perspectives that are relevant to the theme and cite the reference. Sometimes, for a theme, several studies could be cited to interpret it. Discuss the similarities and differences to show the value of the findings to the body of knowledge.

If you find no studies dealing with a particular finding, then it could be a unique finding that your study has brought to light. Discuss the contextual factors for the unique finding to help readers understand how it advances or sets aside a theory or perspective.

In this chapter, you can present a conceptual model (with or without a visual model) by bringing together the themes and sub-themes to make sense. Discuss every component of your model in comparison to the existing models in the literature. Finally, summarize the key contribution of your study to the body of knowledge in theology/religious studies.

Chapter 6 in Quantitative Dissertation/Thesis

The discussion chapter in quantitative dissertation, presents a summary of results in non-statistical terms. Start with restating the purpose and research questions/hypotheses. Cite the studies to discuss the similarities and differences with your results and make your comments. Indicate how your results differ or are similar and offer reasons for the same. Discuss the unexpected results and offer explanations for the cause, which could be because of errors in sampling or instrumentation or research design or situational contingencies. State clearly whether the hypothesis was rejected or supported. The results reflect the reality on the ground and must be interpreted from a theological/religious perspective. You show the importance of your study in contributing to the existing knowledge base.

Chapter 6 in Mixed Methods Dissertation/Thesis

For mixed methods dissertations, you will integrate the findings from qualitative research with the results of quantitative research and interpret them in comparison to the literature and theological/religious perspectives. Show how the mixed methods strategy led to new insights and deeper understanding of the problem.

Chapter 7: Conclusions and Recommendations

This chapter must clearly state how the research questions were answered. Present the aim and research questions of the study and state the main claim or the thesis statement, which is the answer to the primary research question. Then briefly present the answers to the sub-questions and show how the purpose of the study was achieved in your research. State the significant contribution made by your research to theology or religious studies and to the larger body of knowledge across disciplines and state your insights or comments based on your experience of conducting this study.

Present the theoretical and theological implications drawn from the findings as well as the practical implications. Scholars of theology and religious studies will be interested in the theoretical implications, while church officials and religious leaders will be interested in the practical implications. Ground the implications and recommendations in the findings/results. Discuss the relevance of the conclusions and show how they apply to a wider context. Researchers from theology tend to sermonize the practical implications, but practical implications are to be based on the specific findings of the study and logically grounded in the findings.

Present recommendations for further research. State the limitations of the study, which also shows that you are capable of being self-critical of your work. However, you should not give ammunition to the examiners by overstating the limitations (Bryman 2016).

References

You must list all the sources you have cited in the dissertation/thesis in the references section. Based on the referencing style, the title of this section could be "References" or "Works Cited" or "Bibliography." You must strictly follow the referencing style recommended by your department or institution; each referencing style has a specific format. Using a software program for reference management makes it easier to format in any style. Cross check the in-text citations/footnotes with the reference list/bibliography for consistency. Make sure all the cited studies are listed in the references/bibliography.

Appendices

The appendices are a section of the dissertation/thesis in which you can place information that is relevant but not appropriate for including in the main body. If you have only one document, then the title should be "Appendix," otherwise "Appendices." In the appendices, you may place the consent form, copy of the survey questionnaire, interview protocol, data tables/matrix, permission letters from gatekeepers/authorities, and the ethical approval form. Each appendix must start on a new page with a title and an identification number/letter. Each appendix must be referred to in the main body.

Writing a Professional Doctorate Dissertation

The purpose of a PhD degree and professional doctoral degree differs, and so will their research reports. PhD research advances knowledge whereas, professional doctorate advances professional practices in the field. A PhD report presents the advancement of knowledge produced in the research with practical implications. Contrarily, a professional doctoral research report presents a solution to a real problem faced in professional practice. The primary aim of professional doctorates such as Doctor of Education (EdD), Doctor of Nursing (DNP), and Doctor of Social Work (DSW) is to apply the existing knowledge to solve a problem they face in their professional practice.

In theological studies, professional doctorates include Doctor of Ministry (DMin), Doctor of Missiology (DMiss), Doctor of Intercultural Studies (DIS), and Doctor of Pastoral Theology (PThD). All these degrees could be broadly classified under practical theology; however, the orientation of each degree is located in the subdisciplines of theology. Professional doctoral report in theology presents a case for the integration of certain theology/theory and practice for resolving a problem in ministry context. Professional doctorate research can use qualitative or quantitative or mixed methods strategies to offer solutions for problems in ministry practice, which could enhance Christian ministry practice beyond the research site. For specific differences between PhD and professional doctorate in theology, see table 5.

Table 5: Differences between PhD and Professional Doctorates in Theology

Elements of Comparison	PhD in Theology	DMin/DMiss/DIS/PThD
Purpose	Advancement of knowledge	Application of knowledge
Focus of Research	Conceptual	Practical
Nature of Research	Academic research	Applied research
Orientation	Theory oriented	Praxis oriented
Scientific rigor	Discussing the philosophical assumptions and paradigms Proposing new methodology, interdisciplinary approaches, and justifying the chosen methodology Discussing in detail the plan of execution of the research project	Indicating an awareness of the methods in social sciences Explaining the application of the chosen methods for resolving the problem Discussing in detail the plan of execution to resolve the problem through research
Dissertation/Thesis	Presents a thesis statement with supporting reasons and evidence from literature and data	Presents a solution to a problem in ministry practice with supporting reasons and evidence from literature and data
Originality	Raising a theologically significant and contextually relevant research question Applying new methodology Contributing to existing knowledge in theology	Identifying a significant problem from ministry practice Applying appropriate methods for resolving the problem Offering a solution to a problem in ministry practice, which is transferable

The Association of Theological Schools in its *2020 Standards of Accreditation* says, the outcomes of professional doctorates in theology include, "advanced understandings of, and competencies in, appropriate theological disciplines, behavioral sciences, social sciences, research methodologies, and the integration of those areas in a well-designed doctoral dissertation, written project, culminating report on field-based research, or other summative exercise" (n.d., 8). For some reasons, this document differentiated DMin degree from other professional doctorates in theology and reduced the standard to a "written project" instead of a dissertation as the final product of DMin research. However, DMin students can aim to produce a dissertation at par with other professional doctorates in theology. Professional doctorates in theology draw theory from biblical bases, theological perspectives, and theories from social sciences and apply them to solve a real-world problem in ministry context (Vyhmeister and Robertson 2014). Professional doctorates enable pastors, Christian ministers, and missionaries to apply theological/theoretical knowledge to their ministry context to advance knowledge for the benefit of pastoral ministry, missionary work, pastoral care and counseling, and other domains of ministry. These professional doctorates create an opportunity for those who are in Christian ministry to earn a doctoral degree in their profession.

For a professional doctorate dissertation, you can follow the seven-chapter structure that we discussed above. For writing the front matter, each chapter, and back matter, read the above section on "Writing a Dissertation/Thesis." Here, I am highlighting only the additional features of some chapters in a professional doctorate dissertation that you must be aware of.

Chapter 2 on theological perspective presents the real-world problem in a ministry context with details of contextual factors to let readers understand the problem clearly. Discuss the biblical and various theological perspectives, including differing perspectives of the problem to give a theological overview of the problem.

Chapter 3 on literature review must deal with concepts, themes, and existing theories/explanations associated with the problem from the literature. You must discuss specifically the theology/theory/explanation chosen to solve the problem, which could be from the fields of theology or religious studies or social sciences or other disciplines. In addition, you present a critical analysis of empirical studies related to the problem. However, the literature review chapter need not be extensive, as expected for a PhD dissertation/thesis, but can be limited to engaging the literature related to the chosen theory and relevant to the problem. This must be a critical and coherent essay based on an analysis of the literature, instead of an annotated bibliography.

In chapter 4, you must present the methodology. You must have read a fair number of methodology texts to show your grasp of social research methods for solving real-world problems. Then argue how the chosen research methods are appropriate to resolve the problem or challenge in ministry context. You must demonstrate your ability to apply the chosen methods effectively to find a solution to the problem by discussing in detail about carrying out each step in the research process, which includes research design, sampling, procedures for data collection, techniques for data analysis, and steps for establishing the validity/ credibility of your solution.

Chapter 6 on discussion interprets the findings/results in the light of chapter 2 (theological perspective) and chapter 3 (literature review), which is similar to the discussion chapter in a PhD dissertation. As a professional doctorate researcher, you come with rich experience from your ministry practice, which is a key element in interpreting the findings/ results. Therefore, you must incorporate your ministry experience as a reflective exercise to interpret the findings. You can interpret the findings reflectively based on your personal experience about the findings. Here, you can narrate an incident or instance from your experience to support your interpretation or offer further clarity on a finding.

Seminaries vary in their requirements for the completion of a professional doctorate and writing a dissertation; you must adhere to them.

Writing a Journal Article

Journals accept articles based on original research. Having an article published in a peer-reviewed journal places you in the company of specialists on your topic. During or after your PhD research, work out a plan to publish a journal article or multiple articles based on your research.

Rework the dissertation chapters into a journal article. You can convert your dissertation into several articles or a single paper. However, the material must be completely revised to fit the requirement of a journal article. Journals cannot publish lengthy articles. Therefore, you can plan for a single article by trimming down the literature review and methods chapters. Present only the key findings/results to demonstrate the significant contributions of the study to theology and religious studies, or focus on one aspect of your research and present the findings with supporting material as required.

When you submit an article to a journal, you will receive valuable review comments from the reviewers; you can incorporate the suggestions so as to be accepted by the journal. Sometimes articles are rejected simply because they do not fall within the scope of the journal. You must look for a top journal related to your topic for submitting your article. Even if the top journal rejects your manuscript, the review comments are helpful in revising your manuscript. After revising, submit the manuscript to second-line journals and your paper is likely to be accepted. Thus, you enter the community of scholars.

Each journal prescribes its reference style for submissions and follows a pattern of reporting, which must be strictly adhered to. The basic structure of a manuscript for a journal article based on social research includes: title page, abstract with key words, introduction, methods, findings/results, discussion, and references. The introduction covers the literature review. The methods chapter must be tightened to present only the essentials. You present only the key findings/results needed to demonstrate the significant contributions made to the field of study.

Title Page

The title page presents the title of the paper, the author's name and credentials, and an author's note/bio. Peer-reviewed journals require the authors to anonymize to hide the identity and affiliation of the author. In this case, the authors are required to provide the identity and credentials in a cover letter or a separate title page. For online submissions, the manuscript management system captures your identity and delinks from the manuscript for blind review.

Abstract

The abstract is a concise summary of the paper in 250 words. Follow the guidelines given above for writing an abstract for a dissertation/thesis.

Keywords: Below the abstract, list the keywords to be used for indexing the article.

Introduction

The introduction briefly describes the issue, locates the study in the literature, and presents the aim of the study concisely. The literature review from a dissertation/thesis is reduced in length and presented as the introduction of the article. The introduction of a quantitative study presents the research questions or hypotheses, while the introduction of a qualitative study presents the research questions. The mixed methods introduction introduces the research questions for both streams of research.

Methods

The methods section presents the paradigms, methodology, and methods chosen to conduct the study. Follow the guidelines given for writing a chapter on methodology for a dissertation/thesis but present the material succinctly.

Findings/Results

The findings section for a qualitative study presents the major themes with subthemes substantiated by excerpts from the qualitative data. You may have to be selective in presenting the themes instead of attempting to present all findings. You may deal with only the themes that are directly answering your research questions.

The results section for a quantitative study presents statistical data tables. Here, you present both descriptive and inferential statistical results.

Discussion

The discussion section presents the interaction between the findings/results and the literature. Compare the findings with literature by specifically referring to them and citing the literature. In a quantitative study, state whether the hypotheses were supported, and in a qualitative study state how the data answered the research questions. Discuss the theoretical implications of the study and make recommendations for future research.

References

All sources cited in the paper are listed under references and formatted according to the style followed by the journal.

The paper must carry a running head, which is a short title of the paper, and page numbers. Before submitting a manuscript to a journal, read the guidelines for submissions carefully and ensure that you have followed all the requirements.

Chapter Summary

This chapter dealt with writing a masters' or PhD dissertation/thesis, professional doctorate dissertation, and journal article. You have learned the basics of research writing: research argument, academic tone, and academic style. Now you know how to write each chapter of your dissertation/thesis and each section for a journal article. A dissertation using social research in theology and religious studies has the following chapters: an introduction, a theological framework or religious perspective, literature review, methodology, findings/results, discussion, and conclusions and recommendations; it includes the front matter, references, and appendix. The construction of Chapter 5 and 6 vary for qualitative, quantitative, or mixed methods study.

You have also explored writing a journal article, which includes a title page, abstract, introduction, methods, findings/results, and discussion, as well as references.

By following the guidelines given in this chapter, you can effectively communicate your research findings and make a contribution to theology, religious studies, and even across disciplines.

Review Questions

1. What is involved in research writing?
2. How to build a research argument?
3. What is academic tone?
4. What is academic style?
5. How to write an abstract?
6. How to write Chapter 1: Introduction?
7. What to write in Chapter 2: Theological Framework or Religious Perspective?
8. How to write Chapter 3: Literature Review?
9. How to write Chapter 4: Methodology?
10. How to write Chapter 5: Findings/Results?
11. How to write Chapter 6: Discussion?
12. How to write Chapter 7: Conclusions and Recommendations?
13. How to write a professional doctorate dissertation?
14. How to write an article for a journal?

Further Help

American Psychological Association. 2020. *Publication Manual of the American Psychological Association 2020: The Official Guide to APA Style.* 7th ed. Washington, DC: American Psychological Association.

Turabian, Kate L. 2013. *A Manual for Writers of Term Papers, Theses, and Dissertations.* 8th ed. Chicago: University of Chicago Press.

Vyhmeister, Nancy J., and Terry Dwain Robertson. 2014. *Quality Research Papers: For Students of Religion and Theology.* 3rd ed. Grand Rapids: Zondervan Academic.

Chapter 9

THE ROLE OF SUPERVISORS AND EXAMINERS

This chapter deals with the role of supervisors and examiners in supervising and examining students who are using social research methods for theology or religious studies. This chapter will help students, supervisors, and examiners in the following ways.

1. This chapter equips students to work with supervisors, by informing them of the expectations of supervisors and face examination by letting them know examiners' expectations about the quality indicators of a dissertation/thesis.

2. It helps supervisors understand the expectations of students, the role of a supervisor in designing and conducting a qualitative or quantitative or mixed methods study, and examiners' expectations about the quality indicators of a dissertation/thesis.

3. The section on the role of examiners prepares examiners to know the domains and the quality indicators of each domain that determine the quality of a dissertation/thesis using social research methods in theology/religious studies and the type of questions suitable for assessing qualitative, quantitative, and mixed methods dissertation/thesis.

Student-Supervisor Relationship

Supervising as a Calling

Supervising the research of a student scholar in one's specialization is fulfilling and rewarding because the student could well emerge as a specialist. A good supervisor helps students develop their research and develops the student as a researcher (Kearns and Finn 2017). Supervising students may enable a professor to contribute more to the field of study through research and by shaping successive generation of scholars.

Supervisors play a vital role in helping students shape their research interests, identifying theoretical frameworks, choosing a methodology, producing quality research proposals, conducting their studies successfully, and writing quality dissertations/theses. At a later stage of the research, "the supervisor becomes a colleague and the relationship becomes less asymmetrical than it was" (Phillips and Pugh 2010, 119). A supervisor is like a coach who helps students excel in their research.

Students' Expectations of a Supervisor

Many students have a misconception that the supervisor is an omniscient scholar who knows everything about students' topics. Supervisor's specialization and research interest may cover broad areas of students' research topics. This does not mean that they necessarily know everything about your topic. However, supervisors are qualified to supervise because they have done research and established themselves as scholars with several publications. Therefore, they can make your research journey smooth by helping you deal with the challenges and hurdles on the way.

Supervisor's roles in student's research cover five broad domains: developing research skills, offering intellectual support, maintaining a professional relationship, providing administrative guidelines, and offering pastoral care. Nathara Mhunpiew (2013), in a study of the supervisor's roles from the students' perspective, identified fifteen roles. I have rephrased and classified them under five domains and added a few more expectations.

Developing Research Skills
- Cultivating critical thinking
- Guiding in developing the research proposal
- Helping in structuring the dissertation/thesis
- Providing training or suggesting training to acquire skills for

data collection, data analysis, and use of software programs for the research
- Developing research writing skills
- Equipping students for the final viva voce

Offering Intellectual Support
- Pointing to related literature
- Enabling students to advance their knowledge
- Maintaining scientific rigor in research
- Providing timely feedback at different stages of the research
- Offering constructive critical review comments on drafts
- Connecting students to other experts
- Encouraging students to attend seminars and conferences and make presentations
- Facilitating students' publication

Maintaining Professional Relationship
- Being available and accessible
- Helping students to be confident in working with the supervisor
- Enabling students to be independent researchers
- Creating a collaborative environment for research
- Developing a channel of open communication
- Making common goals with a timeline
- Scheduling meetings as per the student-supervisor contract/ agreement
- Overseeing student's timeline for the completion of the dissertation/thesis on time
- Helping students overcome any obstacles
- Not making the student work *for* the supervisor

Providing Administrative Guidelines
- Helping students understand the institutional requirements
- Ensuring adherence to the policies
- Apprising the student of deadlines
- Informing students about funding opportunities

Offering Pastoral Care
Pastoral care refers to social or moral support extended by supervisors to students to deal with their personal problems. Scholars differ on extending pastoral care by supervisors. Some say supervisors should never get involved in the personal and private lives of the students,

while others are of the opinion that they should extend pastoral support (Taylor, Kiley, and Humphrey 2018). However, for theology students, supervisors extend pastoral support which includes spiritual care.

- Developing a quality personal relationship with students
- Being friendly
- Listening to students' problems
- Giving students pastoral support
- Extending social support
- Facilitating social interaction among students, faculty, and other researchers
- Providing prayer/spiritual support (Theology professors)

Supervisors' Expectations of a Student

Supervisors' expectations of a student can be classified under the same five domains discussed above.

Students Acquiring Research Skills

- Practicing critical thinking
- Seeking help in developing specific aspects of the research proposal
- Consulting the supervisor in structuring the dissertation/thesis
- Keeping the eyes open to attend any training to acquire skills for data collection, data analysis, and use of software programs for the research
- Developing writing skills for research writing by attending skills training or taking a module
- Equipping oneself to face the final Viva Voce and practicing the supervisor's advice

Students Seeking Intellectual Guidance

- Debriefing the supervisor about the literature search and asking for the supervisor's advice in finding related literature beyond the field of theology and religious studies
- Discussing any new knowledge gained from the literature or data with the supervisor
- Explaining the steps taken to maintain scientific rigor in the research
- Obtaining review comments for the drafts as per the timeline
- Attending to the feedback given by the supervisor
- Clarifying any critical review comments that are not clear

- Debriefing the supervisor about consulting other experts
- Discussing the plans to attend seminars and conferences and make presentations and debriefing the outcome to the supervisor after the presentation
- Updating the status of the manuscript submitted for publication

Students Maintaining Professional Relationship

- Being passionate about the research that the supervisor may get some of it
- Scheduling meetings periodically and being punctual
- Showing independence in planning and executing the project without seeking the approval of the supervisor for every step
- Considering the supervisor as a collaborator rather than an instructor
- Feeling free to approach and discuss any issue regarding the research with the supervisor
- Striving to achieve the goals set as per the timeline, if not, inform the supervisor about the reasons for the failure and reschedule
- Reporting the completion of the tasks as per the timeline
- Seeking the help of the supervisor to overcome any obstacle
- Feeling comfortable in working with the supervisor
- Being confident in working with the supervisor

Students Obtaining Administrative Guidelines

- Understanding the institutional requirements with clarity
- Adhering to the policy requirements
- Keeping track of the deadlines and meeting them punctually
- Updating the progress periodically
- Taking the help of the supervisor in finding funds

Students Looking for Pastoral Support

- Developing a quality personal relationship with the supervisor
- Having confidence in the supervisor to discuss personal problems
- Being open for socialization
- Making use of the opportunities for social interaction among students, faculty, and other researchers
- Seeking prayer/spiritual support (Theology students)

The Role of Supervisor in Social Research

Supervisor's Role in Choosing a Topic

Supervisors help students identify research questions and problems that are significant enough for a master's or doctoral degree and are based on students' interests. Good supervisors enable students to transform their research interests into potential topics by raising several questions about their interests and pointing them to relevant literature. Some professors may expect students to work on the professor's area of specialization; however, for this to be successful the student must be interested in the same area of specialization. Ultimately, the topic must be based on the interest of the student, otherwise, students may lose self-motivation over time.

Students tend to cover every aspect of a topic in their research, and so need help in narrowing down the research interest to a researchable topic. Helping students use the five levels of funneling exercise is crucial in narrowing down the topic (see Chapter 1).

Some students have the idea that they must find a topic that no one has researched. Here, the professor may point out that a topic with scant literature may not be a good choice for academic research. They can point out that over researched topics can also be investigated by locating the gaps in the literature. Supervisors must make sure that students identify research questions and problems that are significant enough because examiners will reject dissertations/theses that deal with unimportant questions (Lovitts and Wert 2009a).

The supervisor's role in designing a qualitative study is crucial for students. Many students are familiar with quantitative design; therefore, for a qualitative study, they tend to start with a theory and hypotheses. Here the supervisor could help the student understand that because a qualitative study generates new theories rather than testing a theory or hypothesis, students need to formulate one central question and a few sub-questions.

For a quantitative study, students may struggle in formulating hypotheses and there the supervisor's input is valuable. In designing a mixed methods study, students need supervisor's input in choosing appropriate design for answering the research questions.

Students sometimes state the real-world problem as the research problem, and they fail to conceptualize the practical problem. When they present the statement of the problem, they go on to describe the situation in their community or church or institution and claim that the proposed research will solve the problem. They need to be reminded that the research problem is a conceptual one that exists in the literature as gaps. They may also need to be reminded that their research solves only a conceptual problem but that they can offer recommendations to apply the new knowledge to solve a real-world problem.

Supervisor's Role in Engaging Literature

Supervisors can encourage students to look for conceptually relevant studies. Students struggle in identifying relevant literature because field-based studies in theology are rare. Students also tend to look for studies closely related to their context and conclude that not many studies deal with the topic or their context. For instance, if the study is about childlessness among married Naga women in Nagaland, the student may search only for studies related to the Naga people, instead of searching for studies that deal with relevant concepts such as childlessness, infertility, childfree, and so on among women in different contexts. Although contextual factors are relevant in identifying literature, conceptual relevance must be the guiding factor in the literature search. They need help in expanding their search from closely related studies to distantly related studies.

Supervisors can also encourage students to expand the literature search beyond the home discipline, thus paving the way for the students of theology/religious studies to interact with social sciences.

Supervisors must be aware of the difference in expectations regarding engaging literature in social research, and guide students accordingly. For a field-based study, the student is expected to refer to and cite only the studies that are useful in defining the gap, framing the research questions/hypotheses, and interpreting the findings. Therefore, the reference list/bibliography for a dissertation based on social research has fewer pages than a theology dissertation per se. This is contrary to the expectation of theology research, which requires the student to refer to and cite literature extensively and comprehensively.

Supervisors must ensure that students have a combination of literature from their region and other parts of the world. Many scholars from the West show little interest in non-Western studies, although a few are keen to engage in them. Some professors from the majority world insist on engaging literature mainly from their region while being indifferent to Western sources. Unless majority world scholars critically engage Western sources, their contribution will be confined to their context. On the other hand, findings from a culturally and religiously diverse context can offer valuable alternative perspectives to Western theories and models. Therefore, studies from the majority world with diverse religious and cultural contexts have much to contribute to global academia.

Supervisor's guidance is very much needed for students in defining the research problem. Students struggle in finding the gaps in the literature, which leads to a poor definition of the research problem, or they may claim the existence of gaps in the literature without offering evidence from the literature by citing the studies.

Students need help in engaging literature critically. Students tend to summarize the studies instead of critically analyzing them to build their argument in the review. In a study of supervisors' experience, Onius Mafa and Tichona Mapolisa (2012) found that the students were struggling in finding related studies, identifying closely related studies, critically analyzing the strengths and weaknesses of methodologies, synthesizing the literature, referring to outdated studies, acknowledging sources, and referencing. The supervisor's role in helping students engage the literature critically would solve these issues. When students are trained to engage literature critically, they could define the research problem clearly by establishing the gaps in the literature, offer a conceptual or theoretical framework with clarity, and produce a quality research report. See Chapter 2 for more on literature review.

Supervisor's Role in Sampling

Supervisors must ensure that the student's sample size is suitable for the chosen research strategy, and that they have formulated the criteria for selection of the participants based only on the purpose of the research. Supervisors could offer clarity on sampling related to qualitative and quantitative studies to help the study be scientifically rigorous.

In qualitative studies, which deal with narrative data, requiring in-depth analysis, a large sample size results in the superficial analysis of data. Supervisors must ensure the sample size is suitable for the qualitative approach chosen by the student.

In qualitative research, which uses purposive sampling, students may not adhere closely to having the research purpose determine the sample. Students are inclined to recruit different kinds of people in their studies. Supervisors must check the selection criteria for the participants before they go for data collection. See Chapter 4 for more on sampling in qualitative studies.

A quantitative study that aims at generalizing the results by testing hypotheses or predicting the relationship between variables uses probability sampling with random selection. In probability sampling, the samples are representative, for which the student must know the population size and have access to the population framework. Probability sampling requires the student to choose a margin of error and a confidence level and use the statistical formula to arrive at a sampling size. However, students are free to use web tools on the internet to calculate the sample size by inputting the required information.

"Random selection" is the most misunderstood term among students, so supervisors need to help students understand the principle and process of this type of selection. Alan Bryman (2016) advises students to report the challenges faced by them in following probability sampling and random selection instead of making a false claim about it. Supervisors must ensure that the student follow the sampling procedures rigorously.

Students may be tempted to extrapolate the results of a study using non-probability sampling to generalize the results. Supervisors could help them understand the limitations of such studies. See Chapter 5 for more on sampling in quantitative research.

Supervisor's Role in Data Collection

Students may need help in determining the kind of data required to answer the research questions and using the methods of data collection. Supervisors can guide the students on this based on the chosen research strategy and approaches.

For qualitative research, supervisors must encourage students to use various techniques to collect qualitative data rather than only a single method. Students face challenges in conducting in-depth interviews; the supervisor can check the transcript of the first interview to make sure the student has captured the data required to answer the research questions. For an ethnographic approach, supervisors can encourage students to have periodical interaction with them when they are in the field for participant observation.

For a quantitative study, supervisor's inputs are vital in choosing or designing of an instrument and in establishing the validity of the instrument with a pilot test. Because instrument design is a critical phase in quantitative research, it is highly recommended that students adopt an existing instrument. If the instrument design fails, the project will stall.

Supervisor's Role in Data Analysis

Supervisors' input on data analysis will be helpful to students because the type of data analysis and the time of analysis vary according to the chosen research strategy. Data collection and analysis are done simultaneously in qualitative research, whereas data analysis is done only after the completion of the survey in quantitative research. Students may not be aware of the nuances of some of the techniques used for data analysis.

For a qualitative study, students may do a superficial analysis without digging deeper into the data (Mafa and Mapolisa 2012) and may superimpose themes that do not reflect the data. Supervisor can play the role of an external auditor of the data analysis. They can check the analysis to see whether the student has done a deeper and systematic analysis of the data, the units of meaning reflect the participant's point of view, and that the themes have emerged from the data or have been superimposed on the data. It may not be possible for a supervisor to cross check the analysis of every interview, but such a check at the early stage of the analysis would help the student to pick up the needed skills for a deeper analysis and pay meticulous attention to identify categories of meaning.

Students' use of various statistical tests and interpreting results in quantitative research require the supervisor's scrutiny. The supervisor can check the suitability of the statistical tests for the inferences and generalizability.

Supervisors in theology/religious studies who are not trained in social research methods may find supervising students doing social research challenging. But they can update themselves by reading a few methodology texts on social research and will benefit from working with students who have learned the emerging methodologies or techniques. Some students would have taken a module on social research methods, and with further readings on methodology for their research, would be aware of the techniques and trends in social research methods. Therefore, they are able to educate supervisors and add value to supervisors' knowledge of the emerging methodologies and their impact on the discipline (Phillips and Pugh 2010). Students can cite the methodology texts to educate supervisors on social research methods and the significance of social research methods for theology/religious studies.

Supervisor's Role in Dissertation/Thesis Writing

Offering timely and specific feedback on the draft chapters and full draft dissertation/thesis is vital for students to succeed. Supervisors must communicate to their students about the time required for them to review a draft and stick to it. Giving generic feedback like "very good!" or "very poor!" is meaningless unless it is accompanied by reasons and specific evidence from the draft to support the comment. The supervisor's feedback on draft chapters is actually "feedforward" intended to help the student to improve on future drafts; therefore, the review comments must point out the strengths and weaknesses in the draft with suggestions to improve or revise.

Students doing qualitative dissertations may face challenges in presenting the findings such as working with the allotted word count. The findings chapter occupies a larger space in a qualitative dissertation/thesis because the findings are to be presented with thick descriptions from excerpts of interviews. Supervisors can alert the students who do qualitative research about this so they can plan how to allot the word count by chapters. However, the results chapter of a quantitative study is shorter because the results are presented in tables and graphs. See Chapter 8 for more on writing "Findings/Results" chapter.

Students also struggle with discussing the findings/results with the literature. Students must interpret the findings/results by comparing them with the biblical/theological/religious perspectives (chapter 2), and the literature review (chapter 3). Sometimes, while interpreting the findings in the discussion chapter, students cite studies without referring to the specific aspects. Instead, they should discuss each theme by referring to the specific aspect of the relevant studies. All the studies to which they refer must have already been cited in either chapter 2 or 3. If not, supervisors can advise the students to incorporate them in the literature review before citing them in the discussion chapter. In this way, the latest studies may be included to interpret the findings/results. The studies referred to in the discussion chapter must be cited in the required reference style, instead of simply being cross referenced to the literature review chapter.

In the discussion chapter, students must interpret the findings in comparison to the literature as they present their contribution to knowledge in the field of study. "Failure to discuss and interpret findings means that all the effort, time and resources invested by the student will have been wasted" (Mafa and Mapolisa 2012, 1693). Supervisors must pay attention to this aspect to ensure that the student presents the contribution of the study well.

Supervisor's Role in Research Writing

Skillful supervisors understand the importance of retaining the originality of students' work, and they work with students without imposing their style and perspectives, while helping the student improve their quality of writing. The dissertation/thesis is a piece of work by the student, not the supervisor.

Students will gain a lot from the supervisor's input by providing clean drafts for each review so that supervisors can spend their valuable time in reviewing the contents, instead of being distracted by copyediting and formatting errors. Supervisors are not copy editors; however, they must indicate the flaws in these areas for correction. Students may approach the writing center or an editor for help with copyediting and formatting, instead of expecting the supervisor to do it. Supervisors should make sure a dissertation/thesis moves to the next phase only after the student has attended to the sloppiness in writing.

Institutions expect supervisors to offer several rounds of review on the draft chapters and the full draft of the dissertation/thesis to produce publishable dissertation/thesis. Some institutions do not permit supervisors to review the draft chapters or the full draft of the dissertation/thesis more than once to retain the student's originality. In exceptional situations, in which the drafts require major revisions to reach the acceptable quality, the supervisor may be allowed to do more. Supervisors follow the institutional policy.

Students who are non-native speakers of English may require special attention from their supervisors. They may have done the research excellently but may struggle to write the dissertation/thesis in English, in academic style, because they may not be familiar with the academic tone and style of writing. The quality of the research project depends on various factors, but the final assessment is based on the dissertation/thesis. Therefore, the supervisor, having accompanied the student during the entire research journey, knows the quality of the project and may have to go the extra mile to help students write a quality dissertation/thesis with no presentation errors.

In a dissertation/thesis, presentation errors that display poor writing skills will undermine otherwise excellent or outstanding research (Lovitts and Wert 2009a). Supervisors should make sure such a dissertation/

thesis moves to the next phase only after the student has attended to the issues in writing.

Supervisor's Role in Equipping Students for Viva

Supervisors can ease the stress of the students and build a positive attitude in them by explaining what happens in a PhD defense and clarifying any questions their students have. Institutional policy and practices of PhD defenses vary in institutions, universities, regions, and countries. Some institutions require students to pass the oral defense for the award of a doctoral degree, while in other institutions, the defense is a rite of passage, because the examiners have already approved the dissertation/ thesis. Supervisors must explain beforehand the institutional policies and practices for the defense, so students have clarity.

Supervisors can enlighten the students on the various outcomes of PhD defenses. Normally, a dissertation/thesis is passed with commendation or with minor corrections. Sometimes examiners require a major revision of the dissertation/thesis subject to the approval of the doctoral committee/examiners or may award an MPhil degree instead of a PhD. They rarely reject the dissertation at this stage. The supervisor can explain the criteria for various outcomes to the students.

Supervisors can point to the works of the examiners and encourage students to read and be familiar with the examiners' research interests and methodological preferences in preparation for the viva. Some institutions practice confidentiality in assigning certain examiners to read and another examiner to conduct the viva; the supervisor and the student are unaware of the identity of readers but only come to know the examiner who conducts the viva.

Supervisors can offer tips in preparing the presentation for the defense. Students are inclined to cover every aspect of the research in detail because they have invested many years in the project. They could be encouraged to highlight the reason for choosing the topic, its relevance, methods, the significance of the research with key findings, and contribution of knowledge to the field of study and its implications.

Supervisors can conduct a mock defense or encourage students to do a mock defense with the help of other doctoral students. Supervisors can remind them to be brief and precise in answering questions at a viva. The mock defense could deal with typical questions that are asked in a viva:

1. Why did you choose this topic?
2. What are the main findings/results?

3. What original contribution does your research make to the field of theology/religious studies?
4. What are the strengths and weaknesses of your study?
5. If you were to do it again, how will you do the research differently?
6. What is the theological/theoretical significance of your study?
7. What are the implications of your research for addressing a real-world problem?
8. What is the benefit of your research for the churches/religious communities?

Before the student goes for the defense, the supervisor can boost the confidence and morale of the student by reiterating confidence in the student and reassuring them that they will do well. The supervisor can remind the student about the strengths of the research and something which the student did well in executing the project. This would help reinforce students' self-confidence and belief in themselves before facing the final viva.

The Role of Examiners in Social Research

Dissertation/Thesis Viva

The final examination of a dissertation/thesis is called viva voce or viva or defense or oral examination. The final viva determines whether the student has done the research, written the dissertation/thesis, and can talk about it. A doctoral viva is the "final assessment of *the research, the thesis and the student*" (Murray 2015, 2; emphasis added). Examiners assess whether the research is executed as per the chosen methodology and methods, whether the quality of the dissertation/thesis is acceptable for awarding the degree, and whether the student is able to discuss the research confidently with experts. The viva is an opportunity for students to showcase the significance of the research and the new knowledge generated by their research to experts in the field.

The examiners are chosen based on their expertise on the topic and so are keenly interested in learning about contributions made to their field of interest. Contrary to students' perception that the viva decides whether they are to be awarded the degree, examiners see the viva as a formative assessment where they can offer review comments on improving the dissertation/thesis before the final submission or publication. Generally, examiners do not want to fail a candidate but to help students write a dissertation/thesis that can pass (Mullins and Kiley 2002; Lovat, Holbrook, and Bourke 2008).

The audience of the viva varies from institution to institution. Many do not permit supervisors to sit for the viva, while some permit them to be observers. Some institutions require the student to defend only before a panel of examiners, but others allow the faculty and students of the department/institution, family members, and friends to attend the viva.

Examiners' Expectations

A Clean Presentation

Examiners expect a clean presentation of the dissertation/thesis. This involves strict adherence to the reference style in formatting in-text citations, footnotes, bibliography, following hierarchical numbering, formatting pages, and avoiding typos or textual errors. Students may think presentation errors are not serious because the examiners are only concerned about the contents of the dissertation/thesis. Contrarily, G. Mullins and M. Kiley (2002, 378), in a study of how examiners assess PhD theses, found that examiners consider sloppiness an indicator that "the research itself might not be rigorous and the results and conclusions could not be trusted." They get irritated and distracted by sloppiness and it affects their attitude toward the quality of the research (Golding, Sharmini, and Lazarovitch 2014). On the other hand, a clean presentation creates a positive attitude in the minds of examiners and makes their job pleasant.

Importance of Introduction and Literature Review Chapters

The introduction and literature review chapters are the key areas of the dissertation/thesis for creating a positive attitude in the minds of examiners toward reading the rest of the report. After reading these chapters, examiners make up their minds on whether the student knows what they are saying (Golding, Sharmini, and Lazarovitch 2014; Mullins and Kiley 2002). When they find that the introduction chapter offers clarity on the research and the literature review chapter demonstrates the student's command over the subject, they enjoy reading the rest of the dissertation/thesis. Otherwise, they adopt a critical perspective and look for more problems in the dissertation/thesis. In rare cases, a quality presentation of other chapters can positively change their views.

Original Contribution

Examiners across disciplines look for an original contribution, the adding of new knowledge, made by the research to the field of study. However, no single definition of originality is used in assessing the dissertation/thesis. Originality is about "asking new questions or applying new methods to old or new problems and achieving results that have consequence" (Lovitts 2007, 32). Original contribution in sociology dissertations/theses includes, "original data collection and analysis; the reframing of existing data in a way that casts new light on the topic theoretically, substantively, or methodologically; the bringing together of things in a new way; and the application of theory in a new context" (Lovitts 2007, 273–74). Originality deals with raising new questions, using new methods, and finding solutions to problems.

In their assessment of a dissertation/thesis using social research, examiners must recognize that theology/religious studies students who use social research, make original contributions because they raise new questions, use new methods, and produce new insights that are relevant to the context. Students bring original data from the field that do not exist in the academia, analyze data thematically or statistically, shed new light on the topic theologically, and draw implications that are relevant to the people to transform the real world.

In some instances, examiners undermine field-based studies out of a misconception that theological reflection is the best form of research in theology. For example, a theoretical study on spiritual transformation could be done purely reflecting on biblical and theological perspectives. However, a qualitative study of the lived experience of spiritual transformation could bring new narrative data from the lives of participants to the academic table, which would be available for other studies to use as secondary data. The narrative data offer a new understanding of spiritual transformation, which could advance or modify theologies on spiritual transformation and by interacting with social-psychological theories of personal transformation, the findings could modify social-psychological theories with the spiritual dimension. In this manner, interdisciplinary studies in theology that use social research methods break new grounds for theology/religious studies and advances knowledge across disciplines, which is also relevant to the context.

Therefore, in assessing the original contribution of a dissertation/thesis based on social research, examiners must see whether the student has raised new questions that are relevant to real-life for theologizing and/ or adopted emerging methodologies for innovative solutions. Theology professors must consider these factors in assessing the originality of research that has used social research methods.

The contributions of students who do a field study are to be as highly valued as those made by research based on theological reflection or speculation. Examiners should assess original contributions based on the study's theological or theoretical breakthroughs and practical significance for the community.

Originality of professional doctorates in theology is assessed based on the advancement of knowledge for the practice of Christian ministry in one's context and beyond. Students of professional doctorates may come up with a set of strategies, or models, or solutions or policies that could alter the present practice in their contexts and beyond. The outcome of the research may have a wider impact on Christian ministry.

Coherence

Examiners expect coherence in the structure, internal consistency, and a logical flow of argument in a dissertation/thesis. Examiners look for a clear, logical flow of argument from the introduction chapter to conclusions. "A thesis is crafted into a coherent whole by threading an argument through it . . . connecting the research question with an answer, connecting various subsidiary conclusions and connecting these conclusions with the supporting data, evidence and reasons, and with the background literature" (Golding, Sharmini, and Lazarovitch 2014, 569). Coherence does not leave any loose ends and all threads of arguments are tied up together to support the thesis statement.

Academically Sound

To be considered academically sound, the report must present the thesis statement with no ambiguity, back the arguments with reasons and evidence from the literature or data, highlight the theoretical significance of the research, and draw practical implications directly from the findings. The dissertation/thesis must reveal that the student has critically engaged the literature, deployed methodological rigor in collecting and analyzing data, and maintained logical consistency in the presentation. Examiners expect a dissertation/thesis to be academically sound.

Methodological Rigor

Methodological rigor involves showing that the purpose and nature of the research determined the methodology and research design. A detailed discussion on sampling, methods of data collection, and procedures for data analysis, add methodological rigor to the dissertation/thesis. At the doctoral level, students must discuss philosophy behind the methodology and their theological assumptions. In adopting social research methods for theology/religious studies dissertation/thesis, students must be clear on what they chose to do so and how they did it.

Examiners assess the suitability of the methodology for the purpose of research and examine whether the student has followed the procedures and techniques of the chosen research design.

In theology and religious studies, few examiners are trained in social research. Therefore, on many occasions, professors are appointed as examiners despite their lack of expertise in social research methods. Many are influenced by postpositivism and are familiar with the quantitative paradigm. Therefore, their questions in the viva are based on their limited knowledge of social research methods.

Such instances could place examiners in a bad light. Therefore, I recommend, examiners update themselves on the methodology and research strategy adopted by the student before examining a dissertation/thesis that has used social research methods.

Students face a difficult task in defending their methodological choices and steps in executing the project in front of examiners who have not updated themselves on social research methods. It is especially difficult for students to answer questions pertaining to quantitative research when they have actually done qualitative research. I encourage students to defend their choices and actions by citing methodology texts to demonstrate the scientific rigor of methodology in their research.

Levels of Quality of a Dissertation/Thesis

Examiners assess the level of quality of a dissertation/thesis as follows: outstanding, very good, acceptable, and unacceptable. Institutions offer various criteria to assess the level of quality and provide rubrics. Many scholars (Mullins and Kiley 2002; Golding, Sharmini, and Lazarovitch 2014; Lovitts 2007; Lovitts and Wert 2009a; 2009b) have contributed to the assessment of the quality level of a dissertation/thesis. I have relied on these studies to furnish the following quality indicators for different levels of quality of a dissertation/thesis.

Outstanding
- Addressing new questions/important questions or problem
- Indicating a deeper understanding of theory and its application

to new context/samples
- Engaging new sources
- Using interdisciplinary approach
- Demonstrating theoretical superiority
- Analyzing data systematically and comprehensively
- Interpreting the findings/results appropriately by interacting with the Bible/sacred texts, theologies, and literature
- Presenting sound arguments supported by evidence from literature and data
- Making original contributions
- Altering the existing knowledge
- Pushing disciplinary boundaries
- Offering new directions for research
- Creating interest among the larger community
- Displaying independent thinking and maturity
- Leading to publications in high-impact journals
- Exhibiting coherence from start to finish
- Engaging readers in writing
- Presenting without any sloppiness

Very Good
- Addressing good questions or problems
- Displaying a mastery of the topic
- Using suitable theory
- Employing appropriate methods and sources
- Executing the research well
- Exhibiting technical competence
- Analyzing data solidly
- Interpreting the findings/results properly
- Expanding knowledge with a modest contribution
- Leading to publications in top journals
- Presenting with a few presentation errors

Acceptable
- Addressing questions or problems that are not significant enough but relevant
- Lacking adequate conceptualization
- Summarizing studies instead of critically engaging literature
- Analyzing data and interpreting the results minimally
- Presenting arguments with loose ends
- Lacking originality

- Making moderate contributions
- Leading to publications in low-level journals or conference papers
- Displaying poor skills in organizing
- Revealing poor writing skills
- Showing basic research competence
- Meeting the requirements for the award of the degree

Unacceptable

- Addressing irrelevant questions or problems
- Engaging theory incorrectly or missing theory engagement
- Using incorrect methods
- Analyzing data inappropriately
- Interpreting data improperly
- Drawing inferences and conclusions unsupported by findings/results
- Presenting weak or invalid arguments
- Showing logical inconsistency
- Revealing internal contradictions
- Presenting with typos and syntax errors
- Attempting to plagiarize
- Lacking understanding of conventions of the discipline

The above-mentioned levels of quality indicators are common for all dissertations/theses. Specific quality indicators for qualitative, quantitative, and mixed methods dissertations/theses are discussed below.

Quality of Qualitative Dissertation/Thesis

The domains that determine quality indicators of a qualitative study are choice of topic, critical engagement of the literature, methodological rigor, trustworthiness and credibility, and attention to ethical concerns.

Students who produced qualitative dissertations may be disadvantaged because, on many occasions, as discussed earlier, examiners apply the criteria of quantitative research to evaluate a qualitative dissertation. They may raise questions or make inappropriate comments at the viva like:

- How could you have a small sample size for a study like this?
- What is the hypothesis? It is not stated anywhere.
- This study lacks objectivity and is highly subjective.
- How did you establish validity and reliability?

- Can this study be replicated? Will you get the same results?
- Without numerical data, what is the basis for your claims?

These questions are not suitable for evaluating a qualitative dissertation/thesis.

Scholars across disciplines are concerned about assessing the quality of qualitative studies. Many studies have been done to identify criteria for assessing the quality of qualitative research (Anderson 2017; Elliott, Fischer, and Rennie 1999; Cohen and Crabtree 2008; Aamodt 1983; Rocco 2010; Yadav 2021; Northcote 2012). I rely on these studies to broadly classify the criteria under five domains as a series of questions, which can be used to evaluate qualitative dissertations in theology and religious studies. Any evaluation questions need to be based on these five domains for assessing qualitative studies.

The Choice of Topic

Is it relevant to the field of theology/religious studies? Does it solve an academic puzzle? Is it significant? Is the topic contextually relevant? Is it timely?

Assess whether the study raises new question, pushes the disciplinary boundaries, and uses innovative methods. The topic must be theoretically significant and contextually relevant contributing to theology/religious studies and the community.

Critical Engagement of Literature

Has the student located the study in theology/religious studies with a proper grounding?

The chapter on theological framework/religious perspective must present a detailed discussion of the theological framework or religious-philosophical framework to locate the study in theology/religious studies.

Are the gaps in the literature defined to present the research problem?

The research problem must be defined clearly by presenting the gaps in the literature and justifying the need for the research by citing studies. See Chapter 2 for different kinds of gaps in the literature.

Is the literature critically analyzed and synthesized?

Although qualitative research does not start with theories, the student must take stock of existing theories to interpret the findings. Therefore, students must analyze all theories and models related to the topic and demonstrate critical engagement of the literature.

Methodological Rigor

Are the research questions specific and clear?
Qualitative research deals with one primary/central research question with a few sub-questions that deal with different aspects of the primary question. Qualitative research questions are open-ended.

Is there a discussion on the philosophical paradigm?
A study adopts one of the four paradigms of social research, and it must discuss the philosophy behind the paradigm, especially at the level of doctoral research.

Is the chosen methodology appropriate for the purpose of the study?
The suitability of the particular qualitative approach, such as phenomenology, ethnographic, grounded theory, case study, and narrative for the study, must be assessed.

What are the sampling logic and strategies? What are the criteria for the selection of the participants or documents?
Qualitative research uses purposive sampling in which the purpose of the research determines the selection criteria of the sample. Qualitative researchers use the principle of saturation to arrive at the sample size or go by the suggestions given in the methodology texts for each qualitative approach. The qualitative sample size is small compared to that used in quantitative research. However, a clear description of the selection criteria of participants or documents is required to assess the quality of sampling in a qualitative study.

What are the methods of data collection?
Methods of data collection for each form of data must be clearly described and the methodology chapter must report how the data were collected in the field. The student must report the challenges faced in accessing and collecting data.

What are the procedures and techniques for data analysis?
The student must explain in detail the procedures and techniques for data analysis and report on how the data were analyzed.

Does the findings chapter present thick descriptions to support the findings?
Thick descriptions of the participants' experiences indicate that the student has drawn the findings directly from the data. Some students quantify the findings which is not necessary because the philosophy

behind qualitative research values each participant's experience as real and significant. A lower frequency does not make it insignificant. If a participant's experience does not fit with the dominant theme, it should be considered a special case that requires the attention of the researcher instead of being statistically ignored. However, scholars differ on quantifying qualitative findings and if a student has done it, it is acceptable; but the student cannot over emphasize the themes with a higher frequency against those with a lower frequency. Tables are not important in a qualitative dissertation/thesis, but stories are.

Trustworthiness and Credibility

Is bracketing/epoche discussed?

Bracketing/*Epoche* is a vital factor in qualitative research for adding credibility to the study. Qualitative researchers explicitly state their ideological or theological positions and their perspectives to help readers understand the presence of subjectivity in the interpretation process. This is also known as reflexivity.

What procedures were followed in establishing trustworthiness and credibility?

Because qualitative research is inductive and interpretive, trustworthiness and credibility are the key factors in determining the quality of the research. Qualitative researchers employ triangulation, member check, peer debriefing, and various other steps to establish the trustworthiness and credibility of a study. Students should describe clearly the steps taken to establish the trustworthiness and credibility of their research so that examiners are able to assess them.

Ethical Concerns

Has the student addressed the ethical concerns?

A qualitative study collects data on personal narratives. Therefore, students must take all steps possible to avoid harm to the participants and must address all ethical concerns. They must discuss the steps taken to obtain informed consent, protect anonymity, avoid harm, and secure data protection for examiners to judge them.

Quality of Quantitative Dissertation/Thesis

Scholars are familiar with quantitative research across disciplines; however, assessing the quality of a quantitative dissertation/thesis requires clarity on the nuances of the various aspects to be assessed. I rely on Alan Bryman (2016), Denise F. Polit and Cheryl T. Beck (2018), and Michael Coughlan, Patricia Cronin, and Frances Ryan (2007) for stating the various quality indicators under the following five domains.

The Choice of Topic

Is it relevant to the field of theology/religious studies? Does it solve an academic puzzle? Is it significant? Is the topic contextually relevant? Is it timely?

Assess whether the study raises new question, pushes the disciplinary boundaries, and uses innovative methods. The topic must be theoretically significant and contextually relevant contributing to theology/religious studies and the community.

Critical Engagement of Literature

Has the student located the study in theology/religious studies with a proper grounding?

The chapter on theological framework/religious perspective must present a detailed discussion of the theological framework or religious-philosophical framework to locate the study in theology/religious studies.

Are the gaps in the literature defined to present the research problem?

A quantitative study aims at testing or advancing a theory. Students must identify the gaps in the literature and define them by citing studies. The research problem must be stated by presenting the gaps in the literature.

Is the literature critically analyzed and synthesized?

In quantitative research, the literature review leads to the development of research questions or hypotheses and to the building of a theoretical framework. Therefore, critical engagement of literature includes choosing a theory to test or advance, identifying the variables, and the themes.

Methodological Rigor

Are the research questions or hypotheses specific and clear and directly connected to the purpose of the study?

Based on literature, students must present the research questions and hypotheses with clarity. Quantitative studies using only descriptive statistical analysis do not test a hypothesis.

What are the sampling logic and the strategies?

A quantitative study that aims at generalizing the results to the population must use probability sampling and ensure that the samples are representative. If generalization is not the aim, then students can choose non-probability sampling. Sometimes, non-probability sampling is the only option for the student when every participant may not have a chance of being included in the sample due to the non-availability of the population framework or other reasons. Non-probability sampling may use convenience or quota or cluster sampling (see Chapter 5).

What are the criteria for inclusion or exclusion of the participants?
Quantitative research employs a larger sample size than that used in qualitative research. It uses a sample size formula to arrive at the sample size. The selection criteria for selecting participants must be clearly stated. The dissertation also needs to describe clearly how random selection was used for probability sampling and other forms of selection for non-probability sampling.

What is the research design for data collection and analysis?
The student must state the type of quantitative design adopted for the research, such as survey, quasi-experimental, and experimental.

How was the instrument developed or adopted?
The dissertation must state clearly whether an instrument was adopted from an existing study or a new one was developed. If one was adopted, then the basis for adopting the instrument must be stated with a discussion on the validity and reliability of the instrument. If an existing instrument was modified to suit the purpose of the study or a new instrument was designed for the study, the dissertation must explain clearly the procedures followed to establish the validity and reliability of the instrument.

What are the methods of data collection?
The dissertation must clearly describe the methods of data collection and their use. In a quantitative study, students of theology/religious studies commonly use cross-sectional surveys for data collection. The dissertation must state how the survey was administered, whether online, by email, face-to-face, and so on. The student must report the challenges faced in collecting data and the response rate.

What are the procedures and techniques for data analysis?
The student must explain in detail the procedures, statistical tests, and techniques used for data analysis. Then the student must report how the data were analyzed. Examiners must assess whether the statistical tests and procedures are suitable for the purpose of the study.

Are the inferences and conclusions grounded in the results?
Examiners must check whether the inferences and conclusions are based on the statistical results or overstated. Hypotheses may be supported or

rejected, but students cannot claim that they were proved. Attempting to generalize the results of a study using non-probability sampling is unacceptable.

Reliability and Validity

How are the reliability and validity issues addressed?
Reliability and validity are the vital factors determining the quality of a quantitative study. The dissertation must describe the steps taken to establish the reliability and validity of the instrument. If a pilot study was done, the methodology chapter must state how the results have reshaped the instrument design. See Chapter 5 for different types of reliability and validity.

Ethical Concerns

Has the student addressed the ethical concerns?
The dissertation must discuss the steps taken to address the ethical concerns in voluntary participation, obtaining informed consent, and maintaining confidentiality. The report must demonstrate objectivity in designing the study, data analysis, and interpretation of the results by avoiding bias at every stage, which is vital for quantitative research.

Quality of Mixed Methods Dissertation/Thesis

The criteria for assessing the quality of a mixed methods dissertation combine the criteria used for assessing both qualitative and quantitative research. In addition, a few other areas require examiners' attention.

Rationale for Mixed Methods Research

Has the student stated the rationale for choosing a mixed methods strategy?
Students must offer a robust rationale for choosing the mixed methods research design and the approach. They must state whether they followed convergent or exploratory sequential or explanatory sequential designs for their project.

Integration of the Results

How are the findings and results integrated?
The presentation of the findings/results should accord with the approach chosen for the mixed methods design. In this type of study, the results of both studies must be integrated in the discussion chapter and interpreted in comparison to literature.

Coherence

Is there coherence?

Coherence must be evident in all elements of the research including in the rationale for the mixed methods, research questions, data collection and analysis of both phases, integration of the findings and results, and the conclusions (Creswell and Clark 2018). Students must achieve logical flow and consistency in the design and presentation of the dissertation/thesis.

Chapter Summary

This chapter offered practical tips to students, supervisors, and examiners in dealing with dissertation/thesis using social research. Students have learned what they can realistically expect from their supervisors and what the supervisors expect from them such as, acquiring research skills, seeking intellectual guidance, and maintaining a professional relationship.

Supervisors have understood students' expectations of them, their role in assisting them in designing and conducting research social research for theology and religious studies, and preparing them for the final viva.

Examiners find this chapter useful in knowing the domains and quality indicators for assessing qualitative, quantitative, and mixed methods dissertation/thesis. This chapter discussed the techniques and procedures for assessing the quality levels of a dissertation/thesis such as, outstanding, very good, acceptable, and unacceptable, and presented the parameters for determining the levels, which include a clean presentation, the importance of introduction and literature review chapters, original contribution, coherence, academic soundness, and methodological rigor. Both students and supervisors have understood the quality domains and indicators for assessing dissertations/theses using social research, which would help them address quality concerns from designing the study to facing the viva.

Review Questions

1. What do students expect from supervisors?
2. What do supervisors expect from students?
3. What is the role of a supervisor in social research?
4. How could a supervisor help a student in research writing?
5. How could a supervisor help students prepare for the viva?

6.   What are the expectations of examiners?
7.   What are the different levels of quality of dissertation/thesis?

Further Help

Lovitts, Barbara E., 2007. *Making the Implicit Explicit: Creating Performance Expectations for the Dissertation.* Sterling: Stylus Publishing.

Mhunpiew, Nathara. 2013. "A Supervisor's Roles for Successful Thesis and Dissertation" *A US-China Education Review* 3 (3): 119-122.

Mullins, Gerry, and Margaret Kiley. 2002. "'It's a PhD, Not a Nobel Prize': How Experienced Examiners Assess Research Theses" *Studies in Higher Education* 27 (4): 369-386, http://dx.doi.org/10.10 80/0307507022000011507.

Phillips, Estelle M., and Derek S. Pugh. 2010. *How to Get a PhD: A Handbook for Students and their Supervisors.* 5th ed. Berkshire: Open University Press.

Glossary

bivariate analysis: A statistical analysis to determine the existence of any relationship between two variables and the strength of the relationship.

case study: An approach in qualitative research that investigates a particular case or multiple cases that could be an individual or institution or an event or a program or a process. Case study approach is suitable to study the complexity of a problem. It uses multiple sources of data and analyses the complexity of the phenomenon or examines the issue from different angles.

code: A label or a name a researcher assigns to a unit of meaning or category. Qualitative researchers name a code based on their understanding of the segment of the data or they adopt the words or phrases used by the participants to name a code, which is called in vivo code. For quantitative research, the codes are numerals.

coding: The process of labeling a unit of meaning in the data in qualitative data analysis. A unit of meaning could be an idea or action captured from a word or phrase or paragraph, or even the entire narrative. It involves interacting with the transcripts of interviews or other data by raising questions, comparing them, and deriving and developing concepts. Coding in quantitative research is assigning a numerical value to items in the questionnaire.

concept: A term for an abstract idea used to understand the world or to explain a practice or action or an attitude, or behavior. The intangible idea is given a label that is attached to tangible things. Concepts are also called constructs. Each concept has various components or dimensions that need to be identified based on the chosen theory or literature review.

constructivist paradigm: A worldview based on the philosophy of phenomenology; and constructivism, that says that knowledge is socially constructed in a social context by the process of interpreting and reinterpreting. The constructivist paradigm is suitable for studying lived experiences, beliefs, meanings, and unobservable dimensions of life by using qualitative research.

content analysis: A research tool used in quantitative research to quantify and measure message units in texts. Message units are concepts, themes, portrayals, coverage, tones, and so on. The text could include words presented in verbal or written or printed forms or posted online and images, audio, and videos. Quantitative content analysis quantifies the units of analysis based on predetermined categories, which is different from thematic analysis of qualitative data.

convergent design: An approach used in mixed methods research in which both qualitative and quantitative strategies are used simultaneously to understand how the results converge and are similar. Convergent design values both qualitative and quantitative data equally. The researcher collects data separately, analyzes them separately, presents them separately or parallelly, and finally integrates them.

credibility and trustworthiness: Criteria used in qualitative research for establishing the accuracy and reliability of the findings, for assessing how close the findings are to the reality of the world of the participants and their perspectives, and are dependable. Qualitative researchers commonly use triangulation and member check to establish the credibility and trustworthiness of their research.

delimitations: The constraints on a study set by a researcher. The scope of a topic may be broad, but the researcher sets a limit by excluding some of the potentially relevant aspects/factors of the topic. Thus, the researcher restricts the scope of the investigation.

ethnographic approach: An approach in qualitative research for studying social behavior of a group that shares common culture. Ethnography aims to describe the complexity of a group's culture by studying their beliefs, language, and behaviors to find patterns, social organization, and worldviews. It tries to capture the big picture of a culture by collecting every detail on every aspect of the cultural life of a community.

experimental method: A type of quantitative research in which the independent variable is manipulated to examine its effects on the dependent variable. In an experimental study, the researcher randomly assigns the samples to an intervention or experimental group, which receives the treatment or intervention, and the control group, which does not receive any intervention. The researcher takes measurements twice, once before the intervention (pretest) and once after the intervention (posttest). If the experimental group scores higher in posttest, then it is concluded that the intervention caused the changes. Experimental designs are common in natural sciences but not in the fields of theology and religious studies.

explanatory sequential design: A two-phase study used in mixed methods research. In the first phase, quantitative research is completed and in the second phase, qualitative research. Quantitative research takes priority over qualitative research in this design.

exploratory sequential design: A two-phase study used in mixed methods research. In the first phase, qualitative research is used to explore a research problem, followed by quantitative research to explain the relationship between variables related to the problem. In this design qualitative research has priority and the study identifies themes and variables for developing an instrument to be tested in quantitative research.

focus group interview: A form of a semi-structured interview used to elucidate data from a group. It keeps the focus of discussion on the research theme, and the researcher assumes the role of a moderator. The composition of a group is normally five to ten who share an experience. The aim is not to get a consensus but to get multiple narratives and diverse perspectives.

grounded theory: An approach used in qualitative research to generate theories from data and is suitable for studying a process or action. The grounded theory approach largely depends on interview data of individuals who have experienced being part of the process or action. In addition, the researcher can collect data through observations, documents, photographs, audio, and other digital forms related to the phenomenon under study. The grounded theory approach is suitable for generating grounded theology based on the lived experiences of people.

hypothesis: A prediction of the relationship between variables. Quantitative research uses a hypothesis to test a theory or generalize the results to the population. Qualitative research does not start with hypotheses but ends with generating several hypotheses.

in-depth interview: *See* Qualitative Interview

limitations: The constraints relating to the research design that affect the study and over which the researcher has no control.

literature for research: Research-based journal articles and monographs provide evidence from the field or from literature to support a claim. Researchers must use research-based publications for the literature review and to build their arguments in a research report.

literature review: A critical examination and assessment of the literature to identify relevant theories, models, concepts, and themes on a topic and to use them to set the stage for the research. A literature review establishes the gaps in the literature and offers a basis for the researcher to revise or modify or reinterpret or advance existing knowledge.

measurement in quantitative research: The process of quantification of attributes in a data set. Measurement reveals the extent to which two concepts are related and how it varies among the sample. To measure a concept, the researcher needs indicators that are tangible items that are directly or indirectly observable.

member check: A step taken in qualitative research to establish the credibility of the research. As part of the qualitative analysis, the researcher takes the findings or themes back to a few participants to check whether they accurately reflect the participants' experiences. When they do, the findings or themes reflect the real world of the participants.

memoing: Process of writing notes on one's reflection while analyzing qualitative data. Memoing and coding are parallel steps in qualitative analysis. Memoing is a phase that lets the researcher move from coding to writing the research report; memos are the link between data and the final report.

mixed methods research: A research strategy that combines qualitative and quantitative research to minimize the limitations of each strategy and to augment the strengths of both strategies. By systematically collecting and rigorously analyzing different data sets in a single study, the researcher integrates the findings to answer the research questions holistically.

narrative approach: An approach in qualitative research that gathers and analyzes stories narrated by individuals and those told by others about lived experiences. It is suitable for studying the experience of an individual or a small group.

nominal scale: A scale used in quantitative research to name the variables that are categorical or mutually exclusive, like gender, religious affiliation, race, caste, and so on.

non-probability sampling: A technique used by researchers to select sample using their subjective judgment. The sample is chosen non-randomly and is used in quantitative research when a sampling frame is not available or when the population size cannot be defined accurately or when generalizability is not the aim of a study. Qualitative research always uses non-probability sampling.

ordinal scale: A scale used to rank the order of variables in quantitative research. We attribute numerical values to each category by maintaining the level of importance from lower to higher.

original contribution: The adding of new knowledge in a field made by identifying new problems, asking new questions, and using new methods.

paradigm: A worldview based on philosophical assumptions through which one sees the world. For social research, the researcher adopts one or more paradigms based on key concerns for selecting the research strategy and approaches.

participant observation: The main method of data collection for ethnographic approach in qualitative research. Participant observation is done through field work, which immerses a researcher in the daily lives of the participants for a longer period. The researcher collects all information about specific behaviors, practices, and events, and also explores how they are placed in the larger picture of the culture and records them as field notes.

phenomenological approach: An approach in qualitative research used to study the lived experiences of individuals. It examines how individuals experienced a particular phenomenon and how they make meaning of their experience.

postpositivist paradigm: A worldview based on the philosophy of postpositivism that believes reality is one and needs to be discovered objectively like scientists discovering something in natural sciences. It relies on empiricism, which claims that knowledge is based on observable and verifiable facts through senses. It uses quantitative research.

pragmatic paradigm: A worldview based on the philosophy of pragmatism, which gives importance to common sense, practical wisdom, workability, and solutions. Pragmatic paradigm believes reality is interpreted differently by individuals and how one's interpretation differs from the other is key to this paradigm. It uses mixed methods research strategy.

probability sampling: The selecting of a sample from a population using random selection to obtain representativeness, in which everyone in the population has a chance of being selected as a sample. This enables the researcher to generalize the results. Probability sampling is used in quantitative research and not suitable for qualitative research.

purposive sampling: A form of non-probability sampling used in qualitative research. For purposive sampling the researcher determines the criteria for selecting participants, based on the purpose of the research. It enables researchers to include only the participants who have experienced the phenomenon and eliminates others who do not share the experience to contribute to the purpose of the study.

qualitative interview: A method of collecting narrative data from participants about their experiences and the meanings associated with them. It is an in-depth conversation between the researcher and the participants about the lived experience being studied. A qualitative interview is neither a simple conversation nor a question-and-answer session but a meaning-making process. They may be semi-structured or unstructured and involve focus groups.

qualitative research: A research strategy for understanding the world of the participants from their own perspectives in their natural settings and carried out by collecting data that are narrative or in other forms and analyzing them thematically. It uses interpretive frameworks to advance or modify the existing knowledge and aims at transforming the world of participants.

qualitative survey: A questionnaire that has open-ended questions giving clear instructions to the participants to narrate their experiences with thick descriptions. It collects every detail about the experience and how they perceive them. The qualitative survey could be conducted in person, or through post/email/online.

quantitative research: A research strategy that collects numerical data using different methods from predetermined samples and analyzes them statistically to offer an explanation indicating the causal nature or the kind of relationship that exists between variables and/or presents a descriptive explanation of the population.

quasi-experimental method: A type of quantitative research that is similar to an experimental method but done in a natural setting, where the participants cannot be randomly assigned to experimental and control groups.

random sampling or random selection: A sampling technique used in quantitative research for probability sampling. This technique ensures everyone in the population has an equal chance of being selected as sample. The simplest way to do random selection is by drawing lots from the sampling frame. Random sampling is not suitable for qualitative research.

reliability: Criteria used in quantitative research to assess consistency in measuring a variable/concept. If the same questionnaire is administered to the same people at different times, it should yield the same results, which would establish the reliability of the instrument.

research: An investigation that deploys scientific methods for collecting credible data and analyzing them to answer questions and solve conceptual problems by producing new knowledge. The new knowledge could be new insights or modified or refined forms of the current knowledge presented in the literature to enhance human life.

research argument: A presentation of a claim supported by reasons and evidence to convince readers that the conclusions are acceptable. A claim is a statement about a fact, which could be contested. Therefore, research argument involves providing reasons as the basis of the claim being made and offers evidence from data or literature to support the claim. The argument also addresses opposing points of view and differing perspectives.

research design: A framework for collecting and analyzing data; it is concerned with the procedures or methods of data collection and analysis used in a research strategy. Research designs vary for qualitative, quantitative, and mixed methods research strategies.

research ethics: Principles used in social research that govern the relationship between the researcher and the participants. They are concerned with how the researcher treats the participants and the data to avoid causing any harm to the participants.

research objectives: Goals stating what will be achieved at the end of the research; objectives are not the anticipated outcome of the research in the real world. Objectives deal with several aspects or components that the researcher intends to cover in the investigation.

research problem: A statement that identifies the gaps in the literature and justifies the need for a study. A research problem is a conceptual statement based on the literature about the issue under investigation, such as missing or inadequate information on a topic. A research problem is different from a practical problem, which may be found in the real world; a research problem is a conceptual problem that is found in the literature.

research proposal: A document that gives a clear picture of every aspect of a research project. It describes the proposed research in detail, argues the need for and the importance of the research, and explains how the research will be conducted.

research questions: Conceptual or abstract questions raised on a topic based on literature to find answers through research. Research questions are not interview or survey questions.

sample: A small set of the larger targeted population. When the data source is people, then the sample is a small number of people out of the many who share an experience or a part of a process, action, or event.

sampling: A process of selecting of data sources that answer the research questions. For quantitative research, when generalization is the aim, it requires probability sampling or representative sampling. Qualitative research uses the principle of purposive sampling.

sampling frame: A list of people who constitute the target population from which the researcher draws a sample for quantitative research.

semi-structured interview: A data collection method in qualitative research in which the interview is partially structured by the research purpose and research sub-questions. In semi-structured interviews, the researcher asks only a few predetermined questions, with the rest depending on the flow of conversation in the interview

snowball sampling: A non-probability sampling technique, type of purposive sampling, used in qualitative research. In snowball sampling, the existing research participants introduce the future participants. This is suitable when the researcher does not know many potential participants for the study.

social research: A scientific investigation that studies people and their world and produces new knowledge concerning the social world by adopting approaches and methods that are accepted in social sciences. It collects and analyzes data from the field to answer questions with evidence. This method is valuable for scholars of theology and religious studies because it lends itself to producing knowledge that may be applied to make life better.

statistical significance: A claim researchers make that the results are true. A researcher cannot be certain that the results based on a sample will be the same for the population. Statistical significance is about the confidence level and the level of risk the researcher will take to claim that the result is generalizable to the population with probability sampling. Researchers commonly choose significance level of 5% chance of not being true to accommodate other factors or sampling error. The significance level is known as alpha (α). When testing a hypothesis, the researcher needs to use a test of statistical significance to support or reject the null hypothesis.

structured observation: A method used in quantitative research to study the social behaviors of people. Structured observation observes specific aspects of the observed, disconnected from the totality of the context. It is highly organized and based on an observation schedule, which defines the rules for observation. The rules of observation are formed based on the focus of the research to identify mutually exclusive categories of behaviors and record them systematically with numerical codes.

survey instrument: A questionnaire used for collecting data in quantitative research. It must cover all research questions, and its validity and reliability must be established through a pilot study.

survey method: A method of data collection in quantitative research that enables a researcher to study a large population. It uses questionnaire for collecting numerical data from a sample (a small number) of the target population to inspect the relationship between variables by using statistical tools to measure the variance, and to offer a descriptive explanation of the sample.

theory: An explanation of how different variables are related and work together. Variables are attributes that are measurable or observable and that vary like age, gender, caste, and income. Quantitative research is guided by a theory, whereas qualitative research is not controlled by a theory but uses literature as broad theoretical base.

transformative paradigm: A worldview that draws its philosophical foundations from theories and philosophies that address oppression, marginalization, power, and social justice. The transformative paradigm is not confined to generating knowledge but is also a framework for research that seeks to transform the world of the participants. The transformative paradigm uses mixed methods research to study people who are oppressed because of their gender, race, or caste, and so on.

triangulation: A technique in qualitative research to establish and increase the trustworthiness of the study by using multiple data sets to identify common themes across the data sets.

trustworthiness: *See* credibility and trust worthiness

univariate analysis: A simple form of statistical analysis that analyzes one variable and offers a descriptive explanation of the sample by presenting the frequency distribution, central tendency, and measures of variation or dispersion. Univariate analysis helps researchers to summarize the data in a meaningful manner revealing patterns.

unstructured interview: A qualitative data collection method used in narrative approach to capture the life story of an individual. A life story interview is not based on a set of questions; hence, no structure guides the interview. The researcher primarily takes the role of a facilitator to let the participant narrate the life story.

validity: A criterion used in quantitative research to determine the accuracy and integrity of the results. Validity ensures the appropriateness of the instrument in measuring a variable accurately. In other words, whether the instrument measures what it intended to measure.

variable: A measurable component of a concept or a construct that varies or changes from one entity to another. For example, age, income, and belief in God, as variables vary from person to person.

References

Aamodt, Agnes M. 1983. "Problems in Doing Nursing Research: Developing a Criteria for Evaluating Qualitative Research." *Western Journal of Nursing Research* 5 (4): 398—402. https://doi.org/10.1177/019394598300500422.

Agyekum, Shadrack. 2021. "The Experiences of Students with Disabilities: A Phenomenological Study of Postsecondary Students in Ghana." Doctoral Dissertation, Lynchburg, VA: Liberty University. https://digitalcommons.liberty.edu/doctoral/ 3038.

Allen, Russell Joseph. 2021. "Students' Evangelical Worldview in Public High School Content Areas: A Phenomenological Analysis." Doctoral Dissertation, Lynchburg, VA: Liberty University. https://digitalcommons.liberty.edu/cgi/viewcontent.cgi? article=3980&context=doctoral.

Alvesson, Mats, and Jorgen Sandberg. 2013. *Constructing Research Questions: Doing Interesting Research*. London: Sage.

American Psychological Association. 2020. *Publication Manual of the American Psychological Association: The Official Guide to APA Style*. 7th ed. Washington: American Psychological Association.

Anderson, Valerie. 2017. "Criteria for Evaluating Qualitative Research." *Human Resource Development Quarterly* 28 (2): 125–33. https://doi.org/10.1002/hrdq.21282.

Archibald, Mandy M., Rachel C. Ambagtsheer, Mavourneen G. Casey, and Michael Lawless. 2019. "Using Zoom Videoconferencing for Qualitative Data Collection: Perceptions and Experiences of Researchers and Participants." *International Journal of Qualitative Methods* 18: 1–8. https://doi.org/10.1177/1609406919874596.

Atkinson, Robert. 2012. "The Life Story Interview as a Mutually Equitable Relationship." In *The Sage Handbook of Interview Research: The Complexity of the Craft*, edited by Jaber F. Gubrium, James A. Holstein, Amir B. Marvasti, and Karyn D. McKinney, 2nd ed., 115–28. London: Sage.

Aveyard, Helen. 2014. *Doing a Literature Review in Health and Social Care: A Practical Guide*. 3rd ed. Berkshire: Open University Press.

Balnaves, Mark, and Peter Caputi. 2001. *Introduction to Quantitative Research Methods: An Investigative Approach*. Reprint. London: Sage.

Banks, Marcus. 2007. *Using Visual Data in Qualitative Research*. London: Sage.

Bhattacherjee, Anol. 2012. *Social Science Research: Principles, Methods, and Practices*. 2nd ed. Textbook Collection 3. http://scholarcommons.usf.edu/oa_textbooks/3.

Boellstorff, Tom, Bonnie Nardi, Celia Pearce, and T. L. Taylor. 2012. *Ethnography and Virtual Worlds: A Handbook of Method*. Princeton: Princeton University Press.

Bohannon, Kathryn Ellen. 2021. "Christian Women's Pornography Usage: The Role of Perceived Addiction, Social Anxiety, Shame, and Grace." Doctoral Dissertations, Lynchburg, VA: Liberty University. https://digitalcommons.liberty.edu/doctoral/ 2841.

Booth, Wayne C., Gregory G. Colomb, and Joseph M. Williams. 2008. *The Craft of Research*. 3rd ed. Chicago: University of Chicago Press.

———, Gregory G. Colomb, Joseph M. Williams, Joseph Bizup, and William T. FitzGerald. 2016. *The Craft of Research*. 4th ed. Chicago: University of Chicago Press.

Brinkmann, Svend. 2013. *Qualitative Interviewing: Understanding Qualitative Research*. Oxford: Oxford Univ. Press.

Bruce, Steve. 2018. *Researching Religion: Why We Need Social Science*. Oxford: Oxford Univ. Press.

Bryant, Antony. 2017. *Grounded Theory and Grounded Theorizing: Pragmatism in Research Practice*. Oxford: Oxford Univ. Press.

Bryman, Alan. 2012. *Social Research Methods*. 4th ed. Oxford: Oxford Univ. Press.

———. 2016. *Social Research Methods*. 5th ed. Oxford: Oxford Univ Press.

Charmaz, Kathy. 2006. *Constructing Grounded Theory: A Practical Guide through Qualitative Analysis*. London: Sage.

Clark-Carter, David. 2010. *Quantitative Psychological Research: The Complete Student's Companion*. 3rd ed. Hove: Psychology Press.

Clarke, Adele E. 2005. *Situational Analysis: Grounded Theory After the Postmodern Turn*. London: Sage.

Cohen, Deborah J., and Benjamin F. Crabtree. 2008. "Evaluative Criteria for Qualitative Research in Health Care: Controversies and Recommendations." *Annals of Family Medicine* 6 (4): 331–39. https://doi.org/10.1370/afm.818.

Corbin, Juliet, and Anselm Strauss. 2015. *Basics of Qualitative Research: Techniques and Procedures for Developing Grounded Theory*. 4th ed. London: Sage.

Coughlan, Michael, Patricia Cronin, and Frances Ryan. 2007. "Step-by-Step Guide to Critiquing Research. Part 1: Quantitative Research." *British Journal of Nursing* 16 (11): 658–63. https://doi.org/10.12968/bjon.2007.16.11.23681.

Crain, Margaret Ann, and Jack L. Seymour. 1996. "The Ethnographer as Minister: Ethnographic Research in Ministry." *Religious Education* 91 (3): 299–315. https://doi.org/10.1080/0034408960910303.

Creswell, John W. 2012. *Educational Research: Planning, Conducting, and Evaluating Quantitative and Qualitative Research.* 4th ed. Boston: Pearson.

———. 2013. *Qualitative Inquiry & Research Design: Choosing among Five Approaches.* 3rd ed. London: Sage.

———. 2014. *Research Design: Qualitative, Quantitative, & Mixed Methods Approaches.* 4th ed. London: Sage.

———. 2015. *Educational Research: Planning, Conducting, and Evaluating Quantitative and Qualitative Research.* 5th ed. Boston: Pearson.

———, and Vicki L. Plano Clark. 2018. *Designing and Conducting Mixed Methods Research.* 3rd ed. London: Sage.

———, and J. David Creswell. 2018. *Research Design: Qualitative, Quantitative, and Mixed Methods Approaches.* 5th ed. London: Sage.

———, and Cheryl N. Poth. 2018. *Qualitative Inquiry & Research Design: Choosing Among Five Approaches.* 4th ed. London: Sage.

Dawson, Catherine. 2009. *Introduction to Research Methods: A Practical Guide for Anyone Undertaking a Research Project.* 4th ed. Oxford: How To Books.

Dawson, Lorne L., and Douglas E. Cowan. 2004. "Introduction." In *Religion Online: Finding Faith on the Internet*, edited by Lorne L. Dawson and Douglas E. Cowan, 1–16. New York: Routledge.

De Jong, Gordon F., Joseph E. Faulkner, and Rex H. Warland. 1976. "Dimensions of Religiosity Reconsidered: Evidence from a Cross-Cultural Study." Social Forces 54 (4): 866–89. https://doi.org/10.2307/2576180.

Decuir-Gunby, Jessica T., and Paul A. Schutz. 2017. *Developing a Mixed Methods Proposal: A Practical Guide for Beginning Researchers.* Thousand Oaks: Sage.

Deno, Frank. 2017. "A Quantitative Examination of the Relationship between Servant Leadership and Age on Organizational Commitment in Faith-Based Organizations." Doctoral Dissertation, Lynchburg, VA: Liberty University. https://digitalcommons.liberty.edu/cgi/viewcontent.cgi?article=2606&context=doctoral.

Denscombe, Martyn. 2012. *Research Proposals: A Practical Guide.* Berkshire: Open University Press.

———. 2019. *Research Proposals: A Practical Guide.* 2nd ed. Berkshire: Open University Press.

Denzin, Norman K., and Yvonna S. Lincoln. 2018. "Introduction: The Discipline and Practice of Qualitative Research." In *The Sage Handbook of Qualitative Research*, edited by Norman K. Denzin and Yvonna S. Lincoln, 5th ed., 29–71. London: Sage.

De Vaus, D. A. 2002. *Surveys in Social Research.* 5th ed. Crows Nest, Australia: Allen & Unwin.

De Vaus, D. A. 2001. *Research Design in Social Research*. London: Sage.

DeWalt, Kathleen M., and Billie R. DeWalt. 2011. *Participant Observation: A Guide for Field Workers*. 2nd ed. Lanham: AltaMira Press.

Dillman, Don A., Jolene D. Smyth, and Leah Melani Christian. 2014. *Internet, Phone, Mail, and Mixed-Mode Surveys: The Tailored Design Method*. 4th ed. Hoboken: Wiley.

Eddles-Hirsch, Katrina. 2015. "Phenomenology and Education Research." *International Journal of Advanced Research* 3 (8): 251–60.

Efron, Sara Efrat, and Ruth Ravid. 2019. *Writing The Literature Review: A Practical Guide*. New York: The Guilford Press.

Elliott, Robert, Constance T. Fischer, and David L. Rennie. 1999. "Evolving Guidelines for Publication of Qualitative Research Studies in Psychology and Related Fields." *British Journal of Clinical Psychology* 38 (3): 215–29.

Emerson, Robert M., Rachel I. Fretz, and Linda L. Shaw. 2011. *Writing Ethnographic Fieldnotes*. 2nd ed. Chicago: University of Chicago Press.

Estes, Douglas. 2009. *Sim Church: Being the Church in the Virtual World*. Grand Rapids: Zondervan.

Fetterman, David M. 2010. *Ethnography: Step-by-Step*. 3rd ed. London: Sage.

Fink, Arlene. 2003. *The Survey Handbook*. 2nd ed. London: Sage.

———. 2009. *How to Conduct Surveys: A Step by Step Guide*. 4th ed. London: Sage.

Flood, Gavin. 1999. *Beyond Phenomenology: Rethinking the Study of Religion*. London: Cassell.

Galvan, Jose L., and Melisa C. Galvan. 2017. *Writing Literature Reviews: A Guide for Students of the Social and Behavioral Sciences*. 7th ed. New York: Routledge.

Glaser, Barney G., and Anselm Strauss. 1967. *The Discovery of Grounded Theory: Strategies for Qualitative Research*. New Brunswick: Aldine.

Golding, Clinton, Sharon Sharmini, and Ayelet Lazarovitch. 2014. "What Examiners Do: What Thesis Students Should Know." *Assessment & Evaluation in Higher Education* 39 (5): 563–76. https://doi.org/10.1080/02 602938.2013.859230.

Gorard, Stephen. 2004. *Quantitative Methods in Social Science: The Role of Numbers Made Easy*. Reprint. New York: Continuum.

Gray, Stephen, Alexandra Inglish, Tejinder Singh Sodhi, and Tien-Tsung Lee. 2017. "What Are They Really Selling? A Content Analysis of Advertisements During Religious Television Programming." *Journal of Media and Religion* 16 (3): 104–16. https://doi.org/10.1080/15348423.2017.1361710.

Greetham, Bryan. 2021. *How to Write Your Literature Review*. London: Red Globe Press.

Harris, Annie M. 2016. *Video as Method: Understanding Qualitative Research*. Oxford: Oxford Univ. Press.

Harris, Dave. 2020. *Literature Review and Research Design: A Guide to Effective Research Practice*. London: Routledge.

Harris, William S., Manohar Gowda, Jerry W. Kolb, Christopher P. Strychacz, James L. Vacek, Philip G. Jones, Alan Forker, James H. O'Keefe, and Ben

D. McCallister. 1999. "A Randomized, Controlled Trial of the Effects of Remote, Intercessory Prayer on Outcomes in Patients Admitted to the Coronary Care Unit." *Archives of Internal Medicine* 159 (19): 2273–78. https://doi.org/10.1001/archinte.159.19.2273.

Hayes, Catherine, and John Anthony Fulton. 2015. "Autoethnography as a Method of Facilitating Critical Reflexivity for Professional Doctorate Students." *Journal of Learning Development in Higher Education* 8 (March 2015). https://doi.org/10.47408/jldhe.v0i8.237.

Heiselt, April, and Carl J. Sheperis. 2010. "Mixed Methods Designs." In *Counseling Research: Quantitative, Qualitative, and Mixed Methods*, edited by Carl J. Sheperis, J. Scott Young, and M. Harry Daniels, 187–99. Boston: Pearson.

Hendriks, Vincent M., and Peter Blanken. 1992. "Snowball Sampling: Theoretical and Practical Considerations." In *Snowball Sampling: A Pilot Study on Cocaine Use*, edited by Vincent M. Hendriks, Peter Blanken, and Nico F.P. Adriaans, 17–33. Rotterdam: IVO.

Hennink, Monique M. 2014. *Focus Group Discussions: Understanding Qualitative Research*. Oxford: Oxford Univ. Press.

Iyadurai, Joshua. 2015. *Transformative Religious Experience: A Phenomenological Understanding of Religious Conversion*. Eugene: Wipf & Stock.

Jacobs, Ronald L. 2011. "Developing a Research Problem and Purpose Statement." In *The Handbook of Scholarly Writing and Publishing*, edited by Tonette S. Rocco and Tim Hatcher, 125–41. San Francisco: Jossey-Bass.

Johnson, R. Burke, Anthony J. Onwuegbuzie, and Lisa A. Turner. 2007. "Toward a Definition of Mixed Methods Research." *Journal of Mixed Methods Research* 1 (2): 112–33. https://doi.org/10.1177/1558689806298224.

Kaushik, Vibha, and Christine A. Walsh. 2019. "Pragmatism as a Research Paradigm and Its Implications for Social Work Research." *Social Sciences* 8 (9:255). https://doi.org/10.3390/socsci8090255.

Kearns, Hugh, and John Finn. 2017. *Supervising PHD Students: A Practical Guide and Toolkit*. Adelaide: ThinkWell.

Kimberly, Neuendorf A. 2002. *The Content Analysis Guidebook*. London: Sage.

Kohls, Niko, Anna Hack, and Harald Walach. 2008. "Measuring the Unmeasurable by Ticking Boxes and Opening Pandora's Box? Mixed Methods Research as a Useful Tool for Investigating Exceptional and Spiritual Experiences." *Archive for the Psychology of Religion* 30 (1): 155–87. https://doi.org/10.1163/157361208X317123.

Kozinets, Robert V. 2010. *Netnography: Doing Ethnographic Research Online*. London: Sage.

Kumar, Ranjit. 2011. *Research Methodology: A Step-by-Step Guide for Beginners*. 3rd ed. London: Sage.

Kvale, Steinar, and Svend Brinkmann. 2009. *InterViews: Learning the Craft of Qualitative Research Interviewing*. 2nd ed. London: Sage.

Langdridge, Darren. 2007. *Phenomenological Psychology: Theory, Research and Method*. Essex: Pearson Education Limited.

Langmann, Sten, and David Pick. 2018. *Photography as a Social Research Method.* Singapore: Springer.

Leavy, Patricia. 2014. "Introduction." In *The Oxford Handbook of Qualitative Research,* edited by Patricia Leavy, 1–13. Oxford: Oxford Univ. Press.

LeCompte, Margaret D., and Jean J. Schensul. 2010. *Designing & Conducting Ethnographic Research: An Introduction.* 2nd ed. Lanham, Maryland: AltaMira Press.

Leedy, Paul D., and Jeanne Ellis Ormrod. 2015. *Practical Research: Planning and Design.* Boston: Pearson.

Legg, Catherine, and Christopher Hookway. 2021. "Pragmatism." In *The Stanford Encyclopedia of Philosophy,* edited by Edward N. Zalta, Summer 2021 Edition. https://plato.stanford.edu/archives/sum2021/entries/pragmatism/.

Lester, Ashlie M. 2013. "Religious Similarity and Relationship Quality." Doctoral Dissertation, Columbia: University of Missouri. https://mospace.umsystem.edu/xmlui/bitstream/handle/10355/42963/research.pdf?sequence=1.

Lovat, Terence, Allyson Holbrook, and Sid Bourke. 2008. "Ways of Knowing in Doctoral Examination: How Well Is the Doctoral Regime?" *Educational Research Review* 3 (1): 66–76. https://doi.org/10.1016/j.edurev.2007.06.002.

Lovitts, Barbara E. 2007. *Making the Implicit Explicit: Creating Performance Expectations for the Dissertation.* Sterling: Stylus Publishing.

Lovitts, Barbara E., and Ellen L. Wert. 2009a. *Developing Quality Dissertations in the Humanities: A Graduate Student's Guide to Achieving Excellence.* Sterling: Stylus Publishing.

———. 2009b. *Developing Quality Dissertations in the Social Sciences: A Graduate Student's Guide to Achieving Excellence.* Sterling: Stylus Publishing.

Mafa, Onias, and Tichaona Mapolisa. 2012. "Supervisors' Experiences in Supervising Postgraduate Education Students' Dissertations and Theses at the Zimbabwe Open University (Zou)." *International Journal of Asian Social Science* 2 (10): 1685–97.

Manen, Max van. 1990. *Researching Lived Experience: Human Science for Action Sensitive Pedagogy.* Albany: State University of New York Press.

Mash, Rachel, and Robert James Mash. 2012. "A Quasi-Experimental Evaluation of an HIV Prevention Programme by Peer Education in the Anglican Church of the Western Cape, South Africa." BMJ Open 2 (2): 1–8. https://doi.org/10.1136/bmjopen-2011-000638.

Mason, Jennifer. 2002. *Qualitative Researching.* 2nd ed. London: Sage.

Mason, Mark. 2010. "Sample Size and Saturation in PhD Studies Using Qualitative Interviews." *Forum: Qualitative Social Research* 11 (3). http://www.qualitative-research.net/index.php/fqs/article/view/1428/3027.

Matua, Gerald Amandu, and Dirk Mostert Van Der Wal. 2015. "Differentiating between Descriptive and Interpretive Phenomenological Research Approaches." *Nurse Researcher* 22 (6): 22–27. https://doi.org/10.7748/nr.22.6.22.e1344.

McKenna, Brad, Michael D. Myers, and Michael Newman. 2017. "Social Media in Qualitative Research: Challenges and Recommendations." *Information and Organization* 27 (2): 87–99. https://doi.org/10.1016/j.infoandorg.2017.03.001.

Mendez, Mariza G. 2013. "Autoethnography as a Research Method: Advantages, Limitations and Criticisms." *Colombian Applied Linguistics Journal* 15 (2): 279–87. https://doi.org/10.14483/udistrital.jour.calj.2013.2.a09.

Mertens, Donna M. 2015. *Research and Evaluation in Education and Psychology.* 4th ed. London: Sage.

Mhunpiew, Nathara. 2013. "A Supervisor's Roles for Successful Thesis and Dissertation." *A US-China Education Review* 3 (2): 119–22.

Miles, Anthony D. 2017. "Taxonomy of Research Gaps: Identifying and Defining the Seven Research Gaps." *Journal of Research Methods and Strategies* 1 (1): 1-15

Miles, Matthew B., A. Michael Huberman, and Johnny Saldana. 2014. *Qualitative Data Analysis: A Methods Source Book.* 3rd ed. London: Sage.

Mullins, Gerry, and Margaret Kiley. 2002. "'It's a PhD, Not a Nobel Prize': How Experienced Examiners Assess Research Theses." *Studies in Higher Education* 27 (4): 369–86. https://doi.org/10.1080/0307507022000011507.

Murbach, Kyle. 2019. "Self-Efficacy in Information Security: A Mixed Methods Study of Deaf End-Users." Doctoral Dissertation, Madison: Dakota State University. https://scholar.dsu.edu/theses/335.

Murray, Rowena. 2015. *How to Survive Your Viva: Defending a Thesis in an Oral Examination.* 3rd ed. Berkshire: Open University Press.

Natsis, Eva. 2017. "Encountering the 'Unexpected' in Phenomenological Research: Faith and Belief as Expressions of Spirituality in a Qualitative Study." *International Journal of Children's Spirituality* 22 (3–4): 291–304. https://doi.org/10.1080/1364436X.2017.1340263.

Nel, M., and W. J. Schoeman. 2015. "Empirical Research and Congregational Analysis: Some Methodological Guidelines for the South African Context." *Acta Theologica* 35: 85–102. http://dx.doi.org/10.4314/actat.v21i1.7s.

Neuman, W. Lawrence. 2014. *Social Research Methods: Qualitative and Quantitative Approaches.* 7th ed. Harlow: Pearson Education Limited.

Northcote, Maria. 2012. "Selecting Criteria to Evaluate Qualitative Research." In *Narratives of Transition: Perspectives of Research Leaders, Educators & Postgraduates,* edited by M Kiley, 99–110. Canberra, Australia: The Centre for Higher Education, Learning and Teaching, The Australian National University. https://research.avondale.edu.au/edu–papers/38/.

O'Cathain, Alicia. 2010. "Assessing the Quality of Mixed Methods Research: Toward a Comprehensive Framework." In *SAGE Handbook of Mixed Methods in Social & Behavioral Research,* edited by Abbas Tashakkori and Charles Teddlie, 2nd ed., 531–56. London: Sage.

Ogden, Thomas E., and Israel A. Goldberg. 2002. *Research Proposals: A Guide to Success.* 3rd ed. San Diego: Academic Press.

Oltmann, Shannon M. 2016. "Qualitative Interviews: A Methodological Discussion of the Interviewer and Respondent Contexts." *Forum: Qualitative Social Research* 17 (2): 1–16. https://doi.org/10.17169/fqs-17.2.2551.

Olver, Ian N., and Andrew Dutney. 2012. "A Randomized, Blinded Study of the Impact of Intercessory Prayer on Spiritual Well-Being in Patients with Cancer." *Alternative Therapies* 18 (5): 18–27.

Otto, Rudolf. 1970. *The Idea of the Holy*. Oxford: Oxford Univ. Press.

Pearce, Lisa D., George M. Hayward, and Jessica A. Pearlman. 2017. "Measuring Five Dimensions of Religiosity across Adolescence." *Review of Religious Research* 59 (3): 367–93. https://doi.org/10.1007/s13644-017-0291-8.

Phillips, Estelle M., and Derek S. Pugh. 2010. *How to Get a PhD: A Handbook for Students and Their Supervisors*. 5th ed. Berkshire: Open University Press.

Pickett, J. Waskom. 1933. *Christian Mass Movements in India: A Study with Recommendations*. Cincinnati: Abingdon Press.

Polit, Denise F., and Cheryl Tatano Beck. 2010. *Essentials of Nursing Research: Appraising Evidence for Nursing Practice*. 7th ed. Philadelphia: Wolters Kluwer.

———. 2018. *Essentials of Nursing Research: Appraising Evidence for Nursing Practice*. 9th ed. Philadelphia: Wolters Kluwer.

Pope, Catherine, Nicholas Mays, and Jennie Popay. 2007. *Synthesizing Qualitative and Quantitative Health Evidence: A Guide to Methods*. Berkshire: Open University Press.

Punch, Keith F. 2016. *Developing Effective Research Proposals*. 3rd ed. London: Sage.

Ramsay, Nancy J. 2012. "Emancipatory Theory and Method." In *The Wiley-Blackwell Companion to Practical Theology*, edited by Bonnie J. Miller-McLemore, 183–92. West Sussex: Wiley-Blackwell.

Reed, Tamilia D. 2016. "An Examination of Religiosity, Spirituality, and Psychological Wellbeing Among Pagan Women: A Mixed Method Approach." Doctoral Dissertation, Urbana: University of Illinois. https://www.ideals.illinois.edu/bitstream/handle/2142 /92698/REED-DISSERTATION-2016.pdf?sequence=1.

Research Advisors, The. 2006. "Sample Size Table." 2006. https://www.research-advisors.com/tools/SampleSize.htm.

Ridley, Diana. 2012. *The Literature Review: A Step-by-Step Guide for Students*. 2nd ed. London: Sage.

Robinson, Francis P. 1946. *Effective Study*. New York: Harper and Brothers.

Rocco, Tonette S. 2010. "Criteria for Evaluating Qualitative Studies." *Human Resource Development International* 13 (4): 375—378. https://doi.org/10.1080 /13678868.2010.501959.

Roller, Margaret R., and Paul J. Lavrakas. 2015. *Applied Qualitative Research Design: A Total Quality Framework Approach*. New York: The Guilford Press.

Saldana, Johnny. 2011. *Fundamentals of Qualitative Research: Understanding Qualitative Research*. Oxford: Oxford Univ. Press.

———. 2013. *The Coding Manual for Qualitative Researchers*. 2nd ed. London: Sage.

Salkind, Neil J. 2017. *Statistics for People Who (Think They) Hate Statistics: Using Microsoft Excel 2016*. 4th ed. London: Sage.

Scharen, Christian, and Aana Marie Vigen. 2011. "What Is Ethnography." In *Ethnography as Christian Theology and Ethics*, edited by Christian Scharen and Aana Marie Vigen, 3–27. New York: Continuum.

Seidman, Irving. 2006. *Interviewing as Qualitative Research: A Guide for Researchers in Education and the Social Sciences*. 3rd ed. New York: Teachers College Press.

Silverman, David, and Amir Marvasti. 2008. *Doing Qualitative Research: A Comprehensive Guide*. London: Sage.

Smart, Ninian. 1971. *The Religious Experience of Mankind*. New York: Macmillan.

Smith, Jonathan A., Paul Flowers, and Michael Larkin. 2009. *Interpretative Phenomenological Analysis: Theory, Method and Research*. London: Sage.

Stake, Robert E. 1995. *The Art of Case Study Research*. London: Sage.

Stausberg, Michael. 2011. "Structured Observation." In *The Routledge Handbook of Research Methods in the Study of Religion*, edited by Michael Stausberg and Steven Engler, 382–94. London: Routledge.

Stausberg, Michael, and Steven Engler. 2011. "Introduction: Research Methods in the Study of Religion\s." In *The Routledge Handbook of Research Methods in the Study of Religion*, edited by Michael Stausberg and Steven Engler, 3–20. London: Routledge.

Swinton, John, and Harriet Mowat. 2016. *Practical Theology and Qualitative Research*. London: SCM.

Tashakkori, Abbas, and John W. Creswell. 2007. "Editorial: The New Era of Mixed Methods." *Journal of Mixed Methods Research* 1 (1): 3–7. https://doi.org/10.1177/2345678906293042.

Taylor, Stan, Margaret Kiley, and Robin Humphrey. 2018. *A Handbook for Doctoral Supervisors*. 2nd ed. London: Routledge.

The Association of Theological Schools: The Commission on Accrediting. n.d. *2020 Standards of Accreditation*. Accessed July 19, 2022. https://www.ats.edu/files/galleries/standards-of-accreditation.pdf.

Tom, Andrea M. 2021. "A Quantitative Descriptive Study of the Impact Bible Reading Has on the Lives and Leadership of American Evangelical Church Pastoral Leaders." Doctoral Dissertation, Lynchburg, VA: Liberty University. https://digitalcommons.liberty.edu/cgi/viewcontent.cgi?article=4171&context=doctoral.

Turabian, Kate L. 2013. *A Manual for Writers of Research Papers, Theses, and Dissertations: Chicago Style for Students and Researchers*. 8th ed. Chicago: University of Chicago Press.

Vagle, Mark D. 2018. *Crafting Phenomenological Research*. 2nd ed. New York: Routledge.

Vanderstoep, Scott W., and Deirdre D. Johnston. 2009. *Research Methods for Everyday Life: Blending Qualitative and Quantitative Approaches*. San Francisco: Jossey-Bass.

Villani, Daniela, Angela Sorgente, Paola Iannello, and Alessandro Antonietti. 2019. "The Role of Spirituality and Religiosity in Subjective Well-Being of Individuals with Different Religious Status." *Frontiers in Psychology* 10: 1–11. https://doi.org/10.3389/fpsyg.2019.01525.

Vyhmeister, Nancy J., and Terry Dwain Robertson. 2014. *Your Guide to Writing Quality Research Papers: For Students of Religion and Theology.* 3rd ed. Grand Rapids: Zondervan Academic.

Wall, Sarah. 2008. "Easier Said than Done: Writing an Autoethnography." *International Journal of Qualitative Methods* 7 (1): 38–53. https://doi.org/10.1177/160940690800700103.

Weibel, Michelle L. 2011. "Being Outside Learning About Science Is Amazing: A Mixed Methods Study." Doctoral Dissertation, Las Vegas: University of Nevada. http://dx. doi.org/10.34917/2826478.

Weiss, Martin. 2019. *Writing Scientific Research Proposals: A Practical Guide.* London: Bookboon.

Woodberry, Robert D. 2012. "Missionary Roots of Liberal Democracy." *American Political Science Review* 106 (2): 244–74. https://doi.org/10.1017/S0003055412000093.

Yadav, Drishti. 2021. "Criteria for Good Qualitative Research: A Comprehensive Review." *The Asia-Pacific Education Researcher.* https://doi.org/10.1007/s40299-021-00619-0.

Yin, Robert K. 2003. *Case Study Research: Design and Methods.* 3rd ed. London: Sage.

Index

www.ingramcontent.com/pod-product-compliance
Lightning Source LLC
Chambersburg PA
CBHW070504160726
48003CB00004B/1426